DEEP DIVING

AN ADVANCED GUIDE TO PHYSIOLOGY, PROCEDURES AND SYSTEMS

D0958528

by Bret Gilliam and Robert von Maier
with John Crea and Darren Webb

Copyright © 1992 Watersport Publishing, Inc.
All Rights Reserved

No part of this book may be reproduced or transmitted in any form or by any means, electronic or mechanical, including photocopying, recording, or by any information storage or retrieval system, without permission in writing from the publisher.

Disclaimer

Deep diving is a potentially hazardous practice that can expose the diver to considerable risk including death if practiced incorrectly or with incomplete planning and procedures. It requires specialized training, equipment and experience. This book is not intended as a substitute for the above or for the diver to abandon common sense in pursuit of diving activities beyond his abilities. Although the practice of deep diving has become more widespread, it should be noted that the national scuba training agencies recommend a maximum depth of 130 fsw for recreational sport divers. This book is intended as a source of information on various aspects of deep diving, not as a substitute for proper training and experience. The reader is advised that all the elements of hazard and risk associated with deep diving cannot be brought out within the scope of this text. Those divers that choose to pursue deep diving activities do so at their own risk. The authors neither condone nor advocate deep diving per se, and the book is offered for informational purposes only. The authors, publisher, and manufacturers presented in this book, are not liable for damage or injury including death which may result from deep diving activities, with respect to information contained herein.

Cover photo by Bret Gilliam

First Printing 1992
Watersport Publishing, Inc., P.O. Box 83727, San Diego, CA 92138

Printed in the United States

International Standard Book Number
ISBN 0-922769-30-3

Library of Congress Catalog Card Number: 91-066440
von Maier, Robert and Gilliam, Bret, with Crea, John and Webb, Darren
    Deep Diving
       An Advanced Guide to Physiology, Procedures and Systems

DEEP DIVING

AN ADVANCED GUIDE TO PHYSIOLOGY, PROCEDURES AND SYSTEMS

by Bret Gilliam and Robert von Maier
with John Crea and Darren Webb

Watersport Publishing, Inc.
Post Office Box 83727
San Diego, CA 92138

Dedication

To Parker Turner who lost his life while diving on November 17, 1991
and to the many others who went before and led the way...
we dedicate this book.

Table of Contents

Acknowledgements

The preparation and research necessary to produce this book would have been impossible without the cooperation of numerous individuals who generously gave of their time and expertise to assist with the manuscript.

A special thanks to Tom Mount who provided our foreword, invaluable help in tracking down "lost" historical references, and spent countless hours on the phone coordinating data. Also, a major debt is owed to Michael Menduno who opened the files of *Aquacorps* to us and additionally helped with the photo shoots on advanced high-tech equipment. Bill Hamilton graciously consented to interview and supplied important information on custom tables. Also, for his timely contributions, a word of thanks to Ron Russell.

For interviews in the historical section thanks to Gary Gentile, Sheck Exley, Jim Lockwood, Parker Turner, Dustin Clesi, Hal Watts, Dr. Lee Somers and Tom Mount. Our appreciation goes to Dick Rutkowski for input on NITROX and chamber therapy; and Ed Betts for detailed material on oxygen cleaning and NITROX blending systems.

For bravely consenting to be our photographic models, thanks to Lynn Hendrickson, Michael Menduno, Billy Deans, Lina Hitchcock, Bill Walker, Cathy Lawlor, Lamar English, Dustin Clesi, Rick Nicolini and Mark Leonard. Thanks to contributing photographers Rock Palermo, Wes Skiles, Ned DeLoach, Ken Loyst, Gary Gentile, Tom Packer and Tom Mount.

For their time and valuable input, thanks to Dick Long of DUI, Daniel J. Lenihan and Larry Murphy of the National Park Service. Also, a much needed thanks to Christopher Pyle, Lance Milbrand, and Jimmy Stewart of Scripps Institution of Oceanography.

For assistance in editing and preparing the manuscript, many thanks to Richard Nordstrom, Blake Hendrickson, William Schwantes, Joe Heaney, Dr. Jolee Brunton, Christie Jurney, Evelyn Webb, and Denise Winslett.

A special thanks to Heather McSharry for the many long hours she spent at the computer editing and typing.

And a closing thanks to our courageous publisher Ken Loyst.

Bret Gilliam • *Robert von Maier* • *John Crea* • *Darren Webb*
November 1991

Foreword

I was delighted when asked to write the foreword to *DEEP DIVING: An Advanced Guide to Physiology, Procedures and Systems*. This is a text who's time has come. First, I would like to congratulate both Ken Loyst on behalf of Watersport Publishing, Inc. and the authors of *DEEP DIVING* for the courage to present this text and for being responsible enough to publicly acknowledge its need. This text provides a practical approach to exceeding the current 130 fsw sport diving limit and doubles as a reference manual for all serious minded diving enthusiasts. The wealth of information compressed into these pages bridges the gap from "kindergarten" to "graduate school" for most divers.

DEEP DIVING does not set anyone's limits nor does it endorse or encourage diving to great depths. It does provide vital diver education. *DEEP DIVING* recognizes the existing and growing population of those who exceed the 130 fsw mark and their right to be factually informed of risk, achievement and alternatives. With the knowledge from this text, "sound and prudent judgement" may be made in planning dives and setting personal limitations.

What is it that is so fascinating about depth? Who really knows the answer... Deep diving is embraced by so many of us, yet feared by too many others. There is very little factual evidence to support the "Go Below 130 feet And You Will Die" attitude of organized diving. However, many divers do venture to depth without proper education or knowledge and have unnecessary accidents. It is the resistance of the certification agencies to face facts and reality that contribute to the dilemma of this group. Dedicated deep divers make the effort to seek qualified training and study all of the educational references available with a realistic, versus a theory only, orientation. Due to the cloak and dagger view of depth, information and training has, until this publication, been very difficult to find.

Deep diving, as newly defined by the term *Technical Diving*, has been around for a long time. When I was discharged as a Navy diver in 1961, one of my first discoveries was the world of deep diving and (most often) deep cave diving. To my surprise, I was not alone even in those early days. Hundreds of dedicated New England wreck divers had been routinely exploring wrecks to 150 fsw and deeper. Lee Somers, Rick Frehsee, Al

Giddings, Eugenie Clark, Sylvia Earle and others involved in research in the marine environment (and for recreation) made and still make dives to 200 fsw or below. In cave diving, dozens of us were commonly exploring caves to depths well in excess of 260 feet. In fact both Hal Watts (the first to sanction deep diving courses) and myself (the first to teach cave and deep diving cave courses) were teaching deep air diving to depths of 240 plus in the early sixties.

In the Caribbean, Bret Gilliam, Neal Watson and numerous others including Peter Hughes, made frequent dives into the 200 plus fsw range. By the late sixties and early seventies, the 350 and 400 fsw marks were being explored. Jim Lockwood probably has more dives below 400 feet (147 logged to be exact) than any other man alive. In fact, Jim and Bret Gilliam have regularly dived in the 400 plus fsw range on air at various stages of their careers, Gilliam to the new record of 452 fsw.

Today almost all well known cave divers such as Sheck Exley (record holder on mixed gas in a cave at over 800 feet), Wes Skiles, Jim Lockwood, Bill Main, Bill Gavin, Larry Green, Jim King, Billy Deans, Paul Heinerth, Parker Turner, Steve Gerrard, Dustin Clesi, myself (the list goes on and continues to grow at an accelerating rate) have dived in caves to depths of 200 plus feet on air. Three hundred feet and deeper is not uncommon for the above group. From 1969 through 1976, while I was the Diving Officer at the University of Miami Rosenteil School of Marine and Atmospheric Sciences, we had numerous scientists and graduate students performing weekly research dives between 180 and 240 fsw accumulating thousands of accident free dives. Bruce Chalker, Ph.D., Zidi Goldstein and Dr. William H. Hulet, Ph.D. M.D., worked to 250 fsw on air. In addition to these University of Miami scientists, hundreds of others worldwide performed similar deep diving research with amazingly good safety records. It is interesting to note that 190 fsw is still within the sanctions of the American Academy of Underwater Scientists (AAUS).

The point is: deep diving has been, and continues to be, a reality of diving.

There are limitations due to physical ability, physiological limits, training/education and psychological restraints. However, these limits still allow the diver to exceed the mysterious 130 fsw limit promoted today. Don't get me wrong, 130 fsw is a reasonable depth to begin informing students of the risk factors and to point out the need for more sophisticated training prior to deeper explorations for recreational divers. Indeed, the diving community should establish progressive training from 80 fsw on down through the realistic depths. This recommendation is not due to the limiting factor of narcosis, but rather to a combination of limited bottom time without decompression, possible but not probable impairment by narcosis (until depths of 150 fsw or more are obtained), limited air duration at depth, and the diver's attitude.

Diver education must be significantly greater than the status quo taught in traditional courses. This is necessary for every diver to make prudent judgements and plan dives. A good recommended but not mandatory depth limit is, as proposed by Bill Gleason of *Skin Diver* magazine, 150 fsw. At this depth and deeper, the reality of narcosis is a true factor to be considered. With today's dependable BCD's and the use of dive computers, a safe 150 fsw dive is now a fact. It is even possible with computers to dive a multi-level wall profile to these maximum depths, pull a reasonable bottom time, yet still avoid needing obligatory decompression stops. Of course, I recommend mandatory 15 foot safety stops on all dives.

Isn't it a shame that we who have careers in diver education have locked the industry into stated liability by setting maximums instead of "educating" divers to risk factors at or below these given depths. With understandable risk factors taught, many divers would be even more conservative than they presently are. And those who did venture deeper would have a baseline for proper decision making. Of course, this would require better informed instructors to teach actual deep diving courses, and more technical and practical information as outlined in *DEEP DIVING*.

This should all be combined in progressive depth courses. Depths of 200 to 250 fsw and deeper are really the outer limits for true danger due to narcosis, oxygen poisoning and stress. Miles, in the book *Underwater Medicine* from the early sixties, described dives between 180 fsw and 240 fsw on air as "risk dives" with dives deeper than 240 fsw as "dangerous". From my observations of over thirty years of diving, this description has held up as the most intelligent and true risk analysis for extending air dives.

Depths below 200 fsw should be discouraged, not prohibited, on air. At and beyond the 200 foot mark, deep divers may choose (as many of the previously named divers have) the added safety of mixed gas diving.

As a deep diver, it is great to be out of the closet! It is sad that for years the deep diving community has been viewed by some as reckless renegades, when in fact some of the most safety minded divers one could find fall into this group. Typically, dedicated deep divers are well educated on diving physiology, knowledgeable of their abilities, mentally in tune and aware of themselves, and are more safety and equipment aware than most divers. These folks have learned from experience that a deep dive plan leaves nothing to chance. It has always been disappointing to us that so many well known leaders in diver education and publishing have been actively deep divers, and yet (still) deny it in public!

Are there risks in deep diving? Yes, and for some ultra-deep divers, the price has been their lives. Indeed, some of my best friends, all seasoned deep air divers, have paid that price for attempting long 300 plus feet cave penetration or record attempt dives. For the uninformed diving public, the practice of "ripping off" an ultra-deep dive (with no training, little knowledge and no tolerance build-up) can have devastating results. This point is made obvious as the pages of *DEEP DIVING* are read.

It becomes evident that divers must have adequate knowledge and references to establish personal safe diving habits. This text is the only source currently addressing the overall concept of depth. This leads us to the inevitable question of "how deep is deep?". There will be variations in this definition, but finally, a solid written foundation exists that every diver will want to know about... and needs to know about.

Tom Mount
May 1991

(Tom Mount is an ex-United States Navy diver with over 33 years diving experience. He was the first NACD instructor and is NACD's current Training Director. He is ANDI Course Director #4 and holds Instructor ratings from NAUI, PADI, YMCA and IAND. He has logged nearly 10,000 dives including more than 2000 below 200 feet. Additionally, he has been involved in nine saturation missions and extensive mixed gas diving. He is a well-published underwater photographer and the author of two books on underwater photography, the text Practical Diving, Safe Cave Diving, *and* The Cave Diving Manual.

Introduction

The reader has probably selected this text precisely because he desires more information about deep diving than is addressed in conventional sport diving texts. It should be recognized from the outset that much of the discussion material in the following chapters is geared toward a diver who has made a clear and conscious decision to pursue a type of diving that is beyond what is considered "normal" sport diving limits. This personal decision also burdens the participant with some heavy baggage (mentally and physically). Responsibility for one's actions has to be foremost in the deep diver's mind as he contemplates deeper excursions. In fact, a high degree of self-sufficiency in physical conditioning, equipment systems, and gas volume control is desirable. (For more information along these lines refer to *Solo Diving: The Art of Underwater Self-Sufficiency* by Robert von Maier.) Most experienced deep divers will not be looking for a "buddy" to solve problems for them. Indeed, the "dependent" diver as typically found in much of the actual practice of the "buddy system" is largely absent in deep diver communities.

The emergence of the deep diving sports enthusiast has provoked much controversy. Many take the position of the national certification training agencies that 130 fsw (39.4 m) is the absolute depth limit for sport divers. Recently, limitations as shallow as 100 fsw (30.3 m) have been suggested. Many land-based resort operations in tropical sites have instituted enforced depth limits; the Cayman Association of Dive Operators has advocated the 100 fsw limit. Meanwhile, such restrictions are blissfully ignored by the resort divemaster staffs on their day's off and most live aboard vessels pay only lip service to a depth limit (primarily as a reaction to a potential negligence litigation) .

Sport divers of all experience levels seem to have a universal disregard for current recommended depth levels and anyone who has observed everyday diving routines recently has to admit the reality of deep diving in an ever-expanding segment of the traditional diver population. Bill Gleason, editor of *Skin Diver* Magazine, has come forward in 1990 to editorialize the widespread non-adherence to these depth limits and further to brand them as unreasonably conservative. He logically concludes that a more practical solution is to target a depth limit that sport divers would be more inclined to view as meaningful, say 150 fsw (45.5 m), and to have training programs better address the issue of deeper diving.

Like evolution and all changes in the sport diving industry, sharply polarized perspectives have surfaced and the debate still rages as to even what these more aggressive divers should be called. Egstrom and Bachrach (1990) note, "the problem has been compounded to some degree by a blurring of the distinctions that once differentiated commercial and military divers from the sport diving community. In recent years, increasing numbers of sport (or recreational) divers have entered diving activities that involve decompression... wreck diving necessitated divers staying longer at depths to perform tasks. In addition, some cave divers have developed dive profiles that go as deep as 700 fsw and require the use of helium/oxygen mixtures... It is our position that once a diver enters a decompression schedule dive or uses a mix that is not a standard compressed air mix, the dive should no longer be considered recreational. Even if the purpose of the dive is adventure and recreation, the character of the dive has changed and the diver is now a working diver, subject to all the subsequent demands of needing to know more about operations and equipment than the shallow, "no-decompression", warm water diver has ever considered."

Egstrom and Bachrach, long time researchers into human performance underwater, have hit the nail precisely on the head. Venturing into the realm of decompression, mixed gas and dives on air much below 130 fsw does require far more training and equipment/operational disciplines than most typical sport divers have or are willing to acquire.

Current recognized national training courses in "deep diving" are largely considered inadequate; lacking sufficient time in technical skills and a limited amount of actual dives. Admittedly their stated objectives are to train divers to 130 fsw but many professional instructors question if even that goal is realistically attained. More importantly, the mindset of a graduating "deep diver" may not fully understand how limited his training really is and attempt dives deeper and far beyond his experience. (The authors recommend that anyone interested in pursuing deep diving activities contact one of the specialized training facilities listed in Reference Materials.) Although such observations will possibly be misinterpreted as a slap at the training agencies, this is unintended by the authors. Those groups are consistently improving diver education and training in general, but the "sacred cow" of restricted deep diving "standards" needs review in light of known widespread disregard of current depth limits.

How then do we classify these "non-recreational" divers? Egstrom and Bachrach call them "working" divers but recently a new term has come into almost generic use: "technical" or "high-tech" diving. This seems to get a better grip on the activities of cave divers, wreck divers and tropical drop-off wall divers. All are usually operating beyond sport depths, most are conducting decompression dives regularly and all are producing and using equipment that you will not find on your typical Grand Cayman flat-top tour boat.

Michael Menduno, editor of *AquaCorps* journal, is generally credited with introducing the term "technical diver" to our lexicon and his publication has been responsible for providing a responsible public forum for emerging technologies and field practices. Along with the birth of *AquaCorps*, a new era of specialized "high tech" training centers for advanced divers has been born.

From *AquaCorps*' winter 1991 issue on deep diving: "The question today is not whether 130 fsw should be exceeded. It clearly is already by those willing to accept the risks. Rather the issue is how these dives should be responsibly conducted given the methods and technology at our disposal, particularly at the outside of our envelope. The sport diving community is at... a crossroad. As explained by Dr. R. W. Hamilton, a pioneer who has made significant contributions to commercial diving and now is working with the fledgling technical community, 'In many ways we are re-inventing the wheel. But it's a different wheel.' He wasn't referring to PADI's".

OK, at least we have now defined the playing field and the participants. But, as we'll see, they are not all wearing the same uniforms.

About This Book

"I've always felt at peace with the sea. Even the endless crashing of the waves and the relentless fury of oceanic swells instill in me an inner feeling of calm and determined harmony. And if upon the surface I find such solace, how intensely marvelous the depths must be. I often dream of diving deep with the great leviathans and experiencing their world of sound and liquid darkness."

John David Roberts

Writing a book about deep diving and all the various particulars that accompany it is a difficult task in itself. But combine that with the coordinated efforts (or at least that's what we called it) of four authors, two on one coast of the United States and two on the opposite coast, and the difficult task quickly turns into a monumental project. So be it. Monumental or not, the fruits of that project you now have in front of you, printed and bound - *DEEP DIVING: An Advanced Guide to Physiology, Procedures and Systems.*

The text was conceived and written with advanced divers in mind. That's all well and good, but what exactly does advanced mean? We, the authors, define advanced as a minimum of 125 dives in myriad environments, under various conditions. Now, if you're thumbing through your logbook and counting up the number of dives, etc., be advised that 125 is not by any means a magic number. In fact, 125 dives in and of itself does not a deep diver make. The reader is cautioned and advised to seek proper evaluation from a professional in the deep diving community before attempting any dives over the accepted sport diving limits. The same rings true for staged decompression diving - seek professional training and education first. (See Reference Materials for information about professional training agencies.)

As you work your way through this volume note that the chapters are arranged in a particular order. This arrangement covers one facet (per chapter) of deep diving at a time and is structured so that the proceeding chapter will take-up (in an informational fashion) where the other chapter left off. The book has also been written so that if the reader should desire information about a particular subject, oxygen toxicity for example, they can turn to the respective chapter and procure the necessary information.

Keep in mind that this is a book about deep air diving and not mixed gas per se. However, a chapter on NITROX and a chapter on mixed gas have been included for informational purposes. Additionally, we have included an extensive glossary with over one hundred relevant terms and, as eluded to above, a section entitled Reference Materials that includes information about books, periodicals and deep diving training facilities.

At the risk of being redundant, the authors would like to reiterate the fact that this work is not to be used as a training manual (in lieu of experience and training) for deep divers. Anyone who desires to become involved in deep diving should first honestly evaluate their skills, experience and level of training and education. With this in mind, we sincerely hope that *DEEP DIVING: An Advanced Guide to Physiology, Procedures and Systems* will serve as an educated reference to the diving community.

Chapter 1

History of Deep Diving

"Naturally, like any explorer,
I have been asked what I intended to find,
and whether it made any sense to take unavoidable risks...
I did not expect to find pirate's gold in brass bound boxes.
It's more the feeling of adventure,
the great feeling of putting your foot
where no other has been before."
Dr. George Benjamin

"Once a man has been bitten by the diving bug, he's done for.
For there's nothing that can be done against this mania, either
by fair means or foul. No nook or cranny seems safe from
manfish, no cleft, no cave too deep or too dark. He seems to have
a close affinity with the members of the mountaineering
fraternity. The latter also risk their lives for an experience of a
special kind... For them too, it is not really the rock face or the
mountain that has to be overcome, but their own selves."
Hans Hass

THE RECORD HOLDERS

It's April 5th, 1988 in Tamaulipas, Mexico and even though it's a bright, hot, sunny day Sheck Exley is cold and alone in the dark. Oh yeah, he's also nearly 760 feet deep in Nacimiento del Rio Mante cave system in pursuit of the deepest dive ever accomplished by an independent, untethered, surface to surface diver. Right now he's got a little problem: over 100 feet

17

deeper than a free-swimming diver has ever been and almost 450 feet deeper than his nearest alternate gas source (cylinders staged at 320 fsw), he has paused to check his pressure gauge that monitors the TRIMIX (He / N_2 / O_2) tanks on his back.

Even on mixed gas, there are traces of narcosis at this depth. The small percentage of nitrogen in his mixture has produced a partial pressure this deep equivalent to approximately 260 fsw on compressed air. He has been fighting an upflowing current for over twenty minutes on his descent and time has become a factor. "As I entered the unexplored cave zone, I was concerned about the slower than expected rate of descent. I forced myself not to pick up the pace. Instead of continuing its vertical drop, the crevice began to narrow and run at a 60-degree angle. Flashes of narcosis were becoming more prominent. I glanced at my pressure gauge; the reading hadn't changed since my last check. I banged the unit on the tank. The needle jumped a few hundred pounds lower. Pressure had forced the lens against the needle, but had it stuck again? I had no way of knowing. A projection to tie off on was just below. I passed it and dropped deeper. The tunnel began to flatten out, falling at a 45-degree angle. I looked at the pressure gauge; it showed a third of the gas was gone. Was the reading correct? I had been down just over 22 minutes. It was time to get out."

"My light beam fell on an excellent tie-off 20 or 30 feet down. I took a breath and moved toward the projection, when suddenly a jolting concussion nearly knocked me unconscious. I tried to look behind me for a ruptured valve or hose. There was no leak. Something had imploded from the pressure, but what? I drew another breath and kicked the last eight feet to the tie-off. Quickly I threw two half hitches around the rock, reeled in the loose line and made the cut. My down time was 24 minutes, 10 seconds."

Suspended at 780 feet, Exley has shattered the old mixed gas depth record (set by Germany's Jochen Hasenmayer) by 124 feet. But the surface was still a long way up and the implosion shock was numbing.

"I wanted to move fast from the deep water, 120 feet a minute if possible. The current that I had battled during my descent helped to lift me up the incline. I drew a breath and felt a slight hesitation from the regulator. The next breath came harder. Was I out of air? Again, I hit the gauge on my tank but this time the reading didn't change. If I was forced to use the gas in my belly tank, I would miss all the decompression to 330 feet where my first stage bottle was tied off. I switched over to my back-up regulator and with relief drew a full breath."

Proceeding steadily upward in the chasm, he reaches 520 feet and retrieves his conventional depth gauges where he has tied them off. Beyond this depth he has had to calculate depth by means of a knotted line since no gauges had yet been made to handle such pressure.

"At 520 feet, it was strange to be decompressing at such a depth. I knew that only one person had ever gone deeper. I remained a minute and then began to ascend at the rate of ten feet a minute until I reached 340 feet. When I saw my first stage bottle and knew that I had spare gas around me, I finally began to relax. My stress was gone, but the long decompression stops were only beginning."

For 22 minutes bottom time, he would pay a decompression obligation of nearly ten and half hours followed by thirty minutes breathing pure oxygen at the surface.

"Now with the extra time, I began to search for the cause of the deafening implosion. The source was the large plexiglass battery housing for my primary light. The pressure had been so great that the three-quarter inch lid was forced into the casing crushing the battery pack. Amazingly, the light still functioned."

Sheck completed his decompression uneventfully and surfaced at 9:30 PM wrinkled and exhausted. Hours later, support diver Ned DeLoach broached the inevitable question:

"Will you ever do it again?"

Exley paused and considered his answer, "I don't know."

Only days before his 40th birthday and almost exactly a year later on March 28, 1989, Sheck Exley eclipses his own world record in the same cave reaching 881 feet!

There is good reason that he is considered to be one of the finest scuba divers of all time. But what makes his accomplishments all the more compelling is that he has devoted virtually his entire career to the most challenging diving environment of all: deep caves. A veteran of over 3000 cave dives, Exley is the undisputed king of the hill. But he remains an almost reluctant hero, virtually unknown until recently outside of the cave

Sheck Exley returns from his record dive in Mante to resume a lengthy decompression and retrieve stage decompression cylinders.

photo by Ned DeLoach

and "high tech" communities. In addition to the mixed gas record of 881 feet, he holds the record for longest swimming penetration into a cave: a 10,444 foot push into Chip's Hole, a sinkhole in Tallahassee, Florida. He also set the record for longest scooter/DPV penetration at Cathedral Canyon at 10,939 feet, a distance of over two miles!

Sheck is also a prolific writer with over 100 articles and six books to his credit. He has been honored as a Fellow of the National Speleological Society and was a recipient of the prestigious Lew Bicking Award as America's top cave explorer. Even so, "experts" gave him only 50/50 odds at best to survive the 780 foot dive. His custom TRIMIX tables were totally experimental having been developed by decompression physiology pioneer R.W. "Bill" Hamilton. The computerized tables called for Exley to stage sixteen bottles and then carry four tanks with him for the final drop. Eleven different blends of TRIMIX were used with 52 decompression stops. The following year on the 881 attempt, the skeptics were less vocal. That required 34 stage bottles and thirteen and half hours of decompression. It's strictly limited participation at this level of diving, Sheck essentially can compete only with himself.

Although the mixed gas record changed hands almost annually for a while until Exley made it a one-man-show, the depth record on compressed air set by Neil Watson and John Gruener in 1968 seemed destined to hold up forever.

Both men trained intensely for a year prior to their record dive to 437 feet in the Bahamas. With the benefit of an almost 25 year perspective, their accomplishment is nothing short of phenomenal. Lacking the equipment advantages of high performance regulators and modern buoyancy compensators with power inflators, Watson and Gruener operated against incredible performance deficits. And the attempts of other record seekers offered a hodge-podge of success and tragedy.

photo by Mary Ellen Eckhoff

Sheck Exley donning thermal underwear and dry suit before record dive in Mante cave in Mexico, 1988.

Frederic Dumas, a colleague of Jacques Cousteau, established one of the earliest credible compressed air diving records in 1947 by reaching 307 feet but reported severe narcosis. Four years later, Miami lawyer Hope Root set out to attain 400 feet in the clear blue water of the Gulf Stream. At 52 years of age and with little practical experience in working up to such a great depth, his attempt seems particularly ill-advised.

Hans Hass speaks of Root's quest, "Many menfish, like men on land, have, so to speak, a screw loose. They are daredeviltry personified. But even so, they cannot be described as brave, since courage is the conscious mastery of a fear, quite naturally correlated with danger. Into this category must be placed Hope Root."

The dive plan was for him to enter the water wearing doubles and descend beneath a boat drifting in the current. No descent line was used, so the boat would track his progress and record his depth with an echo sounder (similar to sonar).

A band of local press and representatives from *LIFE* magazine were all present to witness the record. Several underwater photographers joined Root in the water including veteran Jerry Greenberg. Around 70 feet Root paused in the water column and looked back up to the surface perhaps considering his fate. He then began swimming down into the bottomless Gulf Stream canyon. Greenberg followed him below 100 feet and continued snapping photos including a haunting portrait of Root drifting away in clouds of bubbles from his double hose regulator. As he passed the 300 foot level, Greenberg lost sight of him forever.

Meanwhile on the boat, the depth finder etched Root's progress and wild applause broke out as he passed the old record at 330 feet. Continuing his dive to destiny, he paused for almost two minutes at 430 feet (recorded on the echo sounder as a horizontal line at that depth). Then to the amazement of the onlookers, Root dropped another ten fathoms to 490 feet. Hesitating only briefly now, he dived to 500 and on to 650 feet before the echo sounder went out of range. Silence settled on the boat as the horrified witnesses realized that Hope Root would not be coming back. His body was never found.

In 1959, Ennio Falco of Italy reportedly reached an approximate depth of 435 feet but had no means to record it. In a subsequent dive to a lesser depth he drowned during decompression.

In the early 1960's, Jean Clarke Samazen declared, "All sports must have a champion. I want to be the champion of scuba diving." Wearing the ultimate in a cylinder package for his day, he utilized doubles on his back and his chest to reach 350 fsw. The rig was awkward, at best, but provided incredible air volume! An early *Skin Diver* Magazine account described him as "looking like a large sandwich." Hal Watts, who is still teaching advanced deep diving today, beat Samazen's record to 355 fsw.

Tom Mount and Frank Martz, two of the United States' cave diving pioneers, experimented with several 325 feet plus dives in the early sixties eventually setting a new compressed air mark for depth at 360 fsw in 1965. Hal Watts and A. J Muns posted a new official record in 1967 attaining 390 feet. One year later Watson and Gruener were poised on their historical threshold. They knew that narcosis and oxygen toxicity had claimed many of their forerunners. Both men were students of Watts and by 1968, they had discovered the value of "adaptive" dives to reduce these effects. They would descend together down a weighted cable and attach clips to it to certify the depth. Although they reached 437 feet, a new world record, both were so affected by narcosis that they could not recall even clipping on to the cable. When asked what it was like on air at 437 feet, Neil Watson replied, "I don't remember".

One of the last serious assaults to the Watson/Gruener record was planned in 1971 by the well experienced team of Archie Forfar, Anne Gunderson and Jim Lockwood. Sheck Exley, then 22 years old, was

Hal Watts and A. J. Muns after their record dive to 390 feet in 1967.

brought in as a support diver. Lockwood set up a regimen of progressively deeper dives for training purposes near the Andros drop-off walls. Although, the youngest member of the dive team at 21 (Forfar was 38 and Gunderson was 23), Lockwood had the most deep diving experience with numerous dives to 400 fsw and deeper. (In 1991, barring the sudden emergence of a credible challenger, he still remains the record holder for most dives below 400 fsw with almost 150 totaled in his career.)

Lockwood was visiting Tom Mount in pursuit of exploring the virgin "Blue Holes" in that area of the Bahamas when he was introduced to Archie and Ann. They had been making dives in the 380-400 fsw range and a discussion was initiated into the possibility of breaking the Watson/Gruener record. It was decided that they would work together and attempt 480 fsw. During the work-up dives, they made 40 dives below 400 fsw including 25 approaching 450 fsw (as measured by SCUBAPRO's helium depth gauge). They experienced no significant difficulties of impairment during the practice dives and on December 11, 1971 considered themselves ready for the official record attempt.

Forfar had decided to use a weighted cable similar to Watson and Gruener for descent and a "traveler" clip system that would slide down with the divers to record their maximum depth. In 1990, Exley provided this retrospective:

"For this attempt, Archie had designed an ingenious but simple system of drop-way weights to insure their survival. When losing consciousness from narcosis most divers will retain their regulator and continue breathing. All the dive team members had to do was to make sure that their BC's were fully inflated during the descent and hook some weights behind their knees. These would automatically drop away when the legs were straightened if a black-out happened and the diver would float up where I could recover him."

However, on the day of the record attempt things went awry. It was discovered that the clips for the cable would not slide freely. Lockwood discussed the events of that day nearly 20 years later:

"We had an engine block attached as the deadweight on the end of the 480 ft. cable but we had never unspooled the cable prior to the dive. When we did at the dive site we found it had a tendency to bend and sort of 'hockle' and wouldn't hang straight and true. The dive plan had to be changed."

Forfar and Gunderson elected to abandon the fall-away weight system and make the drop with empty BC's. Lockwood stayed with the original system and would descend with his BC inflated.

Lockwood relates, *"I still wanted to use the positive buoyancy safety factor in conjunction with the weighted bar but Archie and Ann had their own ideas and decided not to. Almost immediately into the descent I realized that I was in trouble. The cable was oily and greasy and I got the stuff on my hands. This made it almost impossible for me to get any grip on the inflator valve for the pony bottle that fed air into my BC. I was dropping like crazy because of the weight behind my legs and I could not get anything into my vest to counteract this excessive negative buoyancy. My descent rate was probably in excess of 200 feet per minute. I remember thinking that Archie and Ann were not keeping up with me and I was frantically trying to wipe off my oily hands on my wet suit. This was requiring considerable energy and a lot of stress and eventually at some point I passed out."*

Exley, in his role as safety diver hovering at 300 feet, became witness to the ultimate deep diving nightmare. Somewhere in the depths, Forfar and Gunderson lost control. Lockwood lost consciousness below 400 feet and floated up to Exley who verified that he was okay and then made a heroic attempt to locate the two deeper divers. He descended well below 400 feet in his desperate attempt to save his friends but was unable to rescue them. They were not recovered.

The safety divers had agreed not to go beyond 300 fsw but when it became apparent that Archie and Ann could not come back on their own, each made a personal decision to attempt the rescue. Bill Wiggins and Randy Hylton made a simultaneous effort but were severely impaired by narcosis at 360 fsw and nearly 400 fsw respectively. Exley was left alone and remembers:

"The horror was even worse. From 400 feet on down, I could see Archie and Ann still breathing on the steeply sloping wall. Archie had his head down against the engine block and was still slowly kicking as if he were going down the cable, and Ann was lying on her back about 10 feet off to one side. I started to get severe tunnel vision and it was all I could do just to be able to survive at that depth. The last distance to Archie might as well have been a mile."

Lockwood speculates, "I know I never got that inflator valve open and I think it's possible that I ran into the engine block when I bottomed out the cable. Archie probably was OK at that point but expended so much energy trying to inflate my BC that he succumbed to narcosis himself. Ann would never have left Archie so that would account for their double accident. I was out of it so I don't know what happened, but I have no recollection of anything after about the 400 ft. level and I doubt if I ever got any air in my vest. Archie probably saved my life. I don't even remember floating up to Sheck although he says I gave him the OK sign at that point. I really didn't come around until about the 50 ft. decompression stop."

Two decades later, professional diver Bret Gilliam is preparing to break Watson and Gruener's record which remains intact. All challengers to that record have died trying except Lockwood. Gilliam is unperturbed. He has devoted almost a year of adaptive diving and extensive research in physiological effects of depth on humans and other mammals. His work has included over 600 dives in the previous 11 months with 103 dives below 300 feet. He also has made use of recompression chamber dives to experiment with varying high partial pressures of oxygen to simulate conditions below 400 feet.

Like Exley, Gilliam has been professionally involved with deep diving projects for over twenty years. Since 1958, he has logged in excess of 12,000 dives around the world. Over 2000 of those have been below 300 feet. For 15 years he owned one of the Caribbean's most successful dive operations before selling out in 1985 to spend three years cruising and diving on his 68 foot motor yacht while doing diving and marine engineering consulting projects through his company Ocean Tech. Now (in 1989-90) he is under contract to Ocean Quest International as a corporate executive and Director of Diving Operations for their 487 foot dive/cruise ship. It's the largest sport diving program in the world.

From the outset, he set that ship up to support his "high tech" diving interests and launched a carefully conceived one year project to see if the compressed air record could be targeted with an acceptable assumption of risk.

photo by Lynn Hendrickson

Bret Gilliam prior to "warm-up dive" in adaptive preparation to 452 feet, February, 1990.

"In the beginning, I wasn't even concerned with a record dive. I did not even remember what the record was. Later as I got nearer to it, I went back and looked it up and found that I was getting very close and that kind of jogged my interest. But I was really just getting sick and tired of listening to supposed experts make sweeping statements about deep diving that were so totally inaccurate that I finally just decided to see what I could do; more to disprove the misinformation that was postulated than to prove anything. Hell, at this point, NOAA had Gary Gentile tied up in Federal Court fighting an injunction prohibiting his access and right to dive the Monitor wreck. They had omnipotently informed him that 230 feet was too deep to be dived safely. Here they are

*telling one of America's best deep divers that he can't make what for him
was a routine dive. What a crock!"*

At the time, Gilliam was sponsoring an Ocean Tech study of dive
computers and testing several of the models to their limits with frequent
300 foot plus dives weekly. The ship's on board recompression chamber
facility provided an ideal lab for several experimental dives. By January
1990, he decided that his adaptive level and physical training was sufficient
for a major attempt at depth. A chance meeting with custom table producer
Randy Bohrer provided the basis for air tables to 500 feet.

*"The tables process was involved and required extensive field work.
Randy would cut a table with his recommendations and send it off to me on
the ship. It might take three weeks for me to get it and try it out. He leaned
to a more conservative model and I kept modifying it based upon some
work I had done with the Navy on exceptional exposure proprietary tables
under development back in the early seventies in the Virgin Islands for an
ASW (anti-submarine warfare) project. Most of our work was conducted
observing hydrophones and submarines in the deep canyons between St.
Croix and St. Thomas. This required pushing the 400 ft. plus barrier on
several occasions We had a lot of problems with sharks during
decompression in the open ocean and experimented with all kinds of
theoretical models to shorten our hang times."*

After five months of fiddling with Bohrer's successive offerings,
Gilliam had dramatically altered the decompression schedules to minimal
times with a margin for safety:

*"But we were completely breaking new ground; no one had ever field-
validated air tables to these depths. I felt confident that we were on the
right track and I was having no problems with the extreme profiles I was
running. But it was nice to know that I had the chamber right on-site.
Without that security, I doubt if I would ever have done diving this deep so
aggressively."*

In addition to various instructor affiliations, Gilliam is a licensed
USCG Merchant Marine Master and recompression chamber supervisor.
He directs all treatment protocols and therapy for ship divers and occasional locals who get DCS hits. He has no intention of requiring his own
services.

*"This type of diving is a mental exercise. You have to understand the
physiology and mechanisms of narcosis and oxygen toxicity to survive.
Many academicians dismiss deep diving as suicidal with very little real-
dive experience to justify their arguments. I have an overwhelming respect
for the risks involved and seek to provide every edge I can get through
education and planning. Prolonged facial immersion breathing to institute
the diving reflex and other little tricks are all vital pieces of the equation to
minimize CO_2 in the narcosis and O_2 tox responses."*

He will make his descent at 100 feet per minute only slightly over-weighted. Ten minutes are spent on the surface prior to the dive with his face in the water breathing through a snorkel and then five minutes more with no mask breathing from a spare tank at 15 feet below the boat. Surfacing only long enough to dry off his face, he begins the descent. His heart rate and respiration will drop significantly on the dive. 12 to 15 beats a minute with deep slow ventilations of one to two per minute are typical.

The dive site selected is known as Mary's Place in Roatan. He has picked this spot due because of its near vertical wall configuration offering immediate access to abyssal drop-off depths. The day is Wednesday, February 14, 1990; eleven days after Gilliam's 39th birthday. Visibility is 100 feet at the surface depths and over 200 feet in the deep zone, water temperature is 81 degrees and no current. Conditions are ideal.

Only a handful of staff are aware of the upcoming dive. Just before he enters the water, one safety diver asks if he can borrow Gilliam's gold Rolex watch until he comes back. Another asks for his TV and stereo; a third wants his spacious senior officer's stateroom on the ship. The local Roatan deckhand wants his girlfriend. Gilliam keeps the watch.

His gear is kept to a minimum. A single cylinder pressurized to approximately 100 cubic feet with a high performance regulator attached with DIN fittings. A back-up second stage and two pressure gauge consoles with helium depth gauges calibrated to 500 feet are plumbed into the regulator first stage. Three dive computers with a Casio watch are attached to one console. He discovered by accident that the Beuchat computer will accurately read depth digitally to at least 500 feet. He finds digital gauges far easier to read under the influence of narcosis. The computers will not provide any valid decompression information but their depth gauges and timing instruments will hopefully survive the pressure.

Slipping over the wall, he reaches 300 feet in just under three minutes. His descent picks up slightly now and one computer "locks up" in error mode at 320 feet. A large remora fish that has followed him since the 150 foot level is becoming distracting:

> "Here I am at 300 plus feet dropping like a stone with every nerve and impulse in my body going through a self-check a million times a minute for any warning sign of severe narcosis impairment or O_2 tox, and now I've got some damn friendly fish wanting to play with me! It kept swimming in and out of vision and my eyes didn't want to focus on my instruments and the fish simultaneously. I almost had to abort but it finally moved down towards my thigh and out of my vision path so I decided to ignore it. "

Approaching 425 feet he begins to inflate his BC while timing his inhalations so the regulator would only have one volume demand on it at a time. He drops an eight pound weight belt and it disappears. Because his computers are calibrated in feet of fresh water he has prepared a 3% conversion table so he knows exactly where to stop; in large bold instructions on a slate is written: 464 FT: STOP! He hangs motionless perfectly suspended about five feet from the wall; four minutes and 41 seconds have elapsed since leaving the surface.

There is plenty of ambient light even this deep. He retrieves a slate with ten problems involving math, simple word problems, daily event questions etc. (i.e.: what day is it? what time is it? 3 X 10 X 22 = ? ...) It takes one minute and 40 seconds to work the problems; he has not seen them before and it takes longer to finish than he expected. He slips slightly deeper by two feet and the computer will record 466 feet as the maximum depth. Later, all agree that 452 feet of seawater is a reasonable conversion; a new world record on compressed air by 25 feet.

Six minutes and 20 seconds have ticked off, time's up. Ascent commences at just over 100 feet per minute and he slows to 60 ft./min. at a depth of 100 fsw. The first decompression stop is at 50 feet. One hour and sixteen minutes later he surfaces and breathes pure oxygen at the surface for twenty minutes via demand mask. Although some handwriting flaws are apparent, all the test questions are answered correctly. "I've got lousy handwriting anyway," he replies defensively with a laugh.

"Narcosis is there but not to a level that I was uncomfortable with. Impairment is specific to individuals. O_2 tox is the real unknown; that scares me but I had no problems at all. I planned this dive to preclude virtually all exertions. Perhaps I'm an exception to nature but I suspect my conditioning through long term experience and adaptation due to diving constantly in deep situations plays a far greater role. Calculated risk is the operative phrase here. What is attainable for me is possible because of my commitment to detail and training and total discipline during the actual dive process. I also had a positive mental attitude; I knew I could do it."

Gilliam's plans called for an attempt to 500 feet later but he postponed that after leaving the Ocean Quest contract to pursue other business interests.

"I think that 500 feet would have been possible for me if I had followed closely on the heels of the 452 foot dive. But when I came off the ship, I was away from deep diving for a while and felt that I had lost the adaptive edge I had acquired. And I wanted a chamber overhead. In the right circumstances, I might try it if I had the time to work up to it again. If you could do the drop in five minutes I think you could handle the O_2 exposure. Who knows? No one believed that 450 feet was possible."

Exley and Gilliam conducted record setting dives that were vastly different in many ways but with one common denominator: Both elected

Gilliam's slate taken to 452 feet to remind him that his depth gauge was calibrated in "feet of fresh water" and that he should stop when his depth gauge read 464 feet. He added his sentiments upon reaching the new record depth.

photo by Bret Gilliam

to dive alone, regarding the presence of another diver as a potential liability. And both showed a single-minded intensity of preparation that was unprecedented.

Some critics will pontificate that such dives are reckless, crazy, without purpose... but man's competitive motivation is best exemplified in such individuals. Life is full of challenges: Chuck Yeager breaking the sound barrier to "push the outside of the envelope", Sir Edmund Hillary climbing Mt. Everest "because it's there", and now Sheck Exley and Bret Gilliam diving deliberately to bottomless depths "because it's not there!"

The point of any human performance record is individual and reduced to its simplest form: Doing what others cannot do. And that has to be a personal decision. Dangerous? Yes, extremely so. But the personal risk to these individuals was acceptable to them and their success a triumph. Neither Exley or Gilliam advocate such extreme diving for others. Will those records ever be beaten? Both men think so.

MILESTONES IN TRANSITION

The evolution of deep diving in practice has undergone several distinct generations of popular view and perception. Initial deep diving experimentation by naval divers and early explorers such as Cousteau were linked to a common enough interest: a certain fascination with the unknown. Navy divers needed access to deeper depths for tactical operative purposes and scientist/explorers sought entry to deep water zones for research and documentary applications. There was no stigma applied to deep diving per se; in fact, the element of danger and bravado summoned to challenge the unexplored abyss was greeted with a certain appreciative respect for these fledgling "aquanauts".

The initial penetrations to progressively deeper depths by free-swimming scuba divers quickly showed the severe limitations of these divers due to narcosis impairment. Early accounts by Cousteau and other team members relate romantic anecdotal accounts of narcosis so limiting as to preclude diving much below 150 feet. An examination of their methodology in deep diving sheds sufficient light to reveal serious flaws in dive planning that would never be tolerated by today's standards. But hindsight, of course, has the benefit of 20/20 vision in all circumstances. Dumas, Falco and Cousteau himself none the less continued with deep diving experiments in spite of several tragic deaths to associates.

It would be interesting to note at this point how the sport diving industry came to accept certain "axioms" about diving practice with little awareness of the true process of evolution that came to dictate some of our current "sacred cows". Most recreational diving instructors have all been schooled to accept the Navy recommendation of 60 foot per minute ascent rates and that the Navy tables were "holy writ". Only in recent years has closer examination shown the benefits of slower ascents that are now almost universally advocated. How then did the 60 ft./min. rate come into being? Like so many things that we would like to believe resulted from years of research by learned physiologists in nice white lab coats while surrounded by reams of theoretical and field testing data, the ascent rate was derived by a process a little less complex.

In a workshop meeting in the fifties, a group of various delegates from the Navy met to standardize certain practices for Navy divers. One item of heated discussion centered on ascent rates. The scuba diving faction wanted a 100 ft./min. rate; but the hard hat diver faction subscribed to a 25 ft./min. rate. Actually, to be more accurate the tenders for the hard hat divers wanted the slower rate and for good reason: they were responsible for winching these exceedingly heavy monsters on their stages back aboard ships or diving platforms. Many dive operations of this era still used manual winches to recover divers and the exertion required in such a hoist was considerable. Why do you think Popeye had such well developed forearms? At any rate, it was abundantly clear that the hard hat divers could not be winched aboard at anything close to 100 feet per minute, so a compromise was reached by all parties at 60 feet per minute and it was blindly adhered to by all who followed for over thirty years.

Then there is the supposed depth limit of 130 feet for scuba diving. At a recent international conference on diving safety held in 1991, representatives of the national scuba certification agencies were queried on the basis for the 130 foot rule. Although most admitted that they did not know its origin, all held true to the precept that it was a Navy recommendation and therefore it must be right.

Once again, the Navy reference was subjected to misinterpretation by well-meaning educators. In actual practice the Navy had found that it was not productive to assign a diver to a task deeper that 130 feet since he would have an allowable bottom time of only 10 minutes; scarcely enough time to evaluate an assignment and accomplish any useful work. If he was to do a job effectively this deep it was more efficient to equip him with a surface supplied gas source so he could complete the project and then manage his decompression. Somehow along the way, the sport diving industry misapplied the Navy's proprietary working diver recommendation into a sweeping condemnation of any diving below 130 feet. This has come back to haunt the certification agencies in two ways: 1) Since the depth "limit" is almost universally ignored by all but entry level divers, a significant segment of the sport diving population has been effectively forced into "outlaw" diving profiles and consistently deny deep diving thus distorting actual diving trends and statistics, 2) Increasingly more diving personal injury and wrongful death lawsuits are litigated on arguments of negligence based solely on the depth of the dive exceeding the "safe" limit of 130 feet.

THE ANDREA DORIA EXPEDITIONS

Deep diving has been practiced outside the traditional commercial and Navy communities for almost forty years. In 1956, Peter Gimble called a *LIFE* magazine editor to see if they would be interested in underwater photos of the ocean liner *Andrea Doria* which sunk off Nantucket Shoals following a collision with another ship only the day before. Assured that *LIFE* would purchase any such photos that Gimble could produce, he and Joseph Fox hired a plane and flew to Nantucket where, after considerable difficulty, they were able to charter a local boat to go out to the wreck site.

The wreck was a massive ship, 700 feet in length and displacing almost 30,000 tons. She settled on her starboard side in approximately 250 feet of water. This afforded access to her port side beginning in 160 feet. Gimble used the standard of equipment of his day: double tanks and a double hose regulator with no cylinder pressure gauges. Rubber suits over woolen underwear served as thermal protection in the cool northeast water. Less than 24 hours after her fatal plunge, the ship was still gleaming white as the two divers dropped onto her port rail. Gimble began working with a housed 35 mm Leica camera and had fired off only eight frames before Fox suffered dramatic incapacitation from carbon dioxide build-up. Reacting to his signal, Gimble abandoned his photography efforts and assisted his stricken buddy to the surface where he swiftly recovered. His dive had not been in vain however; the black and white Tri-X film pushed to 1000 ASA by the lab yielded usable shots and Gimble had his exclusive with *LIFE*. Thus was born a lifelong passion for him with the *Doria*.

Gimble would return to the site repeatedly over the years. At the age of 52 in 1981 he mounted an expedition to recover the Bank of Rome safe from the First Class foyer. With 33 days on site, and use of both scuba and saturation divers he successfully recovered the prize. After depositing the safe for dramatic effect in the shark tank of the New York Aquarium it remained for three years. On August 16, 1984 the safe was finally opened before an expectant international television audience. Much speculation had centered on the safe's contents. Would it contain the riches in personal valuables, jewelry and gold that had fueled rumors for twenty five years? Gimble's worst nightmare was that it might simply be empty. But as the door swung open finally, the safe revealed a mother lode of U.S. and Italian currency still neatly bundled in rubber bands. Although no gold bars were found, Gimble's monetary haul had considerable souvenir value. The thousands of bills, each etched by the sea's destructive influence, were marketed encased in plastic mounts with certificates of authenticity. The proceeds would not cover the 1.5 million dollar expedition cost but to Gimble the reward was adequate. He had accomplished what scores of others had attempted in vain. He died three years later.

The fascination with the *Doria* has tempted divers since her sinking. Numerous books and films have been devoted to the subject. (Readers are encouraged to obtain Gary Gentile's fascinating *Andrea Doria – Dive To an Era* available from Gary Gentile Productions, Box 57137, Philadelphia, PA 19111.)

In 1964, the team of George Merchant, John Grich, Paul Heckart and Dennis Morse accomplished what author Gentile describes as "one of the most incredible feats of underwater salvage ever accomplished on scuba. Their goal was to recover the life-sized bronze statue of Admiral Andrea Doria from his stance in the First Class Lounge." Dan Turner, captain of their salvage vessel *Top Cat*, carefully planned out the project while intensely studying the *Doria*'s blueprints. He wanted to enter the hull via the Promenade Deck to gain access from directly above the alcove encircling the statue. The divers made judicious use of explosives to blast away the glass weather shielding and metal framework to penetrate the interior. Careful to remove the blasted wreckage at each stage of the salvage so as to not damage the statue, they eventually established an entrance opening almost eight feet wide and five feet high.

At 210 feet, they found Admiral Doria still holding court to the silent ship. They rigged slings to prevent the statue from falling and then commenced on the laborious job of hack-sawing by hand through the legs of the old boy to free him from his pedestal. The four man dive team worked in shifts on compressed air for several days incurring then unheard of decompression by divers in the open ocean. At one point, the team exhausted their supply of hacksaw blades from the back-breaking work and operations had to be suspended while *Top Cat* steamed over to the Nantucket Lightship to beg replacements. Thus re-supplied the cycle of diver rotation began anew and finally Admiral Doria was freed from his premature watery tomb. Only his feet remained behind.

Weather conditions had so deteriorated by this time that Turner elected to retrieve his dive team without in-water decompression and use the ship's chamber for surface decompression. In spite of the heaving seas, the statue was winched aboard unharmed and eventually found a home in the Sea Garden Hotel in Pompano Beach, Florida. One of the expedition investors, Glenn Garvin, had recently purchased the property and had a special platform built for the bronze relic to preside over a magnificent banquet room seating four hundred people. It was appropriately named the Andrea Doria Room. The Admiral seems happy in his current residence and his amputated feet still adorn the original pedestal 210 feet deep on the wreck.

Four years later, Italian film producer/director Bruno Vailati arrived on the scene to shoot the classic *Fate of the Andrea Doria* with a crew including a young Al Giddings employed as a still photographer and backup movie cameraman. This was the last film team to observe the magnificent navigational bridge which collapsed into the sand shortly thereafter. Vailati's production featured panoramic footage of the entire wreck for the first time and chronicled the reclaiming of the ship by the ocean's inhabitants. Gentile quotes Giddings' relation of that experience in his book, "She is a city once again, more populated now by ten thousand times than during her brief life as a great ocean liner. Sea anemones grow from her rails by the scores, and huge schools of fish of every type swim down her teak decked passageways."

The first serious interest in the wreck by sport divers was organized by Michael de Camp during the summer of 1966. He and a group of other dedicated adventurers shared the cost of chartering the *Viking Starlight* for the inaugural assault on the *Doria*. One year later, northeast deep diving pioneer John Dudas entered the bridge station and recovered the binnacle

photo by Gary Gentile

Tom Packer discovers the bell of the Andrea Doria in 1985. The dive team of Packer, Gary Gentile, Art Kirchner, Mike Boring, Kenny Gascon, Bill Nagle, and John Moyer aboard the dive boat Seeker salvaged the bell after 29 years of entombment and countless searches for the prized artifact.

cover and ship's magnetic compass. History was set the same trip when Evelyn Bartram became the first woman to dive the *Doria*. She would become Dudas' wife shortly in the future.

The *Doria* seemed to inspire creativity in would-be salvors and in 1968 the first saturation expedition was mounted by Alan Krasberg and Nick Zinkowski. Their motivation, as usual, was capture of the fabled chief purser's safe and its valued contents. By use of an underwater habitat, divers could go into saturation and continue working on the wreck virtually indefinitely with one large decompression schedule assumed when the job was completed. This was not a new concept but this application for "treasure salvage" was. The habitat itself was decidedly new; christened the *Early Bird*, it was constructed not of steel but wood! Its builders theorized that its building material would provide more insulation and make occupancy more comfortable. Obviously comfort, like beauty, must be in the eye of the beholder since the habitat was only ten feet long and four and a half feet square. This would be the first use of HELIOX as a saturation breathing gas for wreck salvage. Partially funded by MGM, the project would serve as a theme for a documentary film.

Krasber and Zinkowski were adept at securing an international all-star cast as crew. Giddings was brought in a chief cinematographer, significantly upgrading his status from that of Vailati's filming expedition three months earlier. He enlisted as assistants Chuck Nicklin, a California dive store owner, and Jack McKenney, then an editor with *Skin Diver* Magazine. All three men would go on to fame as celebrated film makers, McKenney with his Dive to Adventure series while Giddings and Nicklin would go big-time with such Hollywood features as *The Deep* and *The Abyss*. Now however, the compensation was not much over meal money. Elgin Ciampi was engaged by *LIFE* to operate an experimental multi-camera "sled" designed by Demitri Rebikoff that would function as a photo-mapping transect. Rounding out the distinguished ensemble was breath-hold diving champion Jacques Mayol of France.

Incredibly, with all this talent, virtually every thing that could go wrong did... in spades. Weather held them at the dock until October after construction delays on *Early Bird* forced them to miss the fair summer sea conditions. Following an abortive attempt to anchor and rough conditions that almost sank the habitat, their support vessel *Atlantic Twin* gave up and headed for the shelter of Martha's Vineyard. With more settled conditions the next day they steamed back to the site but gear failure in the rigging process so hopelessly fouled the support lines to the habitat that it was recovered on board just in time for yet another storm to blow in and force them to heave-to for three straight days.

The dive and camera crew utilized mixed gas which greatly improved efficiency when they were finally able to resume operations after the storm. Oxygen decompression was employed in one its earliest applications by non-military and non-commercial divers. Following a productive day of filming, yet another setback showed up in the form of a double bends accident involving Ciampi and Mayol. Ciampi exhausted his gas supply while wrestling with a malfunctioning camera sled known as a Pegasus. He floated to the surface unconscious following an attempted free ascent and was rescued. Mayol, who was operating the other Pegasus unit, attempted to save both sleds by clipping them together but was unsuccessful and both sank. He arrived on the surface with skipped decompression and was loaded in the ship's chamber with the apparently lifeless Ciampi. Luckily, both responded to recompression therapy.

A combination of more bad weather and continued problems with rigging *Early Bird* to the wreck led to the expedition's backers finally throwing in the towel.

Not to be outdone, a new expedition was put together in 1973 by Don Rodocker and Chris DeLucchi, two ex-navy divers. They called their company Saturations Systems and intended to take up where the trouble-plagued *Early Bird* project left off. Equipped with a custom designed habitat called *Mother*, they joined the race for the *Doria's* safe whose legend now had grown to be reputedly worth over five million dollars! Bob Hollis, founder and CEO of diving manufacturer Oceanic Products, came in as a financial partner with machinist Jack Clark. McKenney returned to direct photography along with Bernie Campoli and Tim Kelly.

Mother was far more sophisticated than *Early Bird* and substantially larger. She also could be handled in a less forgiving seaway and had the capability to operate independent of surface support for up to a week if the diving ship were to be blown off the site. Once again though, the *Doria* seemed to haunt these intrepid professionals in much the same manner as their predecessors.

Initially blown off the wreck, they successfully set up their mooring a day later only to realize they were made fast to the after section of the wreck and would have to start from scratch and re-rig further forward on the main bridge wing. After the time consuming and difficult task of relocating, the habitat severed a main power umbilical with Rodocker and DeLucchi already in saturation. The decision was made to hoist *Mother* aboard and return to port for repairs. Upon reaching the dock, the saturated divers were nearly killed when the crane unloading the habitat accidentally dropped them on the pier. Against all odds, *Mother's* hatch seals held and the decompression continued without further mishap.

Finally on August 8th, a permanent mooring was established in the proper section of the wreck. But after eight days in saturation by Rodocker, DeLucchi and eventually Hollis they discovered that the sea's deterioration to the ship's interior had created an impassable mass of wreckage blocking any reasonable path to the safe. Once again, the *Doria* refused to yield her treasure.

Gimble's 1981 expedition would capitalize on the earlier work of *Mother's* team. Massive holes were cut into the hull and superstructure by Rodocker and DeLucchi; Gimble's team, armed with an even more refined habitat and support ship, leap-frogged on these penetrations to eventually reach the safe. But like a reluctant bride, the honeymoon was disappointing. Gimble spent almost two million dollars on this expedition and recovered only a fraction of his costs.

TWO WRECK DIVER PROFILES

The *Doria* remains a siren beckoning now to the most dedicated wreck divers in the country such as Gary Gentile, a veteran of over 80 dives on the ship since 1974. He has also led the battle for access to such sites as the Civil War era wreck of the *Monitor*. This ironclad steamship lies in 230 feet of water 16 miles off the coast off Cape Hatteras. Gentile was forced into a protracted legal battle with the Federal Government when NOAA decided to deny him the right to dive the historic site. Declared a National Marine Sanctuary in 1975, NOAA's argument boiled down to denying Gentile's repeated permit applications on the grounds that the depth was unsafe for sport divers. He recalls, "It's what I call bureaucratic territoriality. The people at NOAA... feel they own the wreck. They don't want

Gary Gentile, one of the U.S.'s top deep wreck divers, with the bell of the Andrea Doria.

photo by Tom Packer

private sector encroachment. They look upon it as their wreck, and they view me-the public-as a trespasser."

Eventually, Gentile prevailed when the sitting judge ruled in his favor and further found that he and others like him had been improperly classified as sport divers. Shortly after his *Monitor* dives, Gentile moved on to explore the German battleship *Ostfriesland* lying in 380 feet of water. These dives were done on mixed gas with dive buddies Ken Clayton and Pete Manchee.

Wreck divers have traditionally been at the forefront of deep diving trends and no one more so than Billy Deans of Key West, Florida. Deans became interested in diving several deep wrecks including the *Wilkes Barre*, a Navy cruiser deliberately sunk in the early seventies in 250 feet only a short run from Deans' dive shop. After initially exploring the wreck on air dives, he became enthralled with the possibilities of mixed gas and proceeded to set up one of the first and finest "high tech" training centers in the country. His facility offers state of the art TRIMIX, HELIOX, and NITROX advanced diver training and equipment outfitting. His dedication to safety and planning has earned him the reputation as one of the U.S.'s top operational supervisors. In demand as a consultant for wreck expeditions and mixed gas supplier, he has been a principal in projects on the *Andrea Doria*, *U-2513*, and the *Monitor*. The popularity of deep diving and the need for suitable training facilities has enabled his Key West Diver High Tech Training Center to show continued growth.

Deans, like so many of the technical diving community, believes there is no such thing as too much planning or too much practice. He concludes, "If you're not prepared to do it right, you shouldn't be doing it."

THE MIXED GAS PIONEERS

Paving the way for Deans and other mixed gas users today, were early experimenters such as Arne Zetterstrom and Hannes Keller who conducted some of the most daring open water dives with then theoretical gases for divers. Zetterstrom, a Swedish engineer, was fascinated with diving and sought to extend the working depths of divers by manipulating the oxygen content of a gas mixture and replacing the narcotic nitrogen with a more "workable" inert gas. Alternatives such as helium and neon were in such short supply as to be virtually unattainable in Sweden in the early 1940's so Zetterstrom focused on hydrogen as a replacement. It had favorable properties with respect to density, viscosity and narcotic potency but had the major disadvantage of forming oxy-hydrogen gas which is highly explosive if mixed with oxygen percentages in excess of 4%.

He was faced with several operational problems from the outset:
1. A 4% O_2 percentage would not support human life underwater until approaching the 100 fsw depth range.
2. Therefore a "travel" gas mix would need to be utilized to allow the diver to safely travel through the surface to 100 fsw range and back.
3. Now the curve ball... regular air as a travel mix could be used to 100 fsw and satisfy the oxygen requirements. However, if the oxygen-hydrogen mixture were to come into contact with a normoxic air mix, it would create oxy-hydrogen gas and, at least theoretically, the diver would explode. So a third mix, a transition gas mixture, would be necessary to protect the diver.

Zetterstrom decided to use one of the earliest NITROX blends as his transition mix: a 4% oxygen and 96% nitrogen mixture. This would allow a safe bridge between the O_2/H_2 "bottom mix". The diver would switch to the NITROX cylinder at 100 fsw and breathe for a period sufficient to flush out the higher O_2 percentage and then switch again to the "bottom mix". This cycle would be repeated during ascent.

It should be noted that since Zetterstrom manufactured his own hydrogen aboard ship at sea by breaking down ammonia to yield 75% H_2 and 25% N_2, his final mix was actually a TRIMIX of 4% O_2, 24% N_2 and 72% H_2. This was one of the earliest uses of TRIMIX; nitrogen in such reduced percentages was not a narcotic factor. In his experimental dives to 130 fsw he encountered no difficulties but was unpleasantly surprised to discover the highly conductive thermal properties of hydrogen and became uncomfortably cold quickly. Also, the light density of hydrogen, like helium, produced "Donald Duck" speech making voice communications with his surface tenders virtually impossible.

His second attempt would be conducted much deeper. The 300 fsw barrier was largely regarded as the limit of practical diver performance, so deliberately he would test his mixture at 360 fsw. Lowered on a wooden stage by a winch from the stern of his support ship *Belos*, he negotiated his mixture switches flawlessly and reached his planned depth where he reported "slight breathing resistance and the narcotic effect practically nil". His dive was regarded as a huge success with implications for commercial applications and for submarine rescue operations.

On August 7th, 1945, Zetterstrom planned a monumental dive to 500 fsw for the first time, far in excess of any dives successfully attained at that point by any method. Tragically, a breakdown in communications within his surface support team led to disaster.

Once again, he employed the diving stage to control his descent and ascent with prearranged signals and time allotments for his mixture switches and bottom time. All went well on the descent and he reached 500 fsw without mishap. He signaled the surface that he was well and the ascent phase was initiated in accordance with his pre-planned schedule. He was winched up to 166 fsw to begin his decompression when all hell broke loose. He had rigged the stage platform not only with a lifting cable but with two lines on either side to counteract any effects of current or tide. Somehow the tender handling the line to the bow of the ship misunderstood his instructions and winched his end of the platform all the way to within thirty feet of the surface. The stern tenders held steady with the intention of leaving Zetterstrom at 166 fsw. An impossible angle of tilt resulted along with rapid decompression. This resulted in the diver's inability to negotiate gas mixture switches or to conduct normal decompression. The 4% O_2 mix was insufficient to maintain proper oxygenation and Zetterstrom died due to hypoxia and severe embolism.

Zetterstrom had dramatically demonstrated the practicality of his revolutionary gas mixes and shattered the depth record only to fall victim to the ineptitude of his surface support crew.

Hannes Keller began experimental dives in 1959 that would ultimately more than double the depths of Zetterstrom but again with fatal consequences to dive team members. Keller, a Swiss mathematician, joined forces with noted physiologist Albert Buhlmann to explore the highly controversial elements of accelerated decompression in conjunction with helium and oxygen mixtures (HELIOX). Both men could see the financial gain to be made by refining a system to place divers in working situations at incredible depths and bring them back to the surface without unreasonable delays due to decompression obligations. Much of their research was conducted cloaked in secrecy.

Working with a hyperbaric chamber capable of simulating 1500 fsw in November of 1960, Keller prepared for the first practical test of his new gas mixes and decompression schedules. This was to be a dual dive: Keller in the lower "wet" chamber and a team of French doctors in the upper "dry" chamber. Keller, equipped with a battery of diving equipment and varied cylinders for his mixes would dive alone to a simulated depth of 830 fsw! This was beyond conception even to theoreticians at this time. The French team would be exposed to a pressure equivalent to 200 fsw. Keller's rapid compression to twenty-five atmospheres was accomplished in only ten minutes and the consensus opinion of outside observers was that he could not survive such an exposure. However, Buhlmann was in voice contact with him and reported him well at the bottom depth.

An equally rapid decompression to the 200 fsw level of the French team was conducted and Keller opened the connecting hatch to join the doctors in the "dry" chamber. Removing his gear and drying off, he then entered the access lock six minutes later. Following only 30 minutes more decompression, he emerged at the surface! By contrast, the French team exposed to only a maximum of 200 fsw would require twice as much decompression time under their conventional tables. Keller had been over four times deeper.

He would not stop there. The second pivotal dive took place in actual open water conditions in Lago Maggiore and this time, incredibly, he took along a *LIFE* magazine reporter named Kenneth McLeish. They would reach 730 fsw while being lowered on a similar platform stage as utilized by Zetterstrom. This time the top-side commands were personally supervised by Buhlmann to avoid any possible problems in operational execution. The dive required four mixes to be employed and broke the in-water record of 600 fsw held then by British Royal Navy diver George Wookey. In startling contrast to Wookey's decompression time of twelve hours, Keller and McLeish completed their decompression in less than 45 minutes. Keller had proved the validity of his decompression theory and McLeish had forever set a new standard in "on scene" reporting. It's hard to imagine one of today's blow-dried news anchors donning a dive suit to report the story from the sea floor.

The Lago Maggiore dive finally prompted the major financial support Keller and Buhlmann so desperately needed. Funding was now supplied by a group of U.S. corporations including Shell Oil, General Motors and the Navy. Keller announced his goal to reach the average limit of the continental shelf and thus open up the exploration of mining raw mineral deposits and food resources previously unreachable. This 1000 fsw dive was scheduled off Catalina Island in southern California.

A custom built diving decompression chamber named *Atlantis* was constructed capable of carrying two occupants to the sea floor over 30 atmospheres down. It was fitted with two chambers and a connecting lock to allow Keller to exit *Atlantis* and then re-enter and conduct his decompression in the upper chamber. With an ever-mindful eye towards the international press, Keller once again chose a journalist to accompany him. Peter Small, a British newspaperman, was only an amateur diver but had obtained a commission assignment for a substantial fee on the stipulation that he personally write the article.

Hans Hass was a personal friend of Small's and writes of his misgivings about the upcoming dive in *Men Beneath The Sea* (1973):

> *"Peter Small had been married only shortly before this, and his wife, Mary, as attractive as she was energetic, was vital to his resolve, or so it seemed to us. From a long conversation with Peter I got the feeling that deep down in his heart he was undertaking more than he really wanted. I don't mean by this that he was afraid, but that he lacked the freedom from doubt, the confidence of Hannes Keller. Various circumstances soon deprived him of his freedom of choice. {the newspaper commission among them, Ed.} Mary saw in him a hero, there was no escape... Somehow I felt uneasy. Peter was a true Englishman, and did not betray his feelings, but I knew him and all divers well enough to understand him."*

Several practice dives were conducted working up to the 1000 fsw exposure and in the process two bends hits were sustained, one on Hermann Heberlein and one on Peter Small only two days prior to the planned primary dive. Keller and Small had taken *Atlantis* to a depth of 330 fsw and exited to spend over an hour outside on the bottom. Small had a minor hit in his elbow after surfacing and was recompressed. On Monday, December 3, 1962 all was finally ready and the support ship *Eureka* was moved into position where the sea floor was exactly 1000 feet deep. An umbilical hose linked *Atlantis* with the ship down to 330 feet to supply gases and pressurization to the chamber. Beyond this depth the divers were on their own connected only via the steel lifting hawser. Keller had installed back-up cylinders in *Atlantis* to provide extra breathing gas if needed. Each diver was equipped with a back mounted rig capable of providing 15 minutes time. It could be replenished by filling off the back-up cylinders. Unfortunately, it was discovered that the back-up units were leaking and Keller was forced into a difficult decision heavily influenced by the financial pressures of corporate endorsement and the desire to still maintain the secrecy of his mixes and decompression schedules.

> *Keller related to Hass, "Before the attempt, this was the situation: barely enough gas in the equipment carried on the back; on the other hand, the team in top form, weather perfect. Personally, a strong fear that it might be*

all called off. Knowing that one never has perfect conditions, an attempt under perfect starting conditions never happens. Never. There are only adequate starting conditions... Well then, I decided to make the attempt."

His goal was to briefly swim out of the chamber and plant the Swiss and American flags on the bottom. He determined that his primary gas units would allow him a sufficient safety margin to exit the *Atlantis* and return. Upon reaching the planned depth, the divers opened the exit hatch and Keller dropped the short distance to the bottom. But the flags became tangled in his breathing apparatus and it took him over two minute to free himself and drop them. After he and Small successfully closed the hatch he was exhausted. At this point he should have refilled their breathing gear from the back-up cylinders but felt himself passing out. He was just able to activate the compressed air vent to flush the knee-deep water from the tiny chamber before losing conciseness.

The remote television cameras linked the surface crew with the developments on the bottom and they immediately instructed Small to remove his mask and breathe the air atmosphere. This would probably result in his unconsciousness as well but with Keller unable to operate the inside gas selections during ascent, it was felt that Small was better handled in this manner. But Small froze in horror and continued to breathe the deep mix and collapsed shortly thereafter out of camera view.

The tenders quickly raised *Atlantis* to 330 feet where divers were sent down to re-connect the umbilical. But at the 200 fsw level, the chamber proved to be leaking and could not be raised without risking explosive decompression to the occupants. Dick Anderson, a professional California diver, and Chris Whittaker, an English friend of Small's, went down to ascertain the problem but could not locate the source of the leak. To Anderson it seemed that the chamber had solved its problems and the two returned to the surface. Whittaker was not nearly the experienced pro that Anderson was and had difficulty on the ascent with this safety vest. He arrived on the ship with a profuse amount of blood in his mask and thoroughly worn out. The surface crew informed them that the chamber was still leaking.

Since they were the only two safety divers, Anderson knew he would have to go back down but preferred to go alone.

"The boy was not very strong, and rather exhausted. He undid his weight belt and took it over his arm. I nodded to him. In an emergency, he could drop the belt and would then float to the surface. We swam down again. On top of the chamber I signalled to Chris to stay there and wait. I swam down again to the hatch. I had more than enough air and had a good look around... The cover was firmly attached but when I looked very closely I discovered a small crack in it. Something small was stuck there. I tried to

get at it with my knife. Then I simply propped myself on the ladder and pressed myself upwards with my back as hard as I could. I did this for quite a while. Finally the hatch appeared to be sealed. When I swam up... Chris had disappeared. I thought he must have surfaced already since I couldn't see him anywhere. When I got to the top, they asked me where Chris Whittaker was..."

(excerpted from Hass' Men In the Sea)

Whittaker was never found. The *Atlantis* was hoisted aboard and Keller regained consciousness and hastened to cut Small from his dive suit and examine him. He reported to Buhlmann that he was alive. Later he came around and said he was thirsty. Keller got him something to drink while Small briefly spoke to Buhlmann on the phone. He then went to sleep seemingly OK. However, when Keller checked his pulse later he discovered that Small had died. He was stunned at Small's death. Keller was completely fine. The double fatality cast his remarkable achievement in shadow. Hillary Hauser, Dick Anderson's ex–wife, notes in her book *Call To Adventure*:

> *"The Keller dive was an awful paradox. It was a success because one man made a 1000 foot dive and lived, proving that the mysterious mixture of gases had worked. It also was a disaster because of the deaths involved. No one knew whether to cheer or boo. The effect was the same as if Neil Armstrong had landed on the moon and lived, while fellow astronaut Buzz Aldrin had not made it back to Earth. In that case, would the moon landing have been considered a success or failure?"*

Hass speculates that Keller's determination and confidence insured his survival while the less experienced and less motivated Small succumbed. Hass felt that had Dick Anderson been Keller's diving partner no lives would have been lost. With the benefit of hindsight, Keller would have been wise to ensure a more professional companion but Small had performed satisfactorily on the practice runs. Keller remained shaken but undaunted and continues today with consulting work in varying fields of diving and computer technologies. His vision of man's ability to work in extreme depths would provide the basis for commercial and naval systems that followed.

THE HABITAT EVOLUTIONS

That same year saw the introduction of the first significant advances in man's attempts to actually live in the ocean. Habitat and submersible pioneer Ed Link launched two short duration but important projects back to back in August and September of 1962. Using himself as a guinea pig in the first project nicknamed *Trial Link*, he spent a cramped eight hours at 60 fsw in a tiny 11'x3' cylinder in the Mediterranean. Robert Stenuit followed him the following month in the same cylinder now called *Man-in-the-Sea*; this time for two hours at 200 fsw breathing HELIOX. On the heels of Stenuit's dive, came the first of Jacques Cousteau's *Conshelf* missions with two divers spending a week at 35 fsw off Marseilles. Much as the "space race" was heating up, so it seemed the race for advances in underwater saturation habitats moved forward. In 1963, Cousteau followed up dramatically with *Conshelf II* in which seven "aquanauts" lived at 36 fsw on the ocean floor of the Red Sea for a month! During this same mission, Raymond Kientzy and Andre Portelatine spent a week in a specially staged mini-habitat called *Deep Cabin* at 90 fsw allowing them "excursion" dives with virtually no decompression to as deep as 360 feet.

In 1964, Link sponsored his *Man-in-the-Sea II* mission off the Bahamas and the U.S. Navy deployed *Sea Lab I* near Bermuda. A plethora of progressively deeper and longer saturation projects followed including the two month mission of *Tektite* in the Virgin Islands in the late sixties. *Tektite* was utilized for multiple missions and in 1971 marked the first all female aquanaut team led by Dr. Sylvia Earle, now chief scientist for NOAA. Link also produced the venerable *Hydrolab* habitat that began operation in 1966 and into the mid-1980's before being retired to the Smithsonian Institution in Washington D.C. During its operational life it provided an underwater home to literally hundreds of scientists and researchers at its sites in Florida, the Bahamas and finally St. Croix in the Virgin Islands. Ultimately *Hydrolab* was replaced with the massive *Aquarius* habitat now in the process of relocating to a site in the Florida Keys. The saturation habitat fascination tapered off in the mid-1970's and now only a handful of projects remain in existence. Renewed interest is surfacing however as the possibilities of saturation exploration of deep wrecks and cave systems are discussed by the emerging high tech community.

Tragically, Ed Link, one of diving's true technical innovators, would suffer the loss of his son while a team member in *Sea-Link*, a deep diving submersible of his design. In the summer of 1973 during a project sponsored by the Smithsonian off Key West, Florida, the sub became entangled in a cable from a wreck they were exploring. The scuttled destroyer *Fred T. Berry* fouled the *Sea Link* while she was attempting to pick up a fish trap at 351 fsw. All efforts by the sub's crew to extricate themselves proved to no avail. The submersible was configured with two chambers: A forward pilot's station for two crew and an after chamber capable of "locking-out" divers for exterior excursions. In the forward command station Bob Meek and Jock Menzies were surrounded by a large acrylic sphere and remarkably this would prove crucial to their survival. In the after compartment, Clay Link and Al Stover, an expert and highly experienced submariner, were encapsulated in highly thermally conductive aluminum.

Although the Navy dispatched its submarine rescue ship *Tringa* to the site, it was almost 12 hours before it finally was positioned over the trapped sub. A "roving diving bell" was airlifted from San Diego and delivered to the ship where it began its first descent the following morning at 9:20 a.m. At this point, the sub's occupants had been marooned for almost 24 hours. Swift currents in the area hampered the efforts to make contact with *Sea-Link* and time began to run out for the helpless four men. To conserve their precious on-board emergency air supply, the sub crew desperately spread baralyme in their compartments which would act to absorb CO_2 from the increasingly stale atmosphere. However, baralyme is ineffective below 70 degrees F. and in the aft compartment surrounded by the conductive aluminum the temperature rapidly plummeted. Stover and Link attempted to raise the baralyme temperature by spreading it over their exposed skin but this ceased to be effective after a time.

While the rescue crew furiously struggled to hook up with the sub, the trapped men finally turned to their emergency breathing system which supplied air to both compartments. The 36 hour ordeal held little hope that the rescue could be made before the air in the emergency cylinders was exhausted. Stover made a personal assessment of his situation with Link in the lock-out compartment and decided that they held far less chance of survival than Menzies and Meek in the pilot sphere. In the ultimate heroic sacrifice to try to at least save his companions, Stover turned off the emergency air system for himself and Link. Both died before the sub was recovered but the other two men survived.

THE FREE DIVERS

Although this is a book primarily about deep scuba diving, the unique accomplishments of a small cadre of breath-hold divers bears mention in our historical narrative. Also known as free-diving, this esoteric diving form has almost become a lost art among American divers since the early seventies. In the infancy of scuba diving almost every new diver was also an accomplished free-diver. This was fueled by the popularity of competitive spearfishing almost exclusively conducted without scuba gear. This produced many divers capable of routinely diving to depths in excess of 100 feet to hunt fish on near equal terms. Many of the most proficient competitors would chalk up bottom times approaching two and half minutes and reach depths of up to 150 feet.

Bret Gilliam, a member of the Virgin Islands spearfishing team in 1974, recalls his introduction to the real world of free-diving,

> *"I was invited to got out with team captain Dave Coston originally back in '71. Dave was about 38 then, I was about 21, and I figured I would show these old guys a thing or two. Now the water in the Virgin Islands is clear but when we got to the dive site, I couldn't see the bottom. Not wanting to be un-cool since everyone else seemed unconcerned , I warmed up with a couple of dives to 50 or 60 feet but still couldn't see the bottom. Finally, after about a half hour or so of watching from afar as Coston and Carl Butler boated massive snapper and grouper, I swam over to inquire where in hell the sea mount was that they were diving on. I was reduced to the rank of rookie in a heartbeat when they informed me there was no secret; the bottom was right underneath me; only 140 feet. Was I having a problem or something?"*

Others like Carlos Eyles of California, the Pinder brothers, and John Ernst of Florida had similar performances. And this was not simply diving down and coming up. A true free-diver could hunt, shoot and struggle with his catch back to the surface from these depths... all on one breath.

Dave Coston, champion breath-hold spearfisherman, with world record silky shark taken in 1974 off St. Croix, in the Virgin Islands. During the mid 1970's, Coston held over a dozen world records for fish species all taken in depths up to 150 feet.

photo by Bret Gilliam

The interest in competitive free-diving saw the introduction of a whole new form of diving evolve: extreme depth breath hold contests. Probably the earliest record holder would have to be the Greek sponge diver, Stotti Georghios, who swam to put a line on a lost anchor in 1913 with no fins in 200 feet of water.

During Navy testing in 1968, diver Bob Croft set a modern record by reaching 240 feet off Bimini. Al Giddings relates his account of that dive in the book *Exploring the Deep Frontier:*

"I went down using scuba to 250 feet to await Croft's arrival. At that depth the nitrogen in the compressed air I was breathing had a dizzying effect on me. It was incredible enough as it was, suspended in the open sea, an ethereal infinity of blue in all directions. Then Croft came racing down the guideline, skin loose, chest compressed from the pressure. After reaching 240 feet he let go of the weight and hand over hand, no fins, pulled himself back to the surface. It was remarkable to watch him go back to the surface under his own power." Croft's dive lasted just over two minutes.

Jacques Mayol studied marine mammals for 15 years and experimented with a variety of methods to extend his time underwater including yoga and meditational exercises. In 1976, he devised a unique weighted sled on a cable that he held onto with both hands during descents. A hand operated brake could allow him to stop at any depth. Mayol preferred not to use a mask at all since equalizing it would only deplete his breath reserve. Instead he wore specially adapted contact lenses that allowed him to see and allowed him to wear a nose clip. Incredibly, he attained 328 feet on his dive. His dive lasted almost three and half minutes.

He related, "When I am down there, I'm not a man anymore. I'm a sea creature... a diving mammal. I belong in the water." A movie based loosely on his amazing career called *The Big Blue* was released in 1988.

Like the compressed air diving record that held up for 22 years, Mayol's mark seemed untouchable until 1989 when a young Italian woman, Angela Bandino, dropped to 351 feet in breath hold competition. Will the 400 ft. barrier be broken? Probably someday.

THE CAVE DIVERS

The earliest known use of scuba gear in United States caves was in January of 1953 by Frank DenBlykker and Charles McNabb to explore the then unknown depths of Florida's Silver Springs. The pair discovered that the Springs were only the entrance to a large cave system and on that first dive they stumbled onto the petrified remains of the elephant's ancient ancestor, the Mastodon. Cave diving was a little practiced sport in these embryonic days of scuba diving and only a handful of participants could be found struggling through the underbrush and down slippery paths to access the mesmerizing call of the dazzling, clear inland cave systems. Jack "Gil" Favor discovered many other of the now popular caves and was active in cave diving from the early fifties until the mid-sixties.

Sheck Exley made his first cave dive in 1966 shortly after his initial scuba training and was "hooked". Looking back at that period of his life in 1984 he recalls:

"Now, for better or for worse, my life was set; I was a cave diver. Sports heroes such as Tarkenton and Gehrig, and military genius Lawrence of Arabia were now replaced with Watts, Mount and Harper on the list of people I most admired. Hall Watts was the best deep cave diver, Tom Mount had the most cave dives and was the best published, and John Harper was simply the best, period."

Mount began cave diving in 1962 after discharge from a hitch as a Navy officer and UDT diver. His introduction was with Zuber Sink (later renamed Forty Fathom Sink) where he would make numerous dives to 240 ft. to bottom out the cave with Frank Martz, another early cave enthusiast. One of the most outstanding deep caves in Florida is Eagle's Nest. First discovered by Don Ledbetter in 1960, this cave is still unfolding as technology advances.

Ledbetter, along with others such as Lee Somers (now the head of the University of Michigan's diving program and a Ph.D.), explored the "Nest", then known as Lost Sink, to depths of 220 ffw. Later John Harper and Randy Hylton pushed on to 230 ffw with Mount and Martz laying permanent line in to a depth of 250 ffw in 1964. Hal Watts and members of his informal "diving club", the Forty Fathom Scubapro's, would reach 260 ffw while penetrating the upstream cave. In 1965, Mount and Martz set out to attempt to "wall out" (reach the end) of the Nest and with progressive pushes reached depths of 285 ffw. Joined by Jim Lockwood in 1969, they found a small passage that dropped to 300 fsw but did not appear to continue; Lockwood laid line in beyond that depth but ultimately encountered silt too thick to penetrate and that tunnel was abandoned.

The opening to the downstream cave was discovered by Mount and Martz in late 1968. This required the divers to negotiate a very tight restriction in the 280-290 ffw level before opening into a large and beautiful tunnel that is the major system of Eagle's Nest. In the years to follow, Lockwood and Jamie Stone would introduce the use of DPV's (Diver Propulsion Vehicles) and Exley would introduce the practice of multiple stage bottles to effect penetrations hundreds of feet beyond the early explorers. The lines laid by Lockwood and Exley would not be exceeded until the late 1980's when Jim King and Larry Green employed combinations of DPV's, staging and TRIMIX to reach 310 ffw for up to one hour and 18 minutes requiring seven hours of decompression. In Mount's opinion (1991), "The Nest has been explored to the limits of open circuit technology. The use of rebreathers for further exploration is being investigated by King and Green and other members of the Deep Breathing Systems Team. We don't know the ultimate possible penetration or depth."

Cave diving pioneer Tom Mount in 1969. Note equipment of that era including "jerry jug" to be used as a buoyancy compensator.

photo by Frank Martz

Possibly one of the deepest caves is popular Morrison Spring in the Florida Panhandle. This is marked by one of the largest and prettiest headpools at its entrance. In the early 1960's, Atlanta dive instructor Jack Faver, made extensive dives into the system and reported depths attained of 270-350 ffw. Martz and Mount attained 285 ffw in 1965. In 1968, teams led by Hal Watts, John Harper and Randy Hylton made it past an extremely narrow restriction at the 100 ffw level by removing their doubles and squeezing through to discover a fourth room extending to the 240 ffw level. Here they were stopped as the passage narrowed to only a small slit. Speculation that this later team missed a side passage taken by Faver and dive buddy George Krasle, stirs interest that the tunnels were not fully explored. Unfortunately, following the deaths of several divers, the local sheriff had enough and ordered the dynamiting of the passage leading to the third room thus sealing the passages forever.

Other deep cave penetrations included Jim Houtz's dive to 315 ffw into Nevada's Devil's Hole surrounded by Death Valley National Monument, and the Sheck Exley/Joe Prosser descent to 325 ffw in Mystery Sink in Orlando, Florida. Will Waters, Jamie Stone, Jim Lockwood and Exley would be among the first to lead pushes into the infamous Die Polder II sinkhole near Weekie Wachee with Dale Sweet reaching 360 ffw in 1980 on HELIOX accompanied by Lockwood on air. At the time of the dive Lockwood did not know that Sweet was using mixed gas, he had kept it a secret. It would be over 12 years before any extensions to the Lockwood/ Sweet line would be laid; this time by Lamar English and Bill Gavin who were followed by Dustin Clesi and Jim King on TRIMIX and DPV's to a depth of 380 ffw. The group intends to return in the future to continue with rebreathers.

The father of "Blue Hole" diving has to be Dr. George Benjamin of Canada. He became fascinated with the Bahamian blue holes in the late 1960's after trips to the western island of Andros. Local legend and superstition kept natives and divers alike away from this mysterious phenomena until Benjamin began diving in them. Due to the often violent whirlpool effects near the entrance of the holes, it was said that they were occupied by evil spirits or the dreaded "lusca", an octopus-like monster, that would drag fishermen and entire boats below the surface if they ventured too near. Benjamin quickly ascertained that the whirlpool effects were related to tidal cycles and was the first to develop dive plans designed around penetrations during the slack water period.

Since he took up blue hole cave diving at the not exactly youthful age of 50, he prudently decided that some younger assistants might be helpful in making the pushes into the labyrinth tunnels and an invitation was offered to veteran cave explorer Tom Mount to come over from Miami to help with the project. Mount proved an invaluable team member and led the way in Blue Hole #4 to discover the first stalactite formations in 1970.

Jim Lockwood in Picannie Ponds in Australia. Lockwood and Tom Mount completed what is still believed to be the deepest Australian cave dive on air to 320 in 1973.

photo by Tom Mount

Benjamin was something of an equipment inventor on his own, introducing the innovative "Benjamin Conversion" manifold that allowed the use of dual regulators on double tanks but provided the "isolation" capability in the event of a valve or regulator malfunction. The air from the "isolated" cylinder was channeled via his unique cross-over bar so that the second regulator/valve system could still access it. (Although Benjamin has largely been credited with the design, Ike Ikehara was actually the brains behind the manifold system). But Mount arrived on the scene with other custom equipment like high intensity lights and specialized reels that he had not seen before. They were manufactured by Mount's close friend, Frank Martz, another veteran Florida cave diver.

After several months of joint work by Benjamin's team and other American divers recruited by Mount including Ike Ikehara, Sharee Pepper, Dick Williams, Jim Lockwood, Zidi Goldstein and Martz, they had pushed well beyond the limits of Benjamin's earlier projections. In the summer of 1970, an offshoot of Benjamin Cave (#4) was discovered by Tom and Ikehara who squeezed through a major restriction at 240 fsw to enter a totally unexplored passage. Mount recalls:

> "It was kind of a roller coaster tunnel that led down to a depth of 300 feet. Later Dick Williams and I placed permanent line in to 310 feet deep and ran into another restriction that we could just get through. At the end of this tunnel we reached a shaft that dropped out of sight. I leaned over at 330 fsw and shined my light straight down and we couldn't see the bottom. At this point, some thirty minutes had elapsed and narcosis was a complication coming back up the tunnel and through the restrictions. On the exit, I had to assist Dick from 290 feet up to 240 feet. He just sort of gave out; he could kick but there was nothing in his effort and he wasn't making any progress."

In 1971, Mount and Martz discovered yet another deep tunnel with a major restriction beginning at 280 fsw but did not have the opportunity to explore it farther. In September, Martz arrived from Florida determined to push the new tunnel beyond the restriction. He enlisted Lockwood as his dive partner. From the beginning things didn't seem to go well. Martz seemed moody and out of sorts to his friends. Benjamin did not want the dive done since it conflicted with his work projects already scheduled and he considered it to be particularly hazardous. Mount was Martz's best friend and even found himself on the short end of an argument that day when he could never recall a strained word between them before.

Since Benjamin was paying the bills to support the mapping and survey of the Blue Holes, Mount explained that the work projects had to take priority. But Martz was insistent and Mount finally persuaded Benjamin to let the dive go forward. Lockwood and Martz set off together while Mount and Zidi Goldstein went into the north tunnel to extend the lines into that passage. Martz and Lockwood successfully negotiated the constricted passage and went on down to 300 fsw. While tying off a new reel, considerable silt was stirred up in the narrow area and Martz went through the restriction by himself. Lockwood waited, alone. In conversation with Gilliam in 1991, he reflects:

"Frank was a headstrong guy who was one of the country's top expert cave divers. When you dove with him you had to accept certain things like the fact that he was going to do whatever he felt on the dive. I was 21 then and Frank was 35. Frank and Tom were the kings, I looked up to them and would never have thought to question either of them underwater. When Frank went through that restriction, I never saw him again. I thought that he must have come by me in the silt-out and headed to the surface. I finally went through and found only a cut safety line dangling into a blue bottomless void, with my light shining from 325 feet deep I couldn't see any end to that shaft."

Dr. Dick Williams, Tom Mount, and Frank Martz prior to their dive in Eagle's Nest in 1969. In addition to some of the earliest deep penetrations in this site, this trio and Jim Lockwood would make extraordinary dives in the Bahamian blue holes a year later.

Lockwood came back through and encountered Mount and Goldstein in the decompression area and briefly, by slate, conveyed that Martz had disappeared. Tom and Jim returned to the entrance of the south passage in the futile hope that Martz might appear but he was gone forever.

The loss of one of the U.S.'s top cave divers had a numbing effect on Mount and the rest of the Florida team. Two attempts were made by Mount and Lockwood to retrieve the body to no avail. In the notes from the police investigation report, Mount makes this statement:

"Frank Martz was probably one of the best cave divers in the world. He was a NAUI, PADI and NACD certified instructor. He was one of my best friends, and one of the people you think it is impossible for them to die diving. He had done more to develop safe cave diving equipment than anyone, and the cave diving world will miss him, his abilities, his excellent diving equipment and his devotion to the exploration of underwater caves."

52

Phillipe Cousteau and Dr. George Benjamin rigging flares for use in the Cousteau special television movie special on the Bahamian Blue Holes in 1971.

photo by Bret Gilliam

Tom may have been correct in his note that it was impossible to believe that Martz could die in a diving accident. All the team had noted his strange behavior in the time before the dive. Sheck Exley remembers that period:

> "The summer of 1971 was especially noteworthy in Florida. A tiny amoeba had infested the water of many of the lakes and ponds in central Florida. It had been reported only a couple of miles south of Eagle's Nest and I think it's reasonable to assume that this amoeba was there as well. Why so much fuss over a microbe? If the amoeba infects a swimmer or diver, as it did in Florida that year, it was 100% fatal. It caused encephalitis, swelling the human brain so that severe headaches are felt in the early stages, then comes high fever and death a few short weeks after the initial infection. How does it get into the brain? Through the nasal passages. Frank had spent countless hours decompressing with his nose in the water (with no mask) at Eagle's Nest. At Andros, divers soon noticed Frank acting strangely. He seemed moody and depressed, and was intent on doing dives that were especially dangerous."

Lockwood may have been an unwitting buddy to a diver focused on a one-way dive. Mount has voiced the same speculation. Exley concludes:

> "A terminally ill cave diver with no close family ties could scarcely pick a better way to commit suicide: in one of the world's most spectacular underwater caves, at a depth deep enough to insure that his passing would be rendered painless by narcosis and make it very unlikely that his body would ever be found."

The Great Blue Hole of Lighthouse Reef Atoll located some 70 miles off Belize harbored similar superstitions as the Bahamian blue holes. In 1971, the Cousteaus traveled with *Calypso* to explore its uncharted depths for the first time. Widely rumored to be "bottomless", stalactite formations were discovered at a depth of only 140 fsw and with the use of their diving submersible the Blue Hole was bottomed out at just over 600 fsw. Following this expedition, they continued on to the Bahamas to visit

photo: Florida Speleological Researchers, Inc.

Rick Nicolini and Dustin Clesi of Team DiePolder '91 made the farthest and deepest penetrations in that system to pass lines laid in by Dale Sweet and Jim Lockwood almost eleven years earlier.

Almost $50,000 worth of high-tech mixed gas equipment, DPV's, and surface supplied decompression gases were employed on the Team DiePolder '91 push. Here multiple sets of doubles await "staging" into the cave system.

photo: Florida Speleological Researchers, Inc

Benjamin and Mount in Andros to film the local blue holes they were mapping. Ironically, Jacques Cousteau almost was killed in #4 when he got off the line on the way out of the cave.

The Lucayan blue hole, called Ben's Cave, located on Grand Bahama island ultimately proved to be one of the longest cave systems in the world. Sheck Exley would explore another even larger system in Belize on Caye Cawlker. After diving the Great Blue Hole and Ben's Cave in the early 1970's, Bret Gilliam searched in vain for similar formations in the Virgin Islands. But he did discover tunnels cut into the face of the steep north shore drop-off of St. Croix. These began at extreme depths, usually 330 fsw or deeper and penetrated nearly horizontally back into the wall face. Some had entrances as narrow as three feet that extended in more than 200 feet before widening sometimes into rooms that were impossible to measure. They were initially discovered by accident on deep wall dives and were extremely difficult to locate. Due the depths and equipment available in this era, the explorations of these mysterious tunnels were largely discontinued after a DPV failure in one push that almost killed him.

Additional Andros Blue Hole expeditions were undertaken in 1981 and in 1987 by Rod Palmer, Bill Stone and their associates. They succeeded in discovering numerous additional inland blue holes and explored them to depths of 310 fsw with the use of mixed gas and rebreathers. Their discoveries were of dramatic proportions yet they still did not achieve depths beyond those of Mount, Martz, Lockwood, Ikehara and Williams almost two decades before on compressed air.

Currently the fastest emerging technological advances in deep diving are coming from the cave diving fraternity. Individuals like Parker Turner (the Sullivan Connection), Wes Skiles and Bill Stone (the Wakulla project), Larry Green (recent Eagle's Nest penetrations) and Jim King with Dustin Clesi (Eagle's Nest and Die Polder II) are all on the leading edge of progress with mixed gas, DPV's and other developing equipment such as fully redundant rebreathers.

Zale Parry after her record breaking 209 foot dive in 1954. Note the old style dry suits and the double hose regulators that were used in that era.

WOMEN DEEP DIVERS

In a diving niche that is already limited, there have been only a handful of women participants over the years. One of the earliest woman deep divers was Rosalia Zale Parry, who reached 209 fsw off Santa Monica, California in 1954. She enjoyed a long career in diving as an actress and stunt person in such series as Lloyd Bridges' popular hit *Sea Hunt.*

Well known scientists Dr. Eugenie Clarke and Dr. Sylvia Earle pursued research projects in depths far in excess of many men divers during the 1960's. During this same period, Zidi Goldstein and Dr. Sharee Pepper at the University of Miami were involved with open water and blue hole deep diving missions that regularly had them in 300 feet plus depths.

Evelyn Dudas was the first woman to dive the *Andrea Doria* wreck in 1966. Given the harsh conditions and depth of that site, her accomplishment is particularly significant.

photo by Sheck Exley

Mary Ellen Eckhoff, probably the U.S.'s finest women deep diver, prepares for her 400 foot dive in Mexico's Mante cave system. Eckhoff has held all women's cave records for depth and distance penetration since 1978 and has equaled the existing women's record for open water depth at 345 feet.

Another trail blazer has been Mary Ellen Eckhoff, one of the top American cave divers, male or female, of the last twenty years. Since 1978, she has held all of the cave diving depth and penetration records for women in addition to sharing the record for overall penetration at Big Dismal in 1981. Her 5847 foot penetration with Sheck Exley and Clark Pitcairn was the world record that summer. She was also the fourth cave diver in the world to complete more than 1000 cave dives (Tom Mount, Exley and Paul DeLoach were the first), and was the second diver in the world to dive to 400 fsw in a cave (on mixed gas). She is the only female diver to ever dive to 300 fsw in a cave and has "unofficially" equaled the women's open water record of 345 fsw on July 4, 1982 off Grand Turk Island while diving with Exley.

Marty Dunwoody holds the officially recognized women's open water depth record of 345 fsw set December 21, 1988. She trained under Hal Watts methods and is now an active instructor with his Professional Scuba Association in Ocala, Florida. She continues a long line of Watts-trained record holders that dates back to the 1960's.

Both professional instructor Lynn Hendrickson and underwater model Patti Mount are still active deep divers with histories of regular multiple 250 fsw plus dives in a single working day. Hendrickson, who is also a licensed USCG boat captain and recompression chamber operator, has hit 300 fsw plus while Patti is close to the women's record with a 335 fsw dive. Both women find themselves placed in the same diving situations as their men partners and frequently outperform them.

Finally, the ultimate woman deep diver has to be the late Ann Gunderson. During practice dives in working up to the 1971 record attempt in the Bahamas, she made over 40 dives below 400 fsw. Sheck Exley observed her on at least one successful drop to 440 fsw, and her dive buddy Jim Lockwood confirms that Ann made approximately 25 dives in this range. Although, Gunderson never attempted to claim the "shallower" dives in her pursuit of the world record at 480 fsw, there is no dispute to her rightful place in history. Sadly, she was lost on December 11, 1971 pursuing that record with her boyfriend, Archie Forfar. Her "unofficial record" may stand as a women's mark forever.

As we approach the twenty-first century, where will the historical reference be? If the past is a benchmark indicator, it will be deeper, longer and totally unexplored...

PROGRESSIVE WORLD RECORDS FOR UNDERWATER DEPTH

Open Water Dives

Year	Depth fsw	Gas	Location	Diver/s
1945	500	TRIMIX	Mediterranean	Arne Zetterstrom
1947	307	Air	Red Sea	Frederic Dumas
1961	350	Air	Florida	Jean Clarke Samazen
1961	730	HELIOX	Switzerland	Hannes Keller & Ken McLeish
1962	1000	HELIOX	California	Hannes Keller & Peter Small
1963	355	Air	Florida	Hal Watts
1965	360	Air	Florida	Tom Mount & Frank Martz
1967	390	Air	Florida	Hal Watts & A. J. Muns
1968	437	Air	Bahamas	Neil Watson & John Gruener
1971	440	Air	Bahamas	Ann Gunderson *
1988	345	Air	Florida	Marty Dunwoody **
1990	452	Air	Roatan, Bay Islands	Bret Gilliam ***

Cave Dives

Year	Depth ffw	Gas	Location	Diver/s
1955	210	Air	Vaucluse, France	Jacques Cousteau
1956	250	Air	Wakulla, Florida	Gary Salesman & Wally Jenkins
1965	315	Air	Devils Hole, Nevada	James Houtz
1969	335	Air	Sinoia Caves, Rhodesia	Frank Salt
1970	415	Air	Mystery Sink, Florida	Hal Watts †
1970	400	HELIOX	Mystery Sink, Florida	Hal Watts
1983	656	HELIOX	Vaucluse, France	Jochen Hasenmayer
1987	656	TRIMIX	Mante, Mexico	Sheck Exley
1988	780	TRIMIX	Mante, Mexico	Sheck Exley
1988	400	TRIMIX	Mante, Mexico	Mary Ellen Eckhoff ††
1989	881	TRIMIX	Mante, Mexico	Sheck Exley †††

* Unofficial Women's Record	†	Current Men's Air Record
** Current Women's Record	††	Current Women's Record
*** Current Men's Record	†††	Current Men's Mixed Gas Record

Chapter 2

Physiological and Mental Preparation for Deep Diving

"How deep is DEEP?"

Michael Menduno

TYPES OF DIVING

Probably more deep diving is conducted in tropical settings on luxurious coral drop-offs than anywhere else. This is also the most "friendly" atmosphere in which to refine skills given the circumstances of clear, warm water usually blessed with excellent visibility. Typically, divers engage in multi-level excursions attaining the deepest depth for a brief time and then "stepping up" (ascending) to progressively shallower depths. It is a frequent practice for multi-day repetitive dives to be conducted in this manner, and many liveaboard divers will average 5-7 dives per day.

Diving styles vary widely and much discussion has centered on what constitutes "typical" sport diving. At land based resorts, most divers are limited to two dives per day with a possibility of a third. Liveaboards, as previously noted, tend to provide virtually unlimited diving within the constraints of either computers or tables. However, a myth of adherence to a 130 fsw limit has been perpetuated. Upon closer examination of actual logs and giving credence to the preponderance of anecdotal accounts, it becomes clear that considerable doubt must be placed upon statistics that reflect more than limited observation of recommended "limits".

Several surveys, including Gilliam's (1989-90) sampling of 77,680 sport dives, found that as many as 40% of those questioned admitted to routinely diving in excess of 130 fsw (39.4m) and as deep as 200 fsw (60.6m). In the opinion of many industry professional resort divemasters and photojournalists, the 200 fsw level is just as widely surpassed.

To examine the types of diving conducted by recreational divers, we must look at, in order of difficultly, the most common deep endeavors to the more difficult journeys.

Wall Diving

In this type of diving, the easiest or most common, most participants use standard scuba equipment i.e. single cylinders, single BCD's, with some degree of back-up/bail-out system depending on depths. Rarely are multiple cylinder sets used or mixed gas systems employed. This is deep diving and equipment in its purest sense. One of the greatest lures to tropical wall diving is the relative ease of access and convenience to deep spectacular coral formations and marine life. The shallow water zones on top of the walls lend themselves perfectly to multi-level dives and provide optimal decompression "stages" (in many cases, the diver can use portions of the shallow reef for decompression stops without the discomfort of hanging on a line).

Similar "excursion" type deep diving is practiced throughout the world, but most sites do not lend themselves to the easy access of vertical wall formations. Elsewhere, divers must also deal with less forgiving environments such as colder, darker water and restricted visibility.

Wreck Diving

Next on the degree of difficulty index comes deep wreck diving. Most of this activity is regionally centered along the East coast of the United States and presents a wide variety of environmental considerations. Frequently, the Florida wreck diver enjoys warm water and

Deep wreck divers are faced with additional considerations if penetrations are intended to the wreck's interior.

Photo by Bret Gilliam

good visibility, but may encounter stiff current conditions in areas washed by the Gulf Stream. At the other end of the spectrum, the Northeast wreck diver faces numerous obstacles to performance: cold water, bad visibility, swift currents and sites located as much as 100 miles (167km) from port. Additionally, all wreck divers can subject themselves to "overhead" conditions where no direct ascent to the surface is possible.

Cave divers are subjected to the most challenging deep environment including "overhead" conditions where the surface is not immediately accessible in an emergency.

Cave Diving

Finally, we have the deep cave divers. Long considered by many as the gatekeepers of the "lunatic fringe." In fact, cavers do face potentially hostile environmental concerns especially since their habitat of choice is almost totally an "overhead" situation. Currents and cold water can be a factor, although most sites enjoy clear water unless careless divers stir up silt rapidly reducing visibility to zero.

Each type of diving has seen an evolution of preferred equipment and procedures, although many practices will see overlapping techniques. Each presents different mental and physical challenges.

We will discuss the generic considerations for deep diving and urge the reader to seek specific training from qualified sources before attempting the more demanding applications of cave and wreck divers.

PHYSICAL CONSIDERATIONS

Strangely enough, many divers fail to fully recognize the implications that external influences may play in dive planning. This is especially crucial in deep diving activities and we offer the following breakdowns:

Size/Strength:

This is primarily a consideration when the equipment package becomes sufficiently large or heavy to be a performance detriment to women or slightly built men. This is not to say that such divers need to be excluded, but the physical ability to move comfortably on the surface and in the water with heavy, cumbersome gear that may also have considerable drag characteristics, can make certain types of diving very difficult for smaller divers to handle.

Thermal Protection:

Even in tropical waters, the body will rapidly chill after prolonged exposure such as that encountered on extended stage decompression. Be sure to select a suit that will allow a sufficient comfort margin. Dry suits become a requirement for most divers once temperatures drop below 70^0 F (20.9^0 C) due to extended decompression times. Remember, cold is a contributing factor to narcosis, decompression sickness (DCS), fatigue, mental acuity and task performance, and can result in severe dexterity degradation.

Deep divers are frequently exposed to cold water and prolonged decompression "hangs". Dry suits and various thermal underwear like this DUI CF-200 suit are used by many deep divers.

Vision:

Surprisingly, many divers fail to recognize the importance of being able to see well underwater. If you wear corrective lenses on land, get a mask with a prescription-ground faceplate. If you wear contact lenses, wear them while you are diving as well. Older divers may require a bifocal plate to allow comfortable reading of gauges and instruments. It is alarming how many accidents have occurred simply because the diver could not see properly. Divers have missed ascent or anchor lines leading them to decompression stages and some have even missed the dive boat, all due to vision deficits.

Hydration:

The importance of proper hydration has been clearly shown as a means of lessening predisposition to decompression sickness. Avoid carbonated beverages containing caffeine, coffee and alcohol before and after diving. Alcohol has a direct effect tending to shut off Anti-Diuretic Hormones (ADH) and contribute to dehydration. Fresh water and unsweetened apple juice have become the fluids of choice. They should be taken frequently and in sufficient quantity to insure clear urine when passed. If the urination cycle is below normal, you are probably already dehydrated. The old mountain climbers all religiously urinated in the snow before major climbs; dark urine color (and perhaps poor handwriting) were grounds for excluding a climber. The authors highly recommend the excellent series of articles on hydration and flying & diving by Michael Emmerman (see reference section).

Rest:

This should be obvious. But the benefits of proper sleep patterns and non-stressful relaxation play significant roles in our physical performance. If you are tired or suffering from inadequate rest, your ability to deal with task loading and simple common sense decisions may be impaired. The body needs a break to "charge its batteries" and restore full function. Get a good night's sleep before any deep dives, at least eight hours. This can be difficult in some resort settings with "distractions". If necessary, modify dive start times to get fully rested. Burning the midnight oil has no place in deep diving. Avoid any sleep medications as these have been proven to have latent effects during dives in some cases.

Diet:

Practice a well balanced dietary ethic. Many deep divers have found consumption of heavy breakfasts or hard to digest foods to be a factor in narcosis susceptibility. Many consume only light fare such as toast or muffins followed by a heartier meal post-dive. Avoid orange, tomato and grapefruit juices as they will stimulate seasickness in many persons.

Fitness:

Overall physical fitness is definitely desirable. A combination of strength and aerobic exercise is recommended along with a regimen of regular swimming and swimming with fins. Diving is a demanding physical test of endurance in many cases. You should be in sufficient shape to handle surface swims, rescue situations, the underwater demands placed upon your body to perform against current, equipment drag/breathing resistance and the myriad unseen contingencies that can and will ultimately present.

Alcohol/Smoking/Drugs:

How many nails do you want in your coffin? Choose your weapons... Each of these influences various performance functions from decreasing your reactive and reasoning ability to inhibiting gas exchange in the lungs. Suffice it to say that none of the aforementioned will do anything but make your body less efficient. Some studies suggest enormous potential hazards when combined with the effects of pressure.

History:
Any injury that could contribute to poor circulation such as scar tissue, burns or prior surgery should be regarded as a potential DCS problem and will call for a more conservative decompression schedule. Divers with past histories of decompression sickness (DCS) or arterial gas embolism (AGE) should be cleared by a diving physician before resuming dive activity. Diving doctors will be familiar with the precise parameters and current thinking on guidelines for return to diving. Evaluation of a lung injury or categorizing a Type I or Type II DCS hit will normally be beyond the scope of traditional general practice medical professionals.

Free-diving:
Breath-hold diving has virtually developed into a lost skill in the majority of today's divers. But this is one of the best conditioning exercises known. It promotes proper weighting, breath control, economy of exertion and overall "control", both mental and physical. Such expert deep divers as Tom Mount, Rick Freshee, Bret Gilliam and Billy Deans are all accomplished free divers.

MENTAL CONSIDERATIONS
Herein lies hardest part of screening candidates for deep diving since no objective testing has really been established. The reader should note that he is not only covering this chapter as a guide to self-evaluation, but for his intended diving companion as well. Rigorous, demanding training programs are conducted by the U.S. Navy and commercial diving operations with the specific goal of "washing out" unsuitable individuals. No such controls exist within the sport diving community or instructor evaluation programs. If anything, the screening of sport divers and instructors has become less exacting as the industry attempts to broaden its market appeal.

For our purposes, this text is directed at advanced divers, hopefully with sufficient experience (**125 plus dives, in various environments and conditions**) to have mastered the entry level anxieties of dealing with strange equipment, unfamiliar environments and the usual chaos associated with the learning process in recreational divers. Divers should be completely comfortable with equipment handling including assembly, gearing up on a rocking boat or in the water if necessary. The elements of buoyancy control should be routine along with contingency drills for out of air scenarios and other emergencies.

We realize it is possible to attain a certification card that proclaims an individual an "advanced diver" or, God help us!, a "Deep Diver" with less than 15 dives total experience in open water conditions. With just a bit more effort you can become a "Master Diver" (a term once reserved for a handful of the U.S. Navy's elite and most experienced diving supervisors). Oh well... progress.

We want to be prudent in identifying and screening candidates with any of the following behavior patterns: (Some material contained is paraphrased or adapted from Dr. Jefferson Davis' recommendations for the medical

Many divers are not comfortable in confined spaces and should avoid them while diving. This inviting wreck may tend to provoke panic in a claustrophobic diver if suddenly presented with an unanticipated stressful scenario.

evaluation of divers contained in his 1986 edition of Medical Examination of Sport Scuba Divers.)

The Panic-Prone Individual:

One must be at home and comfortable in the water. The most common cause of death in divers is panic and inability to deal with stressful situations underwater. Evidence of high anxiety or past "anxiety attacks" should target a prospective diver as unsuitable. This syndrome includes fainting, hyperventilation, claustrophobic tendencies, etc. Close and confined spaces are easily encountered in cave and wreck diving; if such situations cause undue anxiety they should be avoided. Divers should be comfortable with direct facial immersion in water. Many well-experienced divers have proven susceptible to rapidly progressive panic when deprived of their mask. Please refer to Chapter 3 for a more complete discussion of panic and its manifestations.

The Counterphobe:

This individual may possess a deep-seated fear of the water and keep such phobias well hidden from others. Diving may be an avenue of hopefully overcoming these fears. This attempt at boosting self-confidence may be well-intended but lead to tragic consequences in a true emergency at depth. This syndrome is nearly impossible to identify in advance with any degree of accuracy.

The "Dragooned", Reluctant Diver:

Do not let yourself or anyone else be "finessed" into diving activities that you or they are uncomfortable with. The motivation to participate has to be genuine and not the product of coercion or peer pressure. Likewise, motivation to dive that can be identified as an effort to please a spouse or close friend rather than for the individual's pleasure or satisfaction must preclude involvement in deep diving. If any doubt arises as to the diver's willingness to participate, question him or her privately to determine their true state of mind.

The Buccaneer/Top Gun Candidate:

Typically self-centered, impetuous, cocky and headstrong. Incapable of following directions. Sometimes difficult to separate from a confident, qualified diver that is highly motivated but lacks patience with others less skilled. The former cannot be relied on due to typical selfish diving practices and general disregard for accepted diving plans. Avoid them!

Psychotic Disorders:

Totally a crapshoot here... but a few latent suicidal types do appear from time to time. Beware the diver signing up for the deep wreck dive trip to Truck Lagoon... who didn't buy a round-trip airline ticket.

Ideally, we are looking for divers with maturity (not a function of age, incidentally), intelligence, self-control, common sense and confidence. Our candidate should understand the importance of over-learning skills and procedures, reflex response conditioning and a finely-honed ability to deal with stress.

Mentally, our diver will be logical and motivated to excellence in every phase of dive planning and execution. The diver must be at ease with the situation and anticipate in advance every reasonable contingency. Ultimately, deep diving is more a mental discipline than a physical one. Mount (1979) has suggested an ideal balance to be 60% common sense (mental) and 40% physical ability for overall diving skills, and this applies well for advanced deep diving.

Chapter 3

Stress

*"I don't want to participate in any sport in which my
species is not at the top of the food chain."*

Ken Fonte

*"Stress in diving is probably the central problem in
the accidents and resulting injuries and fatalities
that occur to divers..."*

Art Bachrach and Glen Egstrom

STRESS

Many divers do not seem to place traditional activities in the context of
stress-inducing scenarios. Diving is supposed to be fun, right? The
following passage is excerpted from Bachrach and Egstrom's (1987)
Stress and Performance in Diving:

> *"We will cover your nose and eyes with a rubber and glass cup that will
> give you tunnel vision and prevent breathing through your nose. A snorkel
> which is partially filled with water will increase breathing resistance,
> especially when you work harder. A rubber suit will increase your surface
> area and your buoyancy while creating a restriction over each of the
> body's joints. (A partial adjustment will be made by fastening 15-20
> pounds (6.8-9.1 kg) of lead to your waist.) Fins for your feet will make
> walking more difficult and require more energy when swimming. A
> buoyancy compensation device will provide additional drag, especially
> when it is inflated to increase your buoyancy. Approximately 40-50
> pounds (18.2-22.7 kg) of steel or aluminum will be fixed between your*

shoulder blades by means of a backpack with a series of straps and buckles, which will terminate somewhere under the buoyancy compensator near the weight belt buckle. A regulator with various and sundry hoses and gauges will be attached to the tank and will cause you to breathe against an added resistance both during inhalation and exhalation. Various other items, such as knives, gauges, goody bags, cameras, spear guns, gloves, hoods and booties will be added for your comfort and convenience."

These learned authors (by this humorous accounting) have accurately placed into perspective the realities of the stressful environment that scuba divers willingly subject themselves to. By necessity our sport is equipment intensive and simply donning that equipment can produce levels of stress far in excess of what the average person may be comfortable with. Indeed, divers have been observed to reach heart rates approaching 200 beats per minute, nearly 3.5 times the normal rate, just gearing up!

Deep diving not only subjects the participants to added stress but the deeper environment also makes coping with such performance detriments critical. In our discussions we are most concerned with recognizing the early effects of stress and dealing with the effective management of these stimuli underwater.

Stress is variously defined: McGrath (1970) describes it as "a result of an imbalance between the demands placed upon an individual and the capacity of the individual to respond to the demands." Sells (1970) states "for a situation to be stressful the individual must perceive the consequences of his failure to be important." These two views provide perspectives from both the physical and mental effects and clearly shows the potential for compound stress stimuli to be at work simultaneously in the diver. Smith (1979) provides a succinct overview, "in the context of human behavior, stress might be regarded as a force that tends to break down an individual's ability to perform. Physical stress tends to weaken or injure the diver; psychological stress leads to behavior impairment."

The role of stress in deep diving applications cannot be ignored. Typical reactions to stress include such signs as rapid breathing or hyper-ventilation, the consequence of which should be immediately apparent to our readers. Importantly, stress is so varied to individuals that even what may be considered a "routine" problem can be highly stressful in some divers. Bachrach and Egstrom (1987) describe stress as "basically learned" and this perception is learned through "modeling" behavior. If your mother was afraid of reptiles, this phobia may well be passed along to you subconsciously. Likewise, much of the public has an inherent dread or horror of sharks or moray eels with no actual experience to justify such fear. Experienced resort guides think nothing of hand-feeding eels or swimming with sharks but to the uninitiated the mere appearance of such a creature can rapidly induce stress reactions that can lead to near panic.

We all probably have a few skeletons rattling around in our mental closets, some that we may not have even a vague recognition of. Well experienced divers have reported extreme anxiety in their first encounter with "silting- out" situations in caves or wrecks. Willful control of this stress anxiety through discipline and fall-back on training can prevent escalation to a threat scenario.

SOURCES OF STRESS

"Time pressure" is a classic method used by psychologists to alter experimental testing and induce error by test subjects. Problems that are easily accomplished become increasingly difficult and sometimes impossible if the element of time is introduced as an opponent. Diving, especially deep diving, is time dependent: we only have so much allotment due to constraints of decompression and/ or gas supply.

This emphasizes the importance of dive planning so that orderly progression of the dive is maintained within the dive

Dives into tunnels or caverns are beautiful but can be a potential source of stress to some people with phobias about dark or confined spaces.

envelope calculated. Deviations from the plan can cause rapid acceleration of "time pressure" stress inducements. This is true not only for the dive itself but for pre-dive activities such as gearing up. Do not allow yourself to be hurried into mistakes. How many times have you observed divers entering the water without a mask or without fins? Simply putting the gear on an empty cylinder without checking its pressure happens too often.

"Task loading" is another factor well known to produce errors in performance. Simple enough: give the diver more projects (tasks) to do than he reasonably can accomplish in the time period allotted. Or give him competitive, multiple jobs that require him to do two or more things at the same time. Divers are already burdened with monitoring gauges, keeping track of their position underwater (pure navigation and also depth trim), noting the performance of a buddy, etc. Add to this equation an underwater camera system or duties requiring written observations and we have a fairly well "task loaded" diver before any contingencies may arise. And let's remember that all this activity is being attempted in water deep enough to have effects from narcosis and gas density for breathing purposes.

Environmental considerations such as current, cold water or reduced visibility will all contribute to stress loading. Further, when physical exertion is needed to deal with such environmental detriments over any normal exertion on the dive a compounding of stress factors will result.

Equipment alone can be a primary source of stress inducement simply due to its bulk, weight, drag, etc. Take note of the experienced diver whose gear is streamlined and well organized. This individual will be wearing a BCD selected for its suitability for the dive situation. Tropical wall diving in warm water is far more easily accomplished with a light wet suit (2mm) or dive skin with a neoprene vest. Combining this with the newer editions of BCD's that feature less volume, form fitting styles and a full-foot power fin eliminates the needless bulk of heavier wet suits, booties, etc. Gauges conveniently mounted in a single console with a dive computer provide easy viewing and no distractions of arm or wrist attached devices. Combining the "octopus" second stage into one of the inflator/second stages such as Scubapro's AIR II or SeaQuest's AIR SOURCE further streamlines the diver. A light-weight belt sized for neutral buoyancy at low tank pressures (to facilitate safety and/or decompression stops) completes the package.

Obviously, this equipment package must be modified as we deal with cold water, cave or wreck situations but the emphasis on effective management of equipment should be obvious. Consider the equipment stress of the diver outfitted for deep water mixed gas wreck diving: we see him in a dry suit, dual 120 cubic foot cylinders, redundant regulators and gauges, redundant BCD's and inflators, heavy weight belt, lift bags, decompression reels, and, in many cases, stage bottles of NITROX and O_2 clipped to his rig. This individual may well have in excess of 200 pounds (91 kg) of equipment strapped to him.

All this adds up to a diver who is heavily predisposed to performance limitations before he ever leaves the surface. Indeed, as mentioned in the previous chapter, this individual may already have exceeded his physical limits to safely conduct a dive simply due to the equipment load he has strapped on. Is this a comfortable, relaxed diver? Maybe... but add a rough sea and a pitching boat with a violently surging swim platform or ladder, and unless this diver is a superior physical specimen it will be a major stress loading activity to deal with the equipment and get into the water safely.

This leads into the current debate about what equipment is necessary for deep diving. The authors do have some concerns about recent

The energy necessary to manage unwieldy and heavy gear on a bouncing dive boat can result in equipment stress.

trends that exhibit a fascination for equipment-intensive outfitting far in excess of the practical requirements of the dive. At some plateau, the point of diminishing returns is reached: is carrying 300 cu. ft. of gas effective if the performance detriment by the sheer weight/size/drag of such gear requires the additional gas supply? Gilliam (1990) deliberately chose a single cylinder (100 cu. ft.) and regulator package to lesson his equipment load on his record 452 fsw (137 m) air dive. With proper breathing techniques, etc., he was able to comfortably complete the dive on this reduced rig. He relates, "some would argue that redundancy is a requirement at such extreme depths but with DIN fittings I was not concerned with a regulator failure at the valve. Therefore, the physical stress and distraction of extra equipment to me was not justified. I wanted to carry enough gas with me to do the dive, obviously, but the single 100 provided that for me and I was far more comfortable in the water."

Logically, deep divers must carry the gas volumes necessary to do the dive plan with an adequate safety margin. Extended decompression in colder water will dictate larger gas storage carried by the diver but we caution our readers to carefully weigh the equipment stress load with operational requirements of the dive site.

There will always be debate on what equipment is necessary but a perspective on what is realistically matched to the dive plan must be encouraged. A recent trip to the Florida Keys offered one author this scenario while observing dive passengers:

On a 60 to 90 fsw multi-level dive in May with air and water temperatures in the eighties, one dive team wore the following equipment:

71

Two members used full 1/4 inch wetsuits with hoods, one member a full dry suit. All three wore fully redundant double 105 cubic foot cylinders with isolation manifolds and all were employing NOAA NITROX I as dive mix. The three divers were demonstrating marked pre-dive equipment stress loading just in the process of gearing up and moving around on the dive boat. Additionally, all were severely affected by the discomfort of the thermal suits while waiting to get in the water. In spite of the high ambient temperatures, one diver even made use of a separate suit inflator bottle filled with argon as an insulating gas.

Meanwhile, eight other divers dressed in conventional scuba rigs and lightweight wetsuits or dive skins performed the same dive far more efficiently and they probably had a lot more fun.

A diver's performance is directly affected, either for better or worse, by his equipment selection. Certainly, the dive team discussed above was drastically over-equipped for the site conditions and any reasonable expectation of contingency. They liked using the "high tech" gear even though it was not justified in this application. If the motivation to use this equipment was oriented to practice or to refine skills with it, then its use is completely justifiable. But, if its use is solely based upon fascination with "gear intensive" high-tech attitudes, then its use is misplaced. Given circumstances that present cold water, extensive wreck, or cave penetration, etc., and the gear makes sense. As it happened, the gear set only lessened their performance.

An experienced diver dresses for the occasion as it were. A tuxedo is not required for a backyard barbecue. Veteran divers who have access to the most advanced "technical gear" will not hesitate to simplify a gear set when conditions allow. Gilliam's record dive to 452 feet was focused on a specific goal and was of limited duration. In such extreme depths on air he

Cathy Lawlor demonstrates a well-balanced and streamlined equipment package at 175 fsw in Belize.

Photo by Bret Gilliam

SIGNS OF STRESS

- Rapid breathing, hyperventilation
- "Wild-eyed" look
- White-knuckle gripping; muscle tension
- Rapid, jerky, disjointed movements
- Irritability, unreasonableness
- Fixation, repetitive behavior
- High treading, attempts to leave the water
- "Escape to the surface" behavior
- Stalling – taking too long to suit-up
- Imaginary gear problems or ear problems
- Contact maintenance (e.g. clutching swim ladder, anchor line)

balanced his gas volume needs based upon vast experience against his performance ideals dictated by a stripped down and low-drag configuration gear set. In contrast, Sheck Exley's record mixed gas dive to 881 feet had totally different requirements due to cold water, multiple gas switches, extreme depth and drastically extended decompression time. Both dives were extremely hazardous and conducted solo, but both were successful, in part, by balancing equipment packages to the precise operational need.

Divers should be aware in intimate detail of their personal gas consumption rates at a range of depths and dive situations. Likewise, a consideration of their thermal comfort and suit needs must be plugged into the equipment equation. For Caribbean divers conducting multi-level drop-off wall excursions to depths up to 200 fsw, a single BCD is probably adequate with an oversized single cylinder and a regulator with DIN fittings. Some would like the redundancy of a Y-valve for regulator back-up. Fine... we are still dealing with a manageable gear package. The same dive conducted on a northeast wreck will obviously call for an expanded gear set including doubles, dry suits, etc. But let's always keep in mind the common sense rule of equipment stress: Match your gear set to your operation.

Ego threat stress is significant as well in our dive planning. Smith (1979) notes, "An individual can be effectively destroyed by tearing down self-esteem, pride or ego..." The overextention of capabilities by personal challenge or peer group pressure is a leading contributory factor to deep diving accidents. Individuals must seek at all times to do dives within their own limitations. Gentile (1988) relates the case of an experienced northeast coast wreck diver who elected to sit out the last dive of the day as conditions worsened. Unconcerned by any supposed negative peer reactions, Gentile praises this individual for his good judgement in knowing

73

when to quit.

We must not let perceived ego threats intrude on our good judgement. Divers should not encourage others to participate in deep diving activities with which they are uncomfortable. The emotionally mature diver can abstain from diving in any situation with no attendant ego damage. Smith (1979) puts it best: "The truly mature person can do this even when others may extend themselves further into the situation because of either their superior ability or their own foolishness. The threat to one's ego when one must back away from a challenge can be quite stressful, and tolerance to this stress is important in diving... A diver who is incompetent and knows it may be stressful. An incompetent diver may also be stressful to other divers who know about the incompetency. A diver may even stress companions into death by threatening their ego through constantly challenging them to test their limits to save their pride."

EFFECTS OF STRESS

Even a passing review of the material will demonstrate that sources of stress are varied and quite probably unlimited. Now we shall briefly look at the behavioral mechanics of stress and the resulting "**mental narrowing**". As we heap stress loads on our diver he becomes less sensitive to his environment and less able to intelligently focus on problems. These interferences with mental thought processes manifest in several classic ways:

"**Perceptual narrowing**" whereby the diver is unable to notice or deal with subtle developing aspects of a situation and perceives only the grossest or more obvious elements of a problem. At depth, the effects of such narrowing are more serious. A diver who finds himself unable to maintain neutral buoyancy and continues to fixate on depressing the inflate button of his BCD to no avail has lost the intellectual ability to perceive another solution to his problem.

"**Cognitive or analytical narrowing**" whereby the diver is hampered in his ability to analyze a problem. Example: a diver barely reaches his decompression stage bottle because he was low on air. As he begins his 20 foot (6.1m) stop, he has trouble breathing but the indicated pressure is 2500 psi. Under sufficient stress he may not realize that the valve is not open all the way or that switching to the "octopus" would solve the problem.

"**Response narrowing**" occurs when the diver is unable to focus skills and knowledge upon problems. This typically manifests with loss of poorly learned skills or behavior. Over-learned, reflex action type skills are retained longest. The obvious importance of drills and skill repetition until reactions to certain situations are second nature cannot be overemphasized.

"**Panic**" is usually described as unreasoning fear, the ultimate plateau of mental narrowing. Smith (1979), "As stress increases, the diver's ability to diagnose and respond to them properly may diminish accordingly. In any stressful situation, it is critical for the individual to break out of this escalating cycle as quickly as possible. Early detection is important. Thus, it is desirable to recognize the early symptoms of stress in your own behavior and in the behavior of others before these symptoms reach panic proportions. **Panic is the end of the line. It is usually terminal and contagious.**"

Watch for signs of stress such as "Contact maintainence" – the diver who will not let go of the safety line at the surface.

Photo by Bret Gilliam

SUMMARY

The anticipation of problem situations in a dive and the ability to adopt contingency plans calmly and rationally are vital in deep diving. Experience plays a great role in the individual's ability to deal with stress and to formulate alternative reactions to threat scenarios presented. Over-learning of all relevant skills and complete familiarization with equipment is necessary. If over-learning can be taken to its highest level, then much of the reactive behavior in an emergency will be reflexive and not require conscious thought processes. Smith (1979) notes, "Over-learning takes all doubt out of human performance under stress as far as that particular skill is concerned. This not only greatly reduces the probability of human error on certain tasks but also frees the diver's mind to deal confidently with more complex aspects of the problem."

Stress accompanies us everywhere and is magnified in deep diving activities. Know yourself, know your buddy and/or your diving team. Dive within your limits.

Chapter 4

Nitrogen Narcosis

*"It was hard to admit at the time, but my first face-slamming
experience with narcosis occurred at just 160 feet. I was
crushed; demoralized. Eventually, after about 20 dives, I had
worked my way past 200 feet. I was finally the victor; I had
beaten narcosis, or so I thought . . ."*

Wes Skiles

*"What normally keeps me out of trouble on deep air
dives is fear. It keeps me from being too bold, getting too far
away from the anchor line or getting out of control."*

Gary Gentile

NARCOSIS

Within the context of air diving, the effects of inert gas narcosis are
second only to acute CNS oxygen toxicity in hazard to the scuba diver.
Commonly known as "nitrogen narcosis", this condition is first described
by Junod in 1835 when he discovered divers breathing compressed air:
"The functions of the brain are activated, imagination is lively, thoughts
have a peculiar charm and in some persons, symptoms of intoxication are
present." Early caisson workers were occasional victims of befuddlement

on otherwise simple tasks and some were reported to spontaneously burst into singing popular songs of that period. Much of the mysteries of compressed air impairment remained speculative until Benke zeroed in on elevated partial pressures of nitrogen as the culprit. His observations were reported in 1935 and depicted narcosis as "euphoric retardation of the higher mental processes and impaired neuromuscular coordination".

Other studies confirmed this phenomena and U.S. Navy divers reported narcosis a major factor in the salvage efforts on the sunken submarine *Squalus* in 1939. Working in depths of 240 fsw (72.7 m) in cold water, these divers reported loss of clear thought and reasoning. Several unusual entanglement scenarios resulted and in the normal work process at least one diver was reported to unexpectedly lose consciousness underwater on the wreck. Because of this, the Navy switched to then experimental HELIOX mixtures marking the first major project with this gas. Bennett (1966) first related narcosis to the Greek word "nark", meaning numbness. The Greeks used this in association with the human reactive process to opium which produces drowsiness, stupefaction and a general feeling of well being and lassitude.

At any rate, the best explanation appears to be the Meyer-Overton hypothesis relating the narcotic effect of an inert gas to its solubility in the lipid phase or fat. This is postulated to act as a depressant to the nervous system proportional to the gas amount going into solution. Mount (1979) has expressed the narcotic effect as determined by multiplying the solubility by the partition coefficient. By examining tables of various inert gases compared by solubility and partition coefficient it becomes abundantly clear that nitrogen is one of the least desirable gases in a breathing mixture for divers at depth. The relative narcotic potency is expressed as a number value with the highest number reflecting the least narcotic effect. Argon is extremely narcotic with a value of .43, nitrogen is rated at 1.0 with helium one of the least narcotic at 4.26.

As experienced divers more frequently dive to deeper depths in pursuit of wreck, cave exploration and photographic interests, the subject of inert gas narcosis becomes more ardently debated. Much discussion of narcosis theory among scuba divers has been conducted "underground" by a close-knit community of "high-tech" professional divers without a public forum of information exchange. Narcosis was regarded as an occupational hazard that had to be dealt with in order to gain access to new cave systems, more remote wrecks or the most spectacular drop-off walls.

Due to the controversial nature of deep diving within the traditional sport diving industry, an understandable reluctance to discuss actual diving practices was perpetuated. Little actual "field work" was published and a word of mouth grapevine developed to compare different diving techniques in widely diverse areas. In the late sixties and early seventies three distinctly different segments of emerging "technical" diving were conducting deep air dives. On the cave diving scene individuals such as Sheck Exley, Tom Mount, Frank Martz, Jim Lockwood and Dr. George Benjamin pushed ever deeper with their explorations, while Bahamian and Caribbean groups led by Neil Watson and Bret Gilliam pushed beyond the 400 fsw (121.2 m) barrier for the first time in open water. Simultaneously, a whole new wreck diving cult with Peter Gimble, Gary Gentile, Hank Keatts and Steve Bielenda was coming out of the shadows in the northeast to assault previously unreachable sites such as the *Andrea Doria.*

Published accounts of narcosis experiences were largely limited to cave diving newsletters although Gilliam presented a quasi "how-to" paper on deep air methods in 1974. This presentation at the International Conference on Underwater Education in San Diego stimulated some limited exchange of information between the diverse communities but also focused criticism from national training agencies, etc. The "underground" once again retreated from the harsh glare of sport diver scrutiny and new breakthroughs and techniques reverted to word of mouth communiques. As veteran deep wreck explorer Gary Gentile put it, "you can always tell a pioneer by the arrows in his back!"

In 1990 for the first time, the "technical diver" began to come out of the closet and stay a while, and in-depth discussions of narcosis went public.

Some of the earlier accounts by Cousteau (1947) relate instances of near total incapacitation at depths of only 150 fsw (45.5 m) and cite the supposed "Martini's Law" and the classic broad generalization of "Rapture of the Deep". In reality, the severity of impairment is drastically reduced in well equipped and experienced/adapted divers at greater depth. Narcosis is certainly a factor to be dealt with responsibly by divers, but many texts suggest levels of impairment that are far exaggerated for seasoned practitioners.

Today's diver has the advantage of high-tech scuba gear that can markedly increase his performance. Design evolutions in buoyancy compensating devices (BCD's), scuba regulators, instrumentation, less restrictive and more efficient thermal suits etc., all contribute to his ability to work deeper safely.

The authors would like to emphasize that deep air diving below 220 fsw (60.6 m) is generally not recommended given the alternatives available in today's industry. On high risk or particularly demanding dive scenarios this depth should be adjusted shallower. Many veteran air divers now opt for mixed gas to virtually eliminate narcosis problems. What is the cut-off depth on air? This is clearly subjective and must be answered by the individual diver who considers his own narcosis susceptibility, his objective and his access and financial commitment to mixed gas equipment. Wes Skiles (1990), a highly experienced and respected cave diver, has expressed his preference for mixed gas on any penetrations below 130 fsw (39.4 m). Members of the scientific diving community still practice air dives to 190 fsw (57.6 m) officially (with far deeper dives reported "unofficially"). Gentile, Mount and Gilliam suggest practical air limits of between 250 and 275 fsw (75.7 and 83.3 m) for trained individuals. Mixed gas solves some problems for some people, but it adds several new problems and operational considerations to the equation: expense, extended decompression time etc. For many experienced air practitioners, deep air diving remains a viable choice simply because done with the proper disciplines and training it is a reasonable exercise. That is to say it can be approached with an acceptable level of risk. But new divers venturing beyond traditional sport limits must be fully cognizant of the elements of risk, that deep diving will reduce the margin for error, and the accompanying increased chance for injury or death must be understood. Diving within one's limitations should be etched firmly in the deep diver's memory. Depths below 130 fsw (39.4 m) can be safely explored but such diving cannot be taken lightly.

PREDISPOSING FACTORS OF NITROGEN NARCOSIS

Factors contributing to narcosis onset and severity include:
- ncreased partial pressures of CO_2 (hard work, heavy swimming etc.)
- Cold
- Alcohol use or "hangover" conditions
- Drugs
- Fatigue
- Anxiety or apprehension, FEAR
- Effects of motion sickness medications
- Rate of descent (speed of decompression)
- Vertigo or spatial disorientation caused by no 'UP' reference such as in bottomless clear "blue water" or in severely restricted visibility
- Task loading stress
- Time pressure stress
- Another lesser known contributory factor is increased oxygen partial pressure

Table 4 - 1
Relative Narcotic Potencies

Helium (He)	4.26	*(least narcotic)*
Neon (Ne)	3.58	
Hydrogen (H_2)	1.83	
Nitrogen (N_2)	1.00	
Argon (A)	0.43	
Krypton (Kr)	0.14	
Xenon (Xe)	0.039	*(most narcotic)*

ADAPTATION

Narcosis can be controlled to varying degrees specific to individuals but tolerances can change from day to day. Almost any experienced deep diver will tell you that "adaptation" to narcosis takes place. Bennett (1990) notes, "the novice diver may expect to be relatively seriously effected by nitrogen narcosis, but subjectively at least there will be improvement with experience. Frequency of exposure does seem to result in some level of adaptation." The actual mechanics of adaptation are not clearly understood or proven but most deep divers agree that they will perform better with repeated progressively deeper penetrations on a cumulative basis.

Gilliam (1990) relates no significant impairment at 452 fsw (137 m) for his brief exposure, approximately 4.5 minutes in the critical zone below 300 fsw (91 m). He was able to successfully complete a series of higher math and thought/reasoning problems while suspended at the deepest level. But this is probably the extreme end of adaptation; he dove every week for over a year with never more than a six day lay-off. His 627 dives during this period included 103 below 300 fsw (91 m).

For the diver who regularly faces deep exposures, a tolerance far in excess of the un-adapted diver will be exhibited. A gradual work-up to increasing depths is the best recommendation. (This should not be misconstrued as an endorsement of "reverse profile dives". We refer to making each first dive of the day progressively deeper than the day before to build tolerances, i.e., Day 1: first dive to 150 fsw, Day 2: first dive to 175 fsw, etc. Subsequent dives on Day 1 and Day 2 would be shallower than the first.) This process should be over several day's time if the diver has been away from deep diving for more than two weeks. Adaptation appears to be lost exponentially as acquired so no immediate increased narcosis susceptibility will necessarily be evident but divers are cautioned to exercise great conservatism if any lay-off is necessitated.

THE DIVING REFLEX

Back in the mid-1800's Paul Bert observed pronounced brachycardia (lowered heartbeat) in ducks while diving. Suk Ki Hong (1990) describes "a reflex phenomenon that is accompanied by an intense peripheral vasoconstriction, a drastic reduction in the cardiac output, and a significant reduction of O_2 consumption". Hickey and Lundgren (1984) further noted aspects of the mammalian diving reflex to include "muscular relaxation, astonishing levels of brachycardia, e.g., heart rates 13% of pre-dive levels in harbor seals... and depressed metabolism. All of these adaptations conserve the body's energy stores." Simply put, this reflex serves to apparently slow down most vital, internal functions such as heartbeat and shunt blood from the extremities enabling the diving seal or dolphin to more effectively utilize it's single breath oxygen load while underwater.

Similar responses have been noted in human subjects. Several divers stumbled onto this in the late sixties and began to effectively incorporate facial immersion breathing periods prior to diving. Exley and Watson practiced such techniques and Gilliam became a leading proponent of surface and ten fsw (3.03 m) level extended breathing with his diving mask and hood removed before dives below 300 fsw (91 m) in 1971. He has recorded dramatic reductions in his heart rate and respiration rate by following a protocol of ten minutes facial immersion breathing at the surface, then five minutes at ten to fifteen fsw (3.03 to 4.5 m) from a pony bottle. His pulse has been measured at twelve to fifteen beats per minute and respiration rate dropped to two a minute at deep depths (dive to 405 fsw/122.7 m in 1977). Other divers have adopted varying uses of the diving reflex technique in conjunction with meditation disciplines with significant success. Of the divers using this technique, many report pronounced reduction of narcosis, reduced air consumption and better coordination at depth. Regardless of the scientific proof challenges, the technique is becoming more widespread and its subjective benefits certainly bear closer scrutiny.

EQUIPMENT

At depth the air we breathe has far greater density and can be an operational problem if the scuba regulator is not carefully selected to comfortably deliver adequate volumes upon demand. Breathing resistance can markedly increase onset and progression of narcosis. Many so-called "professional" regulator models will fall sadly short on performance below 200 fsw (60.6 m).

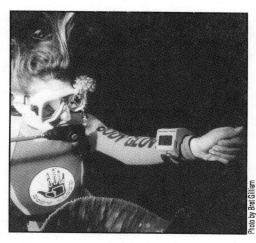

Make certain that your instruments are easy to read at depth under the influence of narcosis.

Photo by Bret Gilliam

Exhalation resistance is a prime factor in breathing control, perhaps more so than inhalation ease. Studies have shown exhalation detriments to be the most significant fatigue element in underwater breathing tests. So how do you choose between the dozens of models offered? Some benchmark can be derived from perusal of U.S. Navy test reports but sometimes results can offer inconclusive appraisals. The Tekna 2100 series unit basically failed the Navy tests for high performance but has been a popular regulator with many experienced deep divers since its introduction. Gilliam (1990) used it on his record setting 452 fsw (137 m) dive in Roatan and reported complete satisfaction. Please refer to Chapter 7 for comments on other suitable regulators.

Now is a good time to insure that you select comparable quality instruments compatible with the depths you anticipate exploring. Keep in mind that many depth gauges and dive computers have depth limitations that will render them useless over normal sport diving ranges. Make certain that the information is displayed in an easily understood format. If you have a hard time deciphering what you are looking at on the surface, imagine the problem at 250 fsw (75.8 m) under the influence of narcosis.

Depth gauges should have large faces and well graduated depth increments so they can be read precisely. Many divers report digital gauges as found in computer models to be far easier to read at depth.

ON THE DIVE

Wreck and drop-off wall divers should use descents undertaken with a negative glide to the desired operational depth and BCD used to quickly attain neutral buoyancy. Do not waste energy using leg kicking to maintain position in the water column. Slow, deep ventilations with minimal exertions will keep CO_2 down and reduces onset and severity of narcosis. Narcosis has been reported subjectively to be most strong when first arriving at depth. Allow yourself a stop-activity period to monitor your instruments and let the initial narcosis effects stabilize.

Diving deep properly is more a mental exercise than a physical one. The diver must constantly be aware of his own limitations to narcosis and not hesitate to abort a dive if impairment becomes unreasonable. If narcosis is severe on descent, slow the rate or stop completely until symptoms are controlled. If possible face an "up" reference at all times such as anchor line or face the drop-off to orient the wall perpendicularly to the surface. This affords more accurate references if you are sinking or rising. If necessary, hold on to the descent line or a drop-off wall outcropping to insure of control of depth while narcosis can be evaluated.

SYMPTOMS

In spite of the warnings of various academicians, it is unlikely that the diver will experience "rapture" or the uncontrollable desire to kiss a fish or dance with an imaginary mermaid. However, there is a wide range of individual susceptibility. Almost all divers will be impaired eventually. This will manifest in many ways.

Most divers are acquainted with traditional depictions of narcosis symptomatology (light-headedness, slowed reflexes, euphoria, poor judgment, even numbness, etc.). But many early symptoms are more subtle. Initially divers will notice, in many cases, a reduced ability to read fine graduations in a depth gauge or watch along with increased awareness of sensitivity to sound such as exhalation and inhalation noise. Perceptual narrowing may limit some divers to successful execution of only limited task loading. Short term memory loss and perceptions of time can be affected. With experience, divers can learn to control these deficits to some extent. But these very real dangers cannot be underestimated. A diver unaware of his depth, bottom time or remaining air volume is about to become a statistic!

Buddy teams need to be more aware of each other in deep dives. Just as frequent scanning of instruments is mandated so is confirmation of your buddy's status. Generally, you should look for him about every three breaths and observe him for any overt signs of impairment. Quick containment of a problem situation in its development is vital to prevent a stressful rescue event that may be difficult to perform at depth.

Gilliam (1972) offered an effective narcosis check between divers. "We were frequently diving very deep with long working bottom times on

Buddy teams need to be more aware of each other on deep dives. Get used to looking for overt symptoms of narcosis and monitor your partner's instruments periodically during phases of the dive. Don't hesitate to abort your dive plan if you feel unduly affected.

Photo by Bret Gilliam

this contract in the Virgin Islands. I had a secret dread of one of our team's divers being overcome without our immediate knowledge. So I came up with a childishly simple hand signal response exercise for use at depth to detect narcosis. If one diver flashed a one-finger signal to another diver, it was expected that the diver would answer with a two-finger signal.

A two-fingered signal was answered with three-fingers; if you really wanted to screw a guy up you gave him all five fingers and then he had to use two hands to come up with a six-finger response. We reasoned that if a diver was not able to respond quickly and correctly to the signal given, then sufficient impairment was presumed to abort his dive. It worked great for us then and I still use it today." Over the years, scores of divers have reported using Gilliam's narcosis signals (also known as The Finger) with success.

Although narcosis effects are generally eliminated by ascent, it is important to understand that many divers will experience some degree of amnesia in their performance at depth. Commercial divers have reported successful completion of a work project to the diving supervisor upon ascent, only to learn later that the objective was not completed at all! Less experienced deep divers will typically not remember their greatest depth or bottom time unless disciplined to record it on a slate prior to ascent. Again, the experienced deep diver will sharply focus on his job objectives and constantly monitor his instruments. Modern devices such as dive computers greatly improve safety controls with maximum depth and time memories as well as decompression planning models.

THE MOUNT-MILNER TEST

In 1965 a research project was conducted by professional diver Tom Mount and psychiatrist Dr. Gilbert Milner to determine the effects of anticipated behavior modeling in diving students with respect to narcosis. Three control groups of four students with equal male/female ratios were trained in identical dive classes except:

TABLE 4.2

NARCOSIS SYMPTOMS

Light-headedness
Euphoria
Drunkenness
Impaired neuromuscular coordination
Hearing sensitivity or hallucination
Slowed mental activity
Decreased problem solving capacity
Overconfidence
Short term memory loss or distortions
Improper time perceptions
Fine work deterioration
Exaggerated movements
Numbness and tingling in lips, face and feet
Stupor
Sense of impending blackout
Levity or tendency to laughter
Depressive state
Visual hallucination or disturbances
Perceptual narrowing
Less tolerance to stress
Exaggerated (oversized) handwriting
Amnesia
Loss of consciousness
Retardation of higher mental processes
Retardation of task performances
Slurred speech
Poor judgement
Slowed reaction time and reflex ability
Loss of mechanical dexterity

Group One was taught that a diver would get narcosis at 130 fsw, and much emphasis was placed on the extremely high probability of narcosis with **severe** symptoms.

Group Two was taught of the existence of narcosis, the symptoms and depths of occurrence beginning at 100 fsw, but were not subjected to an intimidating lecture, as in Group One, that narcosis was an absolute barrier.

Group Three was well educated on narcosis with three full hours of lecture on symptoms, risk, danger and known research. They were told that divers with strong will power as postulated by Miles (1961) could mentally prepare themselves and greatly reduce the effects.

Prior to the open water deep dives all students were given two dives to 30 fsw and two dives to 100 fsw to develop good breathing techniques.

Before the actual dives for testing purposes, the students were taken on a 50 fsw dive where the tests were performed so a mental/dexterity familiarity could be achieved with the format of the test problems. Changes were then made in the test so they could not be performed from memory. The tests consisted of handwriting evaluations, peg board testing, math and ball bearing placement in a long-necked narrow bottle, etc.

In the initial test depth of 130 fsw, divers in Group One had minor to above average narcosis problems while Group Two and Three divers had little affect on test scores.

At the 180 fsw test depth, two Group One divers dropped from the exercise due to severe narcosis problems and were removed from the dive. All Group Two divers were affected although still functioning at about 50% test levels. Group Three divers had minor impairment.

At the 200 fsw test depth, all divers in Group One and two from Group Two were dropped due to severe narcosis and apprehension. Group Three divers actually showed slight improvement in test scores.

At the 240 fsw test depth, one diver was dropped from Group Two and one from Group Three due to severe narcosis. The remaining Group Two diver and three Group Three divers showed levels of impairment but again scores and performance showed improvement over the previous depth level. One diver, a female from Group Three, registered her highest scores on all tests at the 240 fsw level.

Concurrent testing of experienced deep divers showed 7 out of 10 divers with no decrease in performance or scores at the 200 fsw test level. The three divers with decreased performance finished the testing (2 with perfect scores) but required additional time than was usual. At 240 fsw, 5 out of 10 performed all tests with no decreased performance. One diver had problems with the ball bearing test but perfect scores on the peg board, math and handwriting. The other two showed up to 42% deficits and had problems completing the tests.

The obvious conclusions include a subjective validation to both "adaptation" and the negative influence of "modeling" behavior in those groups of divers pre-conditioned that narcosis was inevitable and severe. The Group Three divers with little prior diving experience were satisfactorily still performing a the 200 fsw level and three divers continued to perform (with one showing improvement still) at the 240 fsw test level.

If we teach our children that all dogs will bite, we can safely assume that when presented with a specimen even as lowly as a toy poodle (which should probably be shot on sight anyway), we can expect a high fear index.

Likewise, if we teach our dive students that narcosis is a finite, unyielding biophysical wall, then we can logically expect such conditioning to impair their performance beyond a more realistically educated diver lacking preconceived phobias and suggestions. Education is the key to performance and safety.

CONCLUSION

Depth limitation largely becomes a decision based upon narcosis levels and available gas supply (until the O_2 toxicity range is entered). Most divers will be able to function well in excess of the so-called 130 fsw (39.4 m) limit with even a little practice.

Interestingly, the first edition of the NOAA Diving Manual published in the mid-seventies contained this notation on narcosis: "Experience, frequent exposure to deep diving, and a high degree of training may permit divers to dive on air as deep as 200 fsw (60.6 m)..." Although scientific diving programs and university based research groups generally advocated air diving to around this recommended limit, a significant proportion of dives were conducted in far deeper depths if necessary for observation or collection purposes including dives beyond 300 fsw. The proliferation of "Do as I say, not as I do" mentalities still dominate all factions of the industry primarily for fear of critical condemnation by less realistic "experts".

All divers should exercise prudence and reasonable caution in all aspects of deep diving but particularly so when it comes to narcosis. Experience is vital before attempting progressively deeper dives. (Remember this does not imply "reverse profile" dives.) Ideally, the diver should be seeking out the benefit of training by a competent, well experienced deep diving instructor before a penetration below sport diving depths. Don't try to obtain field experience on your own or with another buddy. The historical record provides too many fatalities or near misses due to narcosis to warrant such a risk.

Chapter 5

Oxygen Toxicity

"Oxygen... a potent hazard if poorly managed."

John Crea

WHAT IS OXYGEN TOXICITY?

Oxygen is the most basic life support system our bodies employ, and yet also has the capacity to cause great harm. Keller (1946) has called oxygen "The Princess of Gases. She is beautiful but has to be handled with special care". We cannot live without it, but in prolonged breathing exposures or in deep depths on standard air scuba systems too much of a good thing can prove fatal.

Thom and Clark (1990) note, "paradoxically, the same gas that is required to sustain life by preventing loss of consciousness and death from hypoxemia has toxic properties that affect all living cells at sufficiently high pressure and duration of exposure." Most divers are familiar with the basic characteristics of oxygen as it occurs in our atmosphere. It is a colorless, odorless and tasteless gas found free in dry air at 23.15% by weight and 20.98% by volume. For discussion purposes, we will consider its volume percentage to be 21%. Interestingly, the relative toxic effects of oxygen are determined not by the percentage in any mixed gas (including standard air at approximately 21% oxygen and 79% nitrogen), but by the oxygen partial pressure (PO_2).

A review of Dalton's Law of Partial Pressures is helpful (The total pressure exerted by a gas mixture is equal to the sum of the partial pressures of the components of the mixture i.e. $P = P1+P2+P3...$ etc.), but put simply, as depth increases a corresponding elevation in the partial pressure of oxygen is achieved and must be considered by any diver planning deeper exposures. At the surface we are naturally adapted to PO_2 at .21 atmospheres absolute (ATA). This is considered the reference point for "normoxic" conditions.

It is important to be aware of certain ranges of tolerance in normal, healthy persons. Most people can maintain proper blood oxygenation down to .16 ATA (16% oxygen in the mix at surface pressure) but dropping much below this will limit performance/endurance and unconsciousness will likely result approaching .1 ATA (10% oxygen at the surface).

As a physics reminder please note that we commonly refer to the percentage of a gas in any mixture as the Fg (fraction of the gas expressed as the decimal equivalent); thusly the FO_2 at the surface can be correctly expressed as .21; Pg or partial pressure of a gas may be expressed as the Fg multiplied by atmospheres absolute or ATA's. Therefore, the PO_2 at 66 fsw is properly expressed as .63 ATA of O_2. This is derived from multiplying .21 (the FO_2 of oxygen in air) by the pressure in ATA's: .21 X 3 = .63 ATA's of O_2. Though the FO_2 will remain constant, the PO2 will increase with depth.

The diver may recall the old reference to the "Ten and Ten Rule" wherein it supposed that blackout will occur if the percentage of either oxygen or carbon dioxide (CO_2) reaches 10% in the gas mixture. This was particularly important to competitive free divers and spearfishermen while holding their breath and attaining depths in excess of 80 to 100 fsw (24.2 to 30.3 m). Many of these individuals could reach far deeper depths through applied disciplines of hyperventilation and adaptation in conjunction with techniques employed to precipitate the "diving reflex" to extend time underwater. This practice, however, is a double edged sword: As depth increased CO_2 was produced by the body's metabolism, and absent any other source the "O_2 storage" was depleted. To a certain degree this was counterbalanced by a corresponding rise in the percentage of CO_2 in the system since this gas is a metabolic waste product as O_2 is burned.

The relationship is important because high CO_2 is a major stimulus to breathe while low O_2 is not. As the diver held his breath, O_2 was consumed and CO_2 eventually said, "Hey buddy, I'll continue to hurt you unless you get back to the surface and get a fresh breath, you idiot!" Now the insidious danger occurs. As the diver ascended, both partial pressures dropped accordingly. His stimulus to breathe was reduced as PCO_2 dropped while his PO_2 could be dropping to dangerous levels.

At some point, the diver passed out from this "latent hypoxia" syndrome or what became commonly known as "shallow water black out". Typically the diver showed no signs or distress and simply went limp, sometimes within ten feet of the surface. Those who were successfully rescued and revived related no warning of the impending blackout or any major stimulus to breathe. But several fatalities were sustained before the problems were identified and the hazards of deep breath-hold diving were well communicated.

CENTRAL NERVOUS SYSTEM (CNS) O_2 TOXICITY
(Paul Bert Effect)

For the free swimming scuba diver, the most immediate dangers with O_2 toxicity are encountered in deeper depths where the PO_2 exceeds 1.6 ATA (218 fsw); in military, commercial and some scientific applications the ideal method of controlling the toxic effects of O_2 are to keep the oxygen dose as near "normoxic" as possible. This is accomplished by controlling the gas mixtures. A typical mix would reduce the oxygen percentage in a deep dive usage and let the elevated pressure raise the PO_2 to normoxic levels. For example, if a diver needed a mix for the 300 fsw (91 m) level the O_2 could be used at only 2% with another inert gas. The affect of 10 ATA's at 300 fsw would produce a PO_2 of .21 ATA, the same as we normally breathe at the surface. The dive supervisor could select a single inert gas such as helium (He) or combine two inert gases such as nitrogen and helium while keeping the O_2 percentage constant. The resulting gas mixes are commonly referred to as HELIOX or TRIMIX respectively. Realistically however, this mix would incur a greater decompression obligation due to the elevated inert gas percentages if oxygen was kept at an FO_2 of .02; a .10 to .15 FO_2 would be more practical. (See Mixed Gas chapter for a more complete explanation).

Since our text is primarily designed for use by deep divers using standard air as the breathing gas, we do not have the luxury of custom mixing our oxygen percentages. Our gas is going to be 21% O_2 and 79% nitrogen and we are stuck with it unless the diver makes the commitment to mixed gas equipment and its attendant responsibilities. As air divers we will be most concerned with the acute phase of oxygen toxicity (sometimes also referred to as oxygen poisoning). Acute O_2 toxicity for well experienced and "depth adapted" divers will ultimately be the deciding factor in penetration limits, not inert gas narcosis.

The central nervous system is primarily affected in the acute phase and the following table will illustrate typical manifestations.

Table 5.1

SIGNS AND SYMPTOMS OF CNS O_2 TOXICITY IN NORMAL MEN *

Facial pallor	Tinnitus and auditory hallucinations
Sweating	Vertigo
Bradycardia	Respiratory changes
Palpitations	Nausea
Depression	Spasmodic vomiting
Apprehension	Fibrillation of lips
Visual symptoms:	Twitching of lips, cheeks, nose, eyelids
Dazzle	Syncope
Constriction of visual field	Convulsions

*Table excerpted from *DIVING MEDICINE* (Bove and Davis, 1990)

In Table 5.2 below the authors have provided a simplified, abridged version to Table 5.1. The reader is directed to note that the first letter of each of the symptoms listed in Table 5.2 spells out the acronym **VENTID**.

Table 5.2

CNS O_2 TOXICITY SYMPTOMS (VENTID)

V ision: any disturbance including "tunnel vision," etc.
E ars: any changes in normal hearing function
N ausea: severity may vary and be intermittent
T witching: classically manifest in facial muscles
I rritability: personality shifts, anxiety, confusion etc.
D izziness: vertigo, disorientation

Even a cursory examination of these effects should illustrate the seriousness of a CNS O_2 hit in deep water. Onset and severity of symptoms do not follow any particular pattern and may vary in an individual diver from day to day. Of particular note is that there may be no warning with less serious symptoms before full convulsion is precipitated. Thom and Clark (1990) observe that "minor symptoms did not always precede the onset of convulsions, and even when a preconvulsive aura did occur, it was often followed so quickly by seizures that it had little practical value".

Many divers have relied on the incorrect supposition that lip twitching or "eye ticks" would provide adequate notice of impending disaster but this has been disproved by chamber tests and direct observation in actual dive scenarios. It is strongly suspected that CNS O_2 toxicity and/or severe narcosis played the major role in the loss of almost a dozen divers in the last two decades while attempting record dives on standard air.

Oxygen convulsions, per se, are not inherently harmful but imagine the implications for an untended diver or even one with a buddy near by. Management of a patent airway and rescue in such an extreme situation is near impossible and the diver will almost certainly drown.

Mount (1991) related a near miss accident he was inadvertently involved in during a deep dive in 1971. He was diving at the 330 fsw level and in control of narcosis with no O_2 toxicity problems when he observed an obviously out of control female diver blissfully pass him with a vigorous kick cycle heading straight down! He gave chase and intercepted her near the 400 fsw (121.2 m) level. Making contact and arresting her plunge required heavy exertion and power kicking strokes to initiate ascent for the pair. "Within seconds after this effort, I had almost complete visual collapse. I found myself looking through a solid red field with black spots; basically blind. I made it up to the 300 fsw level with her and was relieved in the rescue by other divers. By 275 fsw I was getting occasional 'windows' but my vision did not return to normal until past 250 fsw. "

Another account is related by Gilliam (1991) of another close call while diving on a scientific project in the Virgin Islands in 1972. "My regular buddy and I were gathering samples at 290 fsw as part of an on-going survey. We were both well adapted from daily deep diving and routinely worked this depth without difficulty. On this occasion, another scientist diver had joined us at his request. In prior discussions, he had satisfied us that he was familiar

Onset of oxygen toxicity symptoms can occur without warning and with potentially fatal consequences. Lina Hitchcock cruises the top of Sinai Cave at 200 fsw in the Red Sea.

and experienced with deep diving procedures. About seven minutes into the dive we watched him begin hammering away on a coral sample for retrieval and suddenly go limp. I caught him as he started to fall over the drop-off wall and ventilated him with his regulator's purge valve while rapidly ascending. At 190 fsw he completely recovered and began breathing on his own. He was unable to recall anything except beginning work with his hammer. This incident finally stopped the university's practice of forcing outsiders on our professional teams. It was sheer luck that I happened to be looking his way when he passed out".

Most cases of underwater blackout result in death. The dangers of this type of CNS O_2 toxicity cannot be too greatly emphasized. On air, at 300 fsw (91 m) or 10 ATA, the PO_2 has reached 2.1 ATA; this partial pressure will definitely produce toxicity limited only by time and other influences such as elevated PCO_2.

For these indisputable facts, the practice of air diving deeper than 300 fsw (91 m) must be placed in the perspective of assumable risk of sudden death not just injury.

It should be noted that divers routinely push nearly 3 ATA of O_2 in recompression chambers for extended periods. Theoretically, chamber divers are supposed to be at rest but many of the bounce dive profiles practiced by extreme deep air divers include performance plans that essentially have the diver "at rest" in the water with negative descents and controlled buoyant ascents in the toxicity range.

Neither Watson and Gruener (1968) nor Gilliam (1990) suffered O_2 toxicity problems on their record dives to 437 and 452 fsw (132.4 and 137 m) respectively but their times in the critical toxicity zone were limited and they each had practiced exceptional adaptive techniques. (In spite of this, Watson and Gruener reported near total incapacitation due to narcosis.)

Gilliam (1990) believed that adaptation was proven to narcosis as well as to onset of O_2 toxicity and was able to effectively limit narcosis impairment. "But my primary concern from the very beginning was O_2 Toxicity. My tables were based on fast descents and fast ascents in the Toxicity zone. I felt I could tolerate up to five minutes below 300 feet and still get out before the high O_2 would hit me. In retrospect, of course, it worked. Would it work again, who knows?"

Other factors in his success include almost absurdly low respiration and heartbeat rates, repeated progressive deep exposures and limited physical exertion. Like narcosis, O_2 toxicity can be precipitated by higher CO_2 levels generated in work tasks or simply swimming harder. Deep divers need to develop strong disciplines for energy conservation and

94

focused breathing habits. The double whammy of sudden onset and increased severity of narcosis and CNS O_2 toxicity in a stress situation can rapidly accelerate a borderline control situation into a disaster.

The U.S. Navy still conducts oxygen tolerance tests in dry chambers to screen individuals with unusual susceptibility to O_2. However, highly motivated individuals may escape detection anyway. Both Mount and Gilliam have served as chamber supervisors and conducted such tests. In 1991 when interviewed, neither could recall any instances where a pre-screening O_2 tolerance test was failed. The validity of such test protocols remains debated.

The following table (see Table 5.3) gives the oxygen partial pressure limits during working dives as recommended by NOAA. This will provide some parameters for dive planning and is deliberately conservative. The scuba diver should be safe within these limits presuming good physical fitness and no predisposition to toxicity such as heavy smoking habits or asthma conditions. No guarantee of safety can ever be presumed.

Given the growing usage of NITROX mixtures and other mixed gases that may provide oxygen in the mixture at a greater or lessened percentage than that of air at an FO_2 of .21, the following Table 5-4 has been provided as a handy reference for maximum depths on various FO_2 to remain within recommended limits of exposure.

As in the case of Table 5-3 these depths are recommendations based on normal working conditions for the diver. In the case of gases mixed for purposes of decompression, it may possible for some divers to use deeper depths on higher FO_2 values. Consult experts before attempting such higher exposures.

Photo by Bret Gilliam

Exercise, heavy leg-kicking or rapid swimming can all elevate CO_2 and increase deep diver's susceptibility to oxygen toxicity. Notice that this diver exhibits perfect buoyancy control and is able to hang motionless at depth to photograph this soft coral at 215 feet.

CHRONIC OXYGEN TOXICITY
(Lorraine Smith Effect)

This effect was commonly referred to in the past as pulmonary toxicity; Rutkowski makes frequent reference in his lectures to the diver's "pulmonary clock", etc. Recently, the term "whole body" toxicity has also come into use.

This phase of O_2 toxicity is less a problem for divers except in prolonged in-water oxygen decompression or in actual recompression therapy. This "chronic" toxicity is generally associated with longer, low pressure exposures as compared to the high PO_2 values encountered at depth. Due to the limits of extended hyperbaric oxygen breathing, a method of calculating the

Table 5.3

NOAA PO$_2$ And Exposure Time Limits for Working Divers

Feet of Seawater (fsw)	Normal Exposure Limits		
	Oxygen Partial Pressure (PO$_2$) in ATA	Maximum Duration for Single Exposure in Minutes	Maximum Total Duration, 24 Hr Day in Minutes
218	1.6	45	150
203	1.5	120	180
187	1.4	150	180
171	1.3	180	210
156	1.2	210	240
140	1.1	240	270
124	1.0	300	300
108	.9	360	360
93	.8	450	450
77	.7	570	570
61	.6	720	720
	Exceptional Exposures		
281	2.0	30	
266	1.9	45	
250	1.8	60	
234	1.7	75	
218	1.6	120	
203	1.5	150	
187	1.4	180	
171	1.3	240	

individual total O_2 exposure incurred during all phases of a dive was developed. This can also be used to factor decompression and O_2 treatment breathing periods. This measure is known as the Unit Pulmonary Toxicity Dose (UPTD) and tables are available for calculating UPTD's for air, pure O_2 and mixed gases.

Table 5.4

Maximum Depths for a Given FO₂ Given a Limiting PO₂

FO₂	1.4 ATA fsw	1.6 ATA fsw
0.15	275.00	319.00
0.16	255.75	297.00
0.17	238.76	277.59
0.18	223.67	260.33
0.19	210.16	244.89
0.20	198.00	231.00
0.21 (normoxic)	187.00	218.43
0.22	177.00	207.00
0.23	167.87	196.57
0.24	159.50	187.00
0.25	151.80	178.20
0.26	144.69	170.08
0.27	138.11	162.56
0.28	132.00	155.57
0.29	126.31	149.07
0.30	121.00	143.00
0.31	116.03	137.32
0.32	111.37	132.00
0.33	107.00	127.00
0.34	102.88	122.29
0.35	99.00	117.86
0.36	95.33	113.67
0.37	91.86	109.70
0.38	88.58	105.05
0.39	85.46	102.38
0.40	82.50	99.00
0.41	79.68	95.78
0.42	77.00	92.71
0.43	74.44	89.79
0.44	72.00	87.00
0.45	69.67	84.33
0.46	67.43	81.78
0.47	65.30	79.34
0.48	63.25	77.00
0.49	61.29	74.76
0.50	59.40	72.60

Hamilton (1989) notes in his REPEX paper, "The Pennsylvania unit (UPTD) has served well and is based on empirical data; it is the basic unit used in the Repex method. For two reasons, however, we prefer to use an alternative term: OTU or Oxygen Tolerance Dose. First, since we are dealing with operational physiology in managing exposure to oxygen in diving we prefer to refer to these as techniques for 'tolerance' of O_2 exposure, rather than for avoiding O_2 'toxicity'. They are the same thing, but we feel it offers a more positive approach."

The OTU and its predecessors are calculated by the following expression:

$$OTU = t \left[(PO_2 - 0.5) / 0.5 \right]^{0.83}$$

where t is the duration of the exposure in minutes and PO_2 is the oxygen partial pressure in ATA. The 0.5 ATA is the "threshold" below which no significant symptoms develop; even oxygen injured lungs can recover below this level. (Bardin and Lambertsen 1970 and Eckenhoff et al. 1987) The exponent 0.83 was determined to give the best fit to the data on reduction of vital capacity as a function of oxygen exposure. An important benefit of this method is that the units are additive, and the net result of multiple short exposures can be totalled.

These dose tolerances were calculated originally for divers in multi-day saturation missions; scuba divers are urged to consult with experts in O_2 management before attempting any dives where significant OTU doses will be accumulated. Because of the nature of the REPEX operation its algorithm does not devote much attention to acute CNS toxicity specifically. It is intended that divers just stay out of the CNS toxicity zone by staying below 1.5 ATA PO_2. As a general rule of thumb, the daily OTU dose should always be calculated to allow the diver to sustain a full treatment Table 6 (approximately 650 OTU/UPTD) if necessary. Refer to Table 5-3 for suggested exposures at specific depths/ATA PO_2 for scuba divers. By referencing between these two tables, the accumulated OTU dose can be accurately tracked.

For isolated or single day exposures, an 850 OTU dose can be tolerated. Second day exposures drop to a recommended 700 OTU dose level and continue to fall off over multi-day exposures. The reader is referred to Hamilton's original REPEX work for additional information.

Symptoms of chronic pulmonary O_2 toxicity include shortness of breath, fatigue, dry coughing, lung irritation and a burning sensation in the breathing cycle. Pulmonary edema is most common and a marked reduction in vital capacity.

Table 5.5

OTU DOSE BY PO₂ AND AIR DEPTHS

PO$_2$ Atm or Bar	Depth		OTU / Min.
	FSW	MSW	
0.50	45.6	13.8	0
0.55	53.4	16.2	0.15
0.60	61.3	18.6	0.37
0.65	69.1	21.0	0.37
0.70	77.0	23.3	0.47
0.75	84.9	25.7	0.56
0.80	92.7	28.1	0.65
0.85	100.6	30.5	0.74
0.90	108.4	32.9	0.83
0.95	116.3	35.2	0.92
1.00	124.4	37.6	1.00
1.05	132.0	40.0	1.08
1.10	139.9	42.4	1.16
1.15	147.7	44.8	1.24
1.20	155.6	47.1	1.32
1.25	163.4	49.5	1.40
1.30	171.3	51.9	1.48
1.35	179.1	54.3	1.55
1.40	187.0	56.7	1.63
1.45	194.9	59.1	1.70
1.50	202.7	61.4	1.78˙
1.55	210.6	63.8	1.85
1.60	218.4	66.2	1.92
1.65	226.3	68.6	2.00
1.70	234.1	71.0	2.07
1.75	242.0	73.3	2.14
1.80	249.9	75.7	2.21
1.85	257.7	78.1	2.28
1.90	265.6	80.5	2.35
1.95	273.4	82.8	2.42
2.00	281.3	85.2	2.49

R.W. Hamilton, HAMILTON RESEARCH LTD.

Chart of OTU dose by PO$_2$ and air depths. The values in the Table from left are the PO$_2$, depth in fsw or msw diving with air to give that PO$_2$, and the number of OTU per minute at the indicated PO$_2$ level. To calculate a dose, multiply the value in the chart for the exposure PO$_2$ by the number of minutes of the exposure. For exposures at different PO$_2$'s, calculate the dose in OTU for each exposure at a given PO$_2$ and sum the OTU's to get the total exposure.

In treatments in recompression chambers, patient tenders also look for irritability in the patient or unreasonable disposition as early warning signs that dictate an air break in the schedule to allow some relief period. Bennett (1991) has expressed concern over sport divers' use of in-water O_2 decompression as possibly becoming a post-dive factor if treatment should be required later. This relates to the so-called "oxygen box" where a patient reaches the UPTD limit and can no longer tolerate O_2 therapy and leaves the chamber supervisor in a quandary for a viable exit protocol.

Table 5.6

Oxygen Limits for Life Support Systems

ATA O_2

3.0	50 / 50 NITROX Therapy Gas @ 6 ATA (165 fsw)
2.8	100% O_2 @ 2.8 ATA (60 fsw)
2.5	Decompression for Operation Diving (maximum)
2.4	60 / 40 NITROX Therapy Gas @ 6 ATA (165 fsw)
2.0	U.S. Navy Exceptional Exposure to Working Diver
1.6	U.S. Navy Maximum Normal Exposure to Working Diver
.5	Maximum Saturation Exposure
.35	Normal Saturation Exposure
.21	Normal Environment O_2 (normoxic)
.16	Begin Signs of Hypoxia
.12	Serious Signs of Hypoxia
.10	Unconsciousness
<.10	Coma / Death

SUMMARY

Both manifestations of oxygen toxicity can play a role in the deep diver's plan. Of most concern is the extremely dangerous and unpredictable CNS O_2 Tox hit at depth. Divers should exercise extreme caution when venturing beyond the 1.6 ATA range and penetrations beyond 275 fsw (83.3 m) on air are ill-advised except in the most experienced and adapted diver.

Unlike narcosis impairment, where a quantifiable possibility of rescue exists from an alert buddy or self-recognition of problem levels can be relieved by ascent, an O_2 hit can quickly progress to uncontrollable convulsive states and drowning. As divers become more attuned to management of inert gas narcosis, the O_2 toxicity barrier will be the ultimate depth limit.

Chapter 6

Staged Decompression

" It would go a long way toward promoting diver safety if everyone would finally accept that ALL dives are decompression dives."

John Crea

As you venture longer and deeper into the watery depths, you leave the realm of sport diving and along with it the no-decompression limits that you were taught to dive within. Longer and deeper diving moves you into the realm of decompression diving, a realm where planning and careful preparation is essential, and inadequate planning and preparation can literally be fatal.

This chapter will discuss staged decompression, some background physiology, planning considerations, equipment requirements, equipment configuration, utilization of oxygen during decompression, and emergency procedures.

PHYSIOLOGY AND PHYSICS REVIEW

During diving, using compressed air for the breathing mixture, the body takes up the inert gas nitrogen when exposed to higher ambient pressures (resulting in elevated PARTIAL PRESSURES OF NITROGEN). This nitrogen is stored as a dissolved gas in all of the body tissues, with the amounts stored in each type of tissue determined by the blood supply to that tissue and by the solubility of nitrogen in that tissue (these parameters determine the "halftime" for that tissue). After the body has taken up this nitrogen while diving, it must be safely released from the body during ascent in a slow, controlled manner to prevent the development of decompression sickness (consisting of the formation of **bubbles** that can cause great damage to the body, and possibly even permanent disability or death if allowed to occur).

The technique used to allow the controlled removal of nitrogen from the body during ascent is called **Decompression**. Decompression may be accomplished in one of two ways:

I. By a continuous ascent at varying rates (very difficult for most divers to follow precisely).

II. By ascending to pre-calculated depths, and remaining at those depths for a specified length of time to allow excess nitrogen to be removed from the body tissues (as indicated by various decompression tables) until it is safe to ascend to a shallower depth. This procedure is repeated in carefully defined steps until it is safe to ascend to the surface. This is the procedure most commonly used today by the vast majority of divers, the military and commercial dive companies and is referred to as **Staged Decompression.**

Many different tables (DCIEM, U.S. Navy, Royal Navy, etc.) spell out the procedures for this staged decompression, in which the diver stops at pre-determined depths and waits for a specific amount of time to allow nitrogen to exit the body tissues. These tables specify the ascent rate to the first stop, ascent rate between stops, and the body position for decompression. (The U.S. Navy tables specify that the decompression stop depth be measured at mid-chest, as the tables were originally designed for hard-hat divers who ascended in a vertical position. Many articles have discussed the optimal position for decompression, with the consensus being that a horizontal position appears to be best, but if a vertical position is required the decompression stop depth should be measured and maintained according to the U.S. Navy requirements.) These standard tables are almost always designed for use by divers who are breathing air both during the dive and the decompression. (Custom tables are available that incorporate the utilization of other gas mixtures during decompression to produce more nearly optimal inert gas removal.)

It has often been stated that decompression diving carries an increased risk of DCS compared with dives that do not require decompression. Although this is true for many profiles in the U.S. Navy tables (and possibly other tables), it is not necessarily a general truth, as many variables come into play with these dives (however, the U.S. Navy has reported that their tables are inadequate for longer and/or deeper dives requiring significant decompression times). Selection of conservative tables that have been extensively tested should result in a DCS rate during decompression diving comparable to that found during dives not requiring decompression.

If decompression diving is planned it is essential to choose a table that accounts for the conditions of the divers, and of the dive site. If the divers are required to work hard during dive, more decompression will be required. If the dive conditions will result in the divers becoming cold, this will also increase the decompression required. Again, it must be emphasized, a conservative, well-tested decompression table should be utilized during all decompression dives. "I personally recommend either the DCIEM tables or proprietary tables to divers performing deep dives requiring significant amounts of decompression" (Crea, 1991).

PLANNING FOR STAGED DECOMPRESSION

The essentials of staged decompression are readily enumerated:

1) Ascent from the maximum depth to the first decompression stop at an ascent rate as defined by the decompression tables or dive computer in use.

2) Upon reaching the first decompression stop, the diver holds this depth for a given time. After completing the required "hang time," the diver then moves up to the next stop (at the required ascent rate) and repeats the procedure until he reaches the surface.

As seen from the above, the basics of decompression diving appear quite simple. You make your dive and you carry out the required decompression. However, failure to properly perform these "simple" steps can result in injury and/or death. Proper planning is what keeps this procedure a safe and reliable one. The major areas of concern are: 1) Adequate gas supply; 2) Equipment considerations; 3) Abillity to control ascents; and 4) Rate of ascent.

GAS CONSUMPTION CALCULATIONS

It is essential that enough gas be available to allow the diver to complete his scheduled decompression (aborted or omitted decompression increases the risk of development of DCS, and has been known to "ruin a diver's day"). Thus, gas consumption calculations need to be made prior to the dive to assure that adequate amounts of gas will be available for the dive plan. Since you will probably be diving with a buddy, each diver should plan his gas supplies to take into account the possibility of "problems" in which each diver has enough gas for his planned dive decompression, and sharing with his partner. Planning for two times the minimal amount of gas calculated is recommended.

How do you calculate gas requirements? The deep diver should have a good idea of his gas consumption (at the surface at rest). This gas consumption rate (expressed as RMV - respiratory minute volume) is utilized in the rest of the calculations presented here. Surface consumption rates may vary from 0.3 cu. ft./min to as much as 3.0 cu. ft./min.

In order to calculate your air consumption, you must first understand the following term: The "Respiratory Minute Volume (RMV)" is the amount of air consumed in one minute on the surface.

RMV's vary from diver to diver, and a diver's own RMV will change due to variations in his breathing rate. Obviously, if we are anxious, cold, or just out of shape, our breathing rate will be greater than expected. Also, if we are swimming against a strong current, we will be breathing more than at rest.

It follows from the ideal gas law and Boyle's Law, that our RMV will vary with depth. If we double the ambient pressure, we will double our RMV. Thus, if an 80 cu. ft. tank will last 60 minutes at the surface, then it will only last 30 minutes at 33 fsw, 20 minutes at 66 fsw, 15 minutes at 99 fsw, and only last 10 minutes at 165 fsw. The following relationship holds:

RMV x Ambient Pressure (ATA) = Consumption At That Depth

The aspiring deep diver will be well rewarded for taking the time to evaluate his surface consumption rate, as this is the only effective way to estimate his gas requirements for any given deep dive.

Once a RMV has been determined, then the surface equivalent consumption is easily calculated by the following equation:

Total Gas Required = Sum of the Gas Required at Each Stage of the Dive

and
Gas Required at Each Stage = ATA x RMV x Time x Work Modifier

ATA = Pressure at each Stage (ATA) = (Depth x 33)+1
RMV = Respiratory Minute Volume (expressed in cu. ft./minute)
Time = Time in minutes spent at that stage/depth
Work Modifier = A factor by which the gas requirements are multiplied by - reflecting the fact that gas consumption increases with increasing work levels. Suggested work modifiers are as follows:

AT REST	= 1
MILD WORK LOAD	= 1.5
MODERATE WORK LOAD	= 2.0
HEAVY WORK LOAD	= 3.0 − 5.0

Now, the dive is planned (bottom time and decompression requirements). Gas requirements are calculated based on the RMV and anticipated work load. Descent times are treated as if they were included in the bottom time. Ascent rates are calculated by using the average depth and the ascent time as below:

$$AVERAGE\ DEPTH = \frac{(Maximum\ depth + 1st\ Stop\ depth)}{2}$$

This Average Depth is then used in your calculation for gas consumption during ascent (and can be used for extremely deep dive descents). These calculations need to be carried out for every different gas utilized during the dive.

Once you have calculated your gas requirements for your planned dive, then consideration must be made for the "unplanned." Gas supply amounts should be "padded" to allow for emergencies. If you are diving with a partner, then **each diver should plan on having enough gas to support both divers in case of a catastrophic gas supply failure by one of the divers.**

This reserve supply can be calculated by doubling the amount of gas originally calculated. However, this allowance is not enough if you are planning a dive with significant penetrations (i.e., wreck and/or cave diving). For these situations, the cave divers "thirds rule" is more appropriate. One third of the gas supply is allowed for the penetration, one third for the exit, and one third reserved for emergencies. This should allow adequate gas to provide gas for your partner if he suffered a total gas supply failure at maximum penetration or depth.

EQUIPMENT CONSIDERATIONS

Decompression diving can require additional pieces of equipment that are not usually required during no-decompression diving. The key concept in safe deep diving is the concept of **Redundancy**. Simply put, this means that you carry backups of any equipment that is critical for that dive. Usually this refers to redundant regulators, decompression bottles, dive computers or tables, etc. It should not have to be said that **only reliable equipment should be used for deep diving.** If there is any question as to the reliability or performance of any piece of equipment, then it should be serviced prior to utilization for deep diving and tested on a simple dive before being used for deep diving. Failure of dive equipment is usually only irritating during sport diving, but can be critical during deep diving. Deep diving is not the time to be trying out new equipment or borrowed gear. The following is a brief list and description of some of the more common pieces of **extra** equipment used during decompression diving. (Please refer to the Chapter 7 for material on regulator selection, tank valves, etc.)

Bail-Out Bottle (Also known as a **Pony Bottle**) - This is a small scuba cylinder (40 cu. ft.. or less) with regulator attached. Usually this is carried by the diver as an emergency gas source for emergency use during wreck penetrations and/or other "out of air emergencies."

Decompression Line - A decompression line is a line that the divers follow during their ascent and decompression. Quite often, this is the same as the dive boat's anchor line, but ideally is a separate weighted line with 10 foot increments marked. Extra equipment is quite often clipped off on this line (safety bottle, decompression bottles, surface supplied oxygen regulators, fluids and/or food, etc.).

Jonline - A three to six foot long line with one or more hand loops that can be clipped to the decompression line. This line is named after its inventor, Jon Hulbert. By attaching one end of this line to the decompression line and hanging on to the other end, it serves to smooth out the changes in depth that could occur if you were directly attached to the decompression line.

Lift Bag with Line - This is a small (25 - 50 pounds of lift) bag with enough line to reach from your maximum dive depth to the surface. It is utilized whenever the standard decompression line is not available. Upon starting your ascent, the lift bag is inflated and sent towards the surface while you pay out the line. You then ascend this line, and utilize it to allow you maintain a constant depth at each planned stop. This is an extremely comfortable method to use during decompression. If a standard yellow lift bag is used, it not only allows ease of decompression, but it marks your position for the boat that is hopefully searching for you.

Line Reel - A reel with 150 - 1000 feet of braided nylon line. Used by cave divers as a guide line to assure a known exit path, it is also used in this manner by wreck divers when penetrating a wreck. It can also be used

Mark Lenord, Dive Rite president, shows use of one of his custom reels in cave diving application. Such devices are also used as decompression reels for stage decompression in open water.

Photos by Bob Janowski

during decompression to supply a guideline back to the anchor line or decompression line.

Stage Bottles -These are extra single scuba cylinders with regulators. In the usual sense of the phrase, stage bottles are extra cylinders and regulators carried by cave divers to allow farther penetration into cave systems. In decompression diving, stage bottles usually refer to either scuba cylinders attached to the decompression line for use during decompression or carried by the divers to allow the diver to carry out decompression independent from the dive boat.

Tables or Dive Computers - These decompression tools are the heart of safe decompression diving. If diving using computers, then it is highly suggested that two similar computers be utilized (what would you do if your only computer "dies" while inside a deep wreck? Especially if this is the third day of diving utilizing the computer.)

Dive tables should cover the planned dive depths and planned bottom times, plus a good safety margin on either side of the planned depth and time. Also, dive tables used for deep diving should be conservative and well tested over the range of dive depth-bottom times that you are planning to perform.

OXYGEN AND IN WATER DECOMPRESSION

In the last few years, the use of oxygen during decompression has become one of the most discussed topics in the technical diving community. Why use oxygen during decompression? Is in water use of oxygen during decompression safe? How do you set up your equipment to be able to utilize oxygen for in water decompression? These are just a few of the questions that are being asked and although many of the answers are found in medical and diving physiology texts, they are often buried in medical terminology, and sometimes open to interpretation or misinterpretation.

First, some background information on oxygen. Oxygen is a colorless, odorless gas, that comprises 20.99% by volume of the air you breathe. Oxygen has a molecular weight of 31.999, and has a density of 0.08279 lb./cu.ft. All materials that are flammable in air will burn much more vigorously in oxygen. Some combustibles, such as oil and grease, burn with near explosive violence in oxygen if ignited. However, pure oxygen is **Non-flammable** and **Non-explosive**. Gaseous oxygen is usually stored in metal cylinders at a pressure of 2000 psi to 2400 psi. Both steel and aluminum cylinders have been used for storage of gaseous oxygen. (However, Air Products has recently stated that they will not fill aluminum cylinders with oxygen, due to concerns over aluminum oxide formation and potential explosion hazards.) Care must be taken to remove all oils, greases and other combustible contaminants from delivery systems and storage cylinders or replace then with oxygen compatible lubricants before being placed into oxygen service.

The removal of nitrogen from the body after exposure to elevated ambient pressures is based on the **Gradient** between the partial pressure of nitrogen in the tissues in question and the partial pressure of nitrogen in the blood (and ultimately the partial pressure of nitrogen in the lungs). The partial pressure of nitrogen in the blood is in equilibrium with the partial pressure of nitrogen present in the lungs. As you surface, the partial pressure of nitrogen in the tissues and blood exceeds the ambient pressure, and when this pressure difference becomes great enough, then bubble formation occurs (The development of decompression sickness is really much more complex than this, but this simplistic approach is adequate for this discussion. Readers are referred to any of the many diving physiology texts for further discussion of this topic). The pressure of the gas mixture that you are breathing is in equilibrium with the ambient pressure, such that as you ascend, the partial pressure of nitrogen in the lungs is lower than that in the blood or the tissues. When this occurs, gas diffuses from the tissues into the blood, and then is carried to the lungs. At the lungs, the partial pressure of nitrogen in the alveoli is lower than the partial pressure in the blood, and the nitrogen diffuses from the blood into the alveoli and is exhaled.

Any technique that will decrease the partial pressure of nitrogen in the breathing mixture will increase the rate of removal of nitrogen from the blood, and thus from the tissues. This is the rationale behind the use of various gas mixtures that are low or totally lacking in nitrogen during

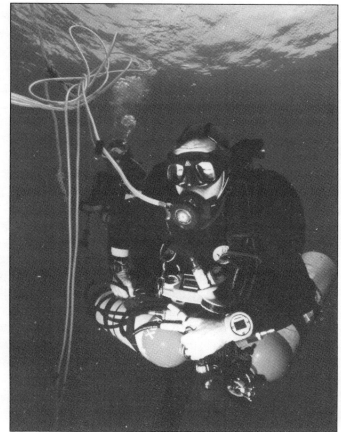

Bill Deans decompressing at 20 fsw on surface supplied oxygen. Note he carries a back-up O_2 cylinder and a NITROX stage cylinder.

Photo by Dan Burton

decompression. With a large nitrogen gradient between the blood and the lungs, you remove nitrogen from the body as rapidly as possible. The easiest way to achieve the greatest nitrogen gradient during decompression is to totally remove nitrogen from the breathing mixture used during decompression.

However, this raises the question of with what gas do you replace the nitrogen? You can replace it with another inert gas, such as helium, but then you are presented with the extremely complex problem of calculating the uptake of another inert gas while removal of the nitrogen is going on, and its influence on our decompression schedule. It is actually possible to accumulate enough helium during decompression from an air dive (if breathing Helium-Oxygen during decompression) to have to consider decompression from the absorbed helium taken up during its use in decompression.

Or, you can replace the nitrogen with a non-inert gas (one that is metabolically active). Oxygen is the metabolically active gas we utilize. Oxygen has several advantages going for its use in this scenario. These are:

I. Using 100% oxygen allows us to have the largest possible nitrogen gradient between the lungs and the blood/tissues, so that nitrogen is removed at the greatest possible rate.

II. Oxygen is used metabolically by the body, and as such is not usually stored in the human body. Thus, you do not usually have to worry about these elevated tissue partial pressures of oxygen contributing to the development of decompression sickness. (In theory, with extremely high partial pressures of oxygen, some contribution to the development of decompression sickness is felt to be possible. However, the partial pressures required are much higher than those encountered if oxygen is utilized only during the 20 ft. and 10 ft. decompression stops.)

III. Oxygen has approximately the same density and thermal characteristics as air, so work of breathing is not changed and heat loss is not a problem. Helium has a high thermal conductivity and chilling is a potential problem with the use of helium in the breathing mixture. (Especially if helium is used to inflate your dry suit.) Not so when oxygen is used for dry suit inflation. (The use of 100% oxygen for dry suit inflation is, however, NOT RECOMMENDED.) No extra insulation needs to be used in the dry suit, and the heat loss via the respiratory tract is approximately the same as with air (heat loss from the respiratory tract is mainly a function of the body supplying humidity to the dry breathing gas, and the heat needed to vaporized the water to provide this humidity must be supplied by the body).

IV. Oxygen is relatively inexpensive compared to most other gases that might be considered for use.

V. Oxygen is the immediate treatment of choice (other than recompression) for decompression sickness, and as such, if you should develop "bubble trouble" during decompression, you are already treating it.

VI. There is a concept called the "Oxygen Window" or "Inherent Unsaturation" that comes into play when oxygen is used to replace the inert gas in a breathing mixture. This refers to several physical laws and the fact that oxygen is utilized metabolically in the body. What it basically

Deep divers are making increasing use of oxygen and/ or NITROX mixtures during decompression. Here are two 80 cubic foot decompression stage bottles rigged and labled for the diver to utilize.

Photo by Bret Gilliam

means is that you can actually remove **more** inert gas (nitrogen when talking about air diving) for the same gradient when breathing oxygen than when breathing any other gas mixture that produces the same gradient for off-gassing. The reasoning behind this is somewhat complex, and we do not have the room in this chapter to cover it adequately. The reader is referred to one of the good diving physiology texts for further explanation.

The use of oxygen to shorten the time required for safe decompression was mentioned as early as 1878 by Bert and again by Ham and Hill in 1905. It has been discussed by Behnke (1969) and used in Japan in caisson workers. Use of oxygen during decompression has been a mainstay of the U.S. Navy's HELIOX procedures. A reduction in decompression time of about 40% is theoretically possible by switching from air to oxygen during shallow decompression stops.

The use of oxygen by many advanced divers is not routinely done to shorten the decompression times that are required (although this is possible with custom designed decompression tables). It is used to increase

Many dive boats provide weighted "decom bars" to assist in decompression.

Photo by Bret Gilliam

the reliability of the tables used and thus reduce the probability of developing Decompression Sickness. Many of the dives made by cave and wreck divers today are in the realm approaching the tested limits of the U.S. Navy air decompression tables, and many dives are into the **Exceptional Exposure Tables** (which are poorly tested, and have an unacceptably high incidence of developing DCS when used). When a diver moves into the deeper or longer schedules of the U.S. Navy Tables, the incidence of Decompression Sickness increases (Thalmann, 1985), and many of the Exceptional Exposure profiles have been tested only on a very limited basis (if at all), and the actual incidence of Decompression Sickness may be much higher than that for the rest of the Navy tables. Thus, by increasing the efficiency of the decompression schedule, the use of oxygen during in water decompression can improve the reliability of the decompression schedule utilized and reduces the risk of developing DCS.

In summary, the use of oxygen during decompression has much to recommend it. It increases the rate of nitrogen off-gassing, and thus increases the reliability and efficacy of the decompression schedule used (if used with standard air tables or with dive computers that were designed for use with air).

Breathing oxygen during decompression increases the gradient for nitrogen removal, and will therefore increase the rate at which pre-existing bubbles will be reduced in size, thus "treating" any bubble formation that might occur during a decompression.

Finally, the use of oxygen in water is not without dangers, and should only be under taken by those divers who have the education and knowledge to utilize this advanced technique safely.

NITROX AND DECOMPRESSION

Along with oxygen, the use of NITROX (within its depth limitations) to "optimize" decompression has seen an increased use in the last few years. The major advantage of NITROX use is that it allows you to get off of compressed air when decompressing at deeper depths, where uptake of nitrogen into the slower compartments continues. Refer to Chapter 10 for more information.

SUMMARY

Ideally, during decompression, we would breathe a different gas at each decompression stop. These different gases would be selected based on the reduction of the amount of inert gas in them and how they are within oxygen toxicity constraints. Since gas switches at every decompression stop are usually not logistically feasible, many divers choose to make one or two gas switches during decompression.

However, the savings from this technique can be slight if the times at deeper decompression stops are minimal. Also, utilization of NITROX and oxygen during decompression must take into consideration of oxygen toxicity limits. Refer to any of the experts in our reference section for advice on the utilization of different gases for decompression.

Chapter 7

Deep Diving Equipment and Self-Sufficiency

*"Take two of everything. My pal Murphy just loves divers.
In fact, you might even think in terms of three...
he and his band of demons are great swimmers."*

Karl Bekker

*"Did you ever look up redundancy in the dictionary?
It says: see redundant."*

Robin Williams

AIR MANAGEMENT SYSTEMS

The issue of air management for the deep diver is a first-line, first-order, concern. No matter what environment one happens to be diving in, not enough air means big trouble. In addition to cylinders being carried in doubles and triples, larger tanks with an increased capacity are also utilized. Specialized valve manifolds and independent systems are quite common. And as one would suspect, it is vitally important for these specialized systems to be managed properly and safely.

The old axiom "proper prior planning prevents piss poor performance" most certainly comes into play for deep divers, particularly in terms of air management. Cave divers and wreck divers adhere to the guidelines spelled out in "The Rule of Thirds". Simply stated, this rule suggests that 1/3 of a diver's air supply be used for cave/wreck penetration (entry), 1/3 be used for exiting the cave/wreck, and 1/3 be left for emergency use. "Cavers", who originated The Rule of Thirds, have very specific applications for this rule. As stated in an article by E. J. Fiorell in *AquaCorps: The Journal for Experienced Divers* (Issue No. 2), "Divers within the open water can always use the surface as a 'bailout' in the event of an air supply problem. But in a cave or any overhead environment, this is not true; all problems encountered during the dive must be handled underwater. As a result, cave divers have had to rethink the problem of how much gas to carry and how best to plan its use."

"The philosophy that has evolved in response is this: A dive partner must have enough air and equipment for both divers to successfully exit the cave if one diver has a catastrophic air loss at the point of furthest penetration."

In its simplest form, this means penetrating the cave no further than the point where the divers have consumed a third of their air supply. When the dive is turned at this point, each diver has two-thirds of his or her original air supply. If one diver then has a catastrophic air loss at this juncture, the other member of the team has a sufficient gas supply to allow both divers to safely exit the cave - at least theoretically."

Whether or not an individual is diving in an "overhead" environment, air consumption and management (as per The Rule of Thirds) are integral parts of proper dive planning for all types of deep diving. This brings us to the issue of specialized equipment. What types of equipment exist and what are the various applications of each?

Listed below the reader will find several types and variations of air management equipment systems. Included with each listing is a brief definition of the device as well as an example of how the equipment can be utilized.

• DIN Fittings:
As far as the high-tech, deep diving vanguard is concerned, the old standard yoke fittings are a thing of the past. Virtually all deep diving rigs incorporate DIN fittings (DIN is an acronym for Deutsches Institut fuer Normung, the German equivalent of the United States' CGA - Compressed Gas Association). These are fittings that are screwed directly into the

cylinder valve (also a DIN connection) and thereby "mating" the regulator's first-stage with the tank valve.

DIN fittings, like the one shown here, are used in cylinders with working pressure in excess of 3000 psi.

Photo courtesy of Sherwood

Aside from the fact that this type of connection allows for the use of a higher pressure cylinder, typically 300 bar (1 bar = 14.504 psi; 300 bar = 4351.2 p.s.i.) is used on 3500 psi service. Also no external o-rings are necessary (DIN fittings incorporate "captured" o-rings) thus decreasing the possibility of a blown o-ring that could conceivably lead to a catastrophic air loss.

• Single Cylinders (Singles):

As the name would suggest, this is a rig that is composed of a single cylinder. For the most part, deep dives are conducted with more than one cylinder, but dives that are fairly short in duration can safely be carried out with a single "bottle". These are dives that usually do not involve excessive depth (over 175 fsw/53m) or stage decompression.

Diving cylinders come in a variety of shapes and sizes from the ubiquitous aluminum 80's (80 cubic feet) that have a working pressure of 3000 psi, to the newer high pressure (HP) steel cylinders (80's, 102's, 120's) that have a working pressure of 3500 psi. In Table 7.1 the reader will find a comparison of the aluminum 80's to the high pressure steel 80's and 102's. The high pressure cylinders come with a standard DIN fitting, whereas aluminum cylinders are not compatible with DIN equipment due to their lower rated working pressure (as mentioned above, DIN rigs typically utilize 3500 psi/300 bar cylinders).

Keep in mind that in addition to the above-mentioned cylinder sizes, there are many others that are in use - some that are no longer being manufactured. The cylinders discussed here, particularly the HP models in connection with deep diving, were chosen because of the fact that they are perhaps a bit more common than others.

Note the size difference between the high pressure 80 cu. ft. cylinder on the right and the standard aluminum 80 cu. ft. cylinder on the left. The high pressure cylinder lends itself to a more compact cylinder package and has more desirable buoyancy characteristics.

Photo courtesy of Discover Diving

SCUBA CYLINDER COMPARISIONS

Table 7.1

SPECIFICATIONS	CYLINDERS					
	STEEL HP 80	STEEL HP 102	STEEL HP 120	STEEL 105	AL 80	AL 90
Volume in Cu.Ft.	84.8	102.6	120	105.5	79.8	88.0
Working Pressure (psi)	3500	3500	3500	2400	3000	3300
Height (valved)	22.0"	27.0"	30.9"	25.5"	26.2"	28.8"
Diameter	7.25"	7.25"	7.25"	7.80"	7.25"	7.25"
Weight (empty)	28.5 lbs.	28.5 lbs.	28.5 lbs.	44.0lbs.	33.5lbs.	35.5lbs.
Buoyancy (empty)	-2.6 lbs	-1.6 lbs	-1.0 lbs	neutral	+3.8 lbs	+2.7 lbs
Buoyancy (full)	-8.6 lbs	-9.3 lbs	-11.3 lbs	-8.2	-2.3 lbs	-3.3 lbs

• Doubles:

Also referred to as twins or duals, this is a cylinder configuration that involves two cylinders (typically dual 80's, 102's, 105's, or 120's). The cylinders are "linked" or "joined" together via a manifold that is mated to the neck of each tank. A standard twin manifold incorporates a single first-stage regulator connector seat and an on/off valve. The latter serves as an on/off mechanism for both cylinders.

Doubles are used to provide the diver with twice the amount of a particular breathing medium than would normally be allowed. Although heavy and bulky, they make it possible for the deep diver to remain at depth for an extended period of time as well as providing him with additional gas for emergency use. The reader is reminded that the use of twins does not negate the need for an additional Emergency Breathing System (EBS).

One particular *disadvantage* of using doubles is that they are comparatively bulky, much heavier, and cumbersome than a single, requiring a little getting use to before an individual will feel comfortable.

Double steel 120 cubic foot cylinders with Genesis isolation manifold and valve protector bar.

• Independent Doubles:

Independent doubles (two cylinders, each with a separate set of regulators and instruments) are composed of a similar configuration to twins. The primary difference is that instead of the manifold providing a single valve and single regulator seat, it supplies the diver with dual valves and two regulator seats. This provides the diver with two completely independent systems: One for primary use and one for emergency backup. By allowing an individual to turn on or off either regulator independently (thus making it possible to keep one regulator and its cylinder shut off and in reserve), it adds an additional margin for safety.

Independent doubles have gained popularity among wreck and cave divers due to the additional "air insurance" that their use provides as well as the fact that they supply the diver with a reserve regulator and cylinder. They are an excellent combination of primary air source and EBS in a single configuration.

• Benjamin Conversion:

Dr. George Benjamin in collaboration with Ike IkeHara designed the first double cylinder isolation manifold in the late sixties. A crossover bar plumbed into the cylinder valve below the valve orifice allowed two regulator systems to be mounted. In the event of a regulator failure or o-ring blow-out, the diver could turn off the supply valve on that cylinder, effectively "isolating" the defective gear. However, the air in the cylinder could still be used via the crossover supply plumbing. *(NOTE: Benjamin Conversions are rarely used today and the reader is advised to have any such rig thoroughly inspected by a qualified equipment technician or someone who is expert in their use and function before the equipment is utilized.)*

• Sherwood Genesis Manifold:

Essentially this is the "manufactured version" of the original Benjamin modification. Originally produced in the late 1970's with a standard valve system it was the first industry response to the need for an isolation manifold. This manifold was produced in response to requests from the active cave diver community and was standard equipment for NOAA's *Hydro Lab* saturation system for scientist aquanauts. Designed and manufactured by Sherwood Scuba, this is a system that goes one step further than the typical independent doubles set-up. Now officially called

the **DIN Double Genesis Manifold**, it employs a unique isolation valve that can be used to isolate either cylinder. The added factor of cylinder isolation represents a truly independent EBS that allows for maximum redundancy. Additionally, it is currently (as of the printing of this text) the only doubles manifold on the market in the United States that incorporates DIN fittings.

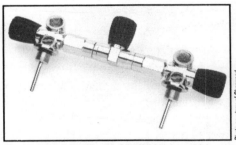

The Sherwood DIN Double Manifold Valve, which allows divers to switch instantly between cylinders.

Photo courtesy of Sherwood

•Crossover Manifold/Yoke:

These were originally designed to quickly equalize the pressure in the cylinders of two divers. They were built for use with 2250 psi tanks and when they were eventually used with 3000 psi tanks they malfunctioned due to the increased pressure. There was a 3000 psi model manufactured, but they were not as common as the 2250 psi model. They were also used to make "doubles" out of two tanks. The danger presented by the use of this type of rig is that if the manifold is accidentally knocked against an overhead obstruction, etc. an air leak could occur, or the seams of the manifold may be damaged and become separated. The crossover manifold/yoke is rarely used today and the reader is advised that they are potentially dangerous and belong on the shelf and not in the water.

Valve/Manifold/Regulator Cage:

This is a cage that is normally constructed of stainless steel and designed to protect the cylinder valve/manifold and the regulator's first-stage from abrasion and/or damage caused by contact with hard surfaces (rocks, wrecks, cave/cavern surfaces, etc.). If the valve/manifold or regulator first-stage were to be accidently slammed into a hard surface, the end-result could be a catastrophic air loss. With the addition of a protector cage this type of emergency can be avoided.

REGULATORS

Choosing a regulator for deep diving is somewhat more involved than choosing one for traditional sport/recreational diving. In *AquaCorps: The Journal for Experienced Divers* (Volume 3/Winter 1991), an excellent article by Ron Russell, a diving equipment manufacturer's representative specializing in high-tech gear, offers a few parameters to consider before purchasing a regulator:

"What's important in a regulator anyway? Apart from the overriding concern in some quarters with the way your regulator color-coordinates with the rest of your gear, I would like to suggest a few basic criteria:

Regulators are one of the most important parts of the deep diving system. Here is a fully-rigged redundant deep diving system, including 120 cubic foot cylinders with Genesis DIN Isolation Manifold, dual regulators, twin Dive Rite back mounted buoyancy compensators, dual BC inflators, valve protector bar, and dual instrument consoles.

Photo by Bret Gilliam

- Performance: how well does the regulator deliver air under various conditions?
- Reliability: how failure-prone is it within your intended parameters of use?
- Maintainability: how easy is it to service and what needs to be replaced at overhaul?
- Safety design: what design features have been included to minimize potential hazards?
- Ergonomics: how well does the regulator fit with human physiology? (Ed. physical requirements?)
- Compatibility: how will the regulator work with the diving system you now have or may acquire in the future?"

The six points listed above are certainly critical considerations for deep divers. Let's now take a closer, more definitive look at the particulars involved with each.

Performance:

This applies to how well the regulator breathes or "performs" at depth. As depth increases it becomes considerably more difficult for the regulator to deliver the air, which has become more dense. Additionally, the more arduous a divers' activity (harder working), the greater the exhalation resistance. (These are both factors which contribute to increased diver fatigue and carbon dioxide build-up.) Another influencing factor involves cylinder pressure; as tank pressure decreases, it becomes more difficult for the regulator to supply air at an efficient rate.

All of the above considerations dictate that the regulator chosen must be able to perform adequately no matter which of them come into play. Any regulator used for deep diving should have a balanced first-stage (diaphragm or piston) and a matched/compatible first- and second-stage. Additional second stages should be designed to work at the same intermediate pressure that the first-stage delivers. (*If the second-stage is designed for a lower intermediate pressure and is used with a first-stage that delivers a higher intermediate pressure, then it is likely to free-flow.*)

Reliability:

This refers to the unit's dependability as well. Does its' track record show that it can perform well, and without incident, at depth? It is critically important for the regulator to be mechanically reliable. Particularly at greater depths, even a small malfunction can turn into a catastrophic air loss.

An excellent means of gaining information about a particular regulator's reliability is to consult a deep diving training facility (See **Training Facilities** in back of book).

Maintainability:

Is the regulator easily repaired if, prior to a dive, a malfunction is detected? This applies to both minor field repairs as well as in-house repairs, overhauls, etc. Also, it is important that spare parts for field repairs and parts for regularly scheduled maintenance be readily available from the distributor or the manufacturer. Other important considerations are: How often does the unit have to be overhauled (once every six months or once every year)? How durable are the second-stage seats? Is it necessary for the regulator to be re-tuned if the diving environment changes (i.e. going from warm, tropical water to cold water)?

Safety Design:

If a problem does occur at depth (such as a first- or second-stage failure or malfunction) are there any safety features built in that would help to avert a full-blown emergency? One such example is the Poseidon regulators that have a built-in over-pressure relief device in the LP hose that connects the first- and second-stages. With this system, if the second-stage should malfunction resulting in free-flowing, the free-flowing air would be vented from the relief device in the hose. In this way, the regulator would still be breathable.

The reader should keep in mind that most, if not all, downstream designed regulators will automatically free-flow and continue to deliver air in the event of a malfunction. However, if this should occur, the diver's air would then be depleted at a much faster rate than normal. Conversely, upstream designed regulators will lock-up and no longer deliver air to the diver in the case of a malfunction.

Ergonomics:

This is a term that has recently been exploited by the automotive industry. It refers to how well the design of a particular product matches the "physical" needs of the consumer. In the case of automobiles, it is usually the comfortability of how the overall car design fits with the human body, to which the term is applied. In the case of a regulator, it again refers to the degree of physical comfort that the device affords. Does the unit contribute to jaw fatigue due to its' design and weight? After extended periods of time in the water (particularly after a long dive and during an even longer decompression) does the unit continue to feel comfortable?

Compatibility:

Is the regulator compatible with the rest of your diving equipment and if you should decide to "upgrade" will it remain as such? Also, is it compatible with the type of diving that you'll be conducting (deep, cave, wreck, ice, etc.) or, in consideration of the above five points, would another choice be more prudent?

In 1987, the United State's Navy Experimental Diving Unit (NEDU) tested a group of regulators to discern the deepest depth at which each regulator would still perform at a physiologically sustainable level of effort (i.e. would still allow the diver to safely continue respiration at a physiologically adequate level). Conversely, this testing was also designed to indicate the point (depth) at which each regulator would fail to deliver an adequate supply of air from the diver's point of view. This is referred to as the "work of breathing" and is measured in RMV (Respiratory Minute Volume). *Note: For more information on RMV, see Gas Consumption Calculations in Chapter 6.*

In Table 7.3, the nine regulators tested are ranked in order of performance from Group A of the Navy tests. The depths listed represent the maximum depth at which each unit was still performing satisfactorily at 1000 psi supply pressure according to the work load applied to it Listed below is the simulated work load (work of breathing) which is derived from the breathing rate, tidal volume and RVM's. These simulated work loads apply in table 7-3 to each regulator at the specified depths.

U.S. Navy Regulator Test Criteria   Table 7.2

Breathing Rate	Tidal Volume	RMV	Simulated Work Load
15 BPM	1.5 Liters	22.5	Light
20 BPM	2.0 Liters	40.0	Moderate
25 BPM	2.5 Liters	62.5	Moderate Heavy
30 BPM	2.5 Liters	75.0	Heavy
30 BPM	3.0 Liters	90.0	Extreme

Table 7.3

REGULATOR PERFORMANCE

	DEPTH (in feet of sea water)					
	33	66	99	132	165	198
Poseidon Thor						
Moderate Heavy	●	●	●	●	●	●
Heavy	●	●	●	●	●	●
Extreme	●	●	●	●	●	●
Poseidon Cyklon 5000						
Moderate Heavy	●	●	●	●	●	●
Heavy	●	●	●	●	●	
Extreme	●	●	●	●		
AGA Divator/U.S. Divers Royal						
Moderate Heavy	●	●	●	●	●	●
Heavy	●	●	●	●	●	●
Extreme	●	●	●	*		
Scubapro MKX G-250						
Moderate Heavy	●	●	●	●	●	●
Heavy	●	●	●	●		
Extreme	●	●	●			
Poseidon Odin						
Moderate Heavy	●	●	●	●	●	●
Heavy	●	●	●	●		
Extreme	●	●	●			
U.S. Divers Pro Diver						
Moderate Heavy	●	●	●	●	●	●
Heavy	●	●	●	●		
Extreme	●	●	●			
AGA Divator/U.S. Divers Conshelf XIV						
Moderate Heavy	●	●	●	●	●	●
Heavy	●	●	●	*		
Extreme	●	●				
U.S. Divers Conshelf SE2						
Moderate Heavy	●	●	●	●	●	●
Heavy	●	●	●	*		
Extreme	●	●				

● Acceptable performance   * Marginal performance

Note A: *The light and moderate work loads categories have been eliminated from this table since all of the above Group A regulators had acceptable performance in those tests.*

Note B: *Other high performance regulators include the Tekna 2100 series and the Zeagel Zepher, but they are not included in this comparison due to their incompatibility with the Navy's test equipment.*

EMERGENCY BREATHING SYSTEMS (EBS)

Remember your Open Water/Entry Level class and the various "rules of scuba" that your instructor taught you? Well if not, here's a brief refresher:

Rule number one - BREATHE CONTINUOUSLY. This can be a difficult rule to follow if your regulator (first/second-stage or cylinder valve) decides to malfunction. It is therefore necessary to provide yourself (or perhaps another member of the dive team who may require assistance) with some form of a back-up system.

(Note: Although sharing air via an Octopus/Alternate Air Source is certainly a viable option, it is not addressed to any length in this text due to the fact that the authors believe in a more logical, realistic line of defense - self-sufficiency and equipment redundancy.)

All deep divers should provide themselves with at least an extra second-stage regulator. Additionally, some means of emergency back-up should be provided for a catastrophic air failure (e.g. first-stage malfunction/failure, torn LP hose, blown cylinder valve o-ring, etc.). The emergency back-up is not only for the diver who is carrying it, but, as referred to above, another member of the dive team may need it as well. The alternate air source, as per the general consensus of the high-tech deep diving community, should be equipped with a hose of at least 5 feet in length - particularly in overhead environments. This is to insure that an out-of-air team member will have sufficient hose length to safely function during ascent or, should the scenario arise, during a decompression "hang". Additionally, when diving in a constricted environment such as a cave or wreck it is often necessary for the divers to exit in single file formation due to the "constriction" of the cave/wreck. A safe-second hose of sufficient length will allow this type of single file exit.

Emergency breathing systems (EBS) are categorized into two groups: Type I Alternate Air Supply and Type II Redundant Air Supply. Type I emergency breathing systems are very different from Type II in that they do not offer air supply redundancy. However, they do offer one form of redundancy - a back-up second-stage regulator. Due to the fact that they don't provide an additional air supply, they are referred to as alternates. Their primary function in the recreational diving community is one of supplying an out-of-air buddy with an octopus/safe-second, or in the case of a primary second-stage failure, to supply the diver with an emergency back-up. Type II systems are referred to as redundant because they offer a completely separate air source. An example of a Type II EBS would be a pony bottle with attached regulators.

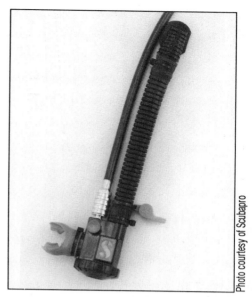

Scubapro's popular Air II illustrates an EBS employing an emergency second stage / inflator.

Photo courtesy of Scubapro

In order to select the appropriate back-up system it's important for the diver to examine exactly what type of coverage and redundancy is needed and then decide which Type II system would best fit the situation. The ideal Type II system would allow the diver to extricate him/herself from an out-of-air situation by ascending at a safe, normal rate (60 feet per minute, or appropriate rate of ascent if a dive computer is used) and avoiding a possible lung over-expansion injury. Another consideration would be staged decompression diving. If a particular back-up system did not allow the diver enough reserve air to make a required stop(s), then it would be considered insufficient. A missed decompression stop is certainly less severe than drowning, but if both can be avoided by diving with the proper equipment, so much the better.

It is also important to take into consideration the *amount* of air that is necessary for the diver to carry. Limiting factors in this equation would be: Personal air consumption, depth, water temperature, overhead environments, arduous activity involved, etc. After considering all of the various factors, the proper Type II EBS could then be selected (e.g. size of pony/bail-out bottle, etc.).

Below in Table 7.4 is a comparison of various Type I and Type II systems as well as what form of emergency coverage they provide along with a few of their individual disadvantages. It was not designed to be a complete representation on emergency breathing systems (EBS), but rather a comparison of some of those most widely used.

Emergency Breathing Systems

Emergency Breathing Systems	Emergencies Covered							Disadvantages
	Out-of-Air Buddy	Out-of-Air Solo Diver	First Stage Failure	Second Stage Failure	Blown O-ring	Ruptured Burst Disc	Shattered Valve	
Type I								
Octopus/Safe **Seconds**	X			X				Can become fouled if not properly secured. Requires additional LP hose.
Scubapro **A.I.R. 2**	X			X				
Sea Quest **Air Source**	X			X				
Zeagle **Octo +**	X			X				
Tekna **Second Wind**	X			X				Currently can only be used with Tekna Power Inflator.
Sherwood **Shadow**	X			X				
Type II								
Submersible Systems **Spare Air 3000**	X	X	X	X	X	X	X	Minimal air supply. Not sufficient for some environments.
Pony Bottles	X	X	X	X	X	X	X	Minimal air supply. Not sufficient for some environments.
Independent Doubles	X	X	X	X	X	X	X	Bulky: size & weight
Sherwood **Genesis Manifold**	X	X	X	X	X	X	X	Bulky: size & weight
Dual Cylinders w/ separate regs & SPG	X	X	X	X	X	X	X	Bulky: size & weight

130

THERMAL PROTECTION SYSTEMS

The deep water environment requires a diver to be properly suited and thus protected against the affects of cold water. Cold water as it is referred to in this text means water that is 75° F (26° C) or less.

In addition to wetsuits, the standard fare of non-cold water divers (Caribbean, South Pacific, etc.), dry suits with thermal underwear are the obvious alternative. They provide the diver with exceptional protection against the elements by keeping all but his hands and head dry (some suits are designed to keep hands and head dry as well) and also allow the individual to be dry at the end of a dive. This is particularly important for repetitive dives, especially if the diver's surface interval takes place in an environment that is less than warm and comfortable.

Affects of Cold Water:

Body heat loss via conductivity in water (water has approximately 25 times the conductive capacity of air) contributes physiologically to a number of negative factors that influence a diver's efficiency. A few of these factors are:

1. Loss of flexibility in the limbs (arms, hands, legs).
2. Overall fatigue and sluggishness.
3. Loss of short-term memory.
4. Greater susceptibility to inert gas narcosis (nitrogen narcosis).
5. Greater susceptibility to decompression sickness.

Affects of Increased Pressure:

With an increase in pressure comes an increase in wetsuit compression. This in turn results in the suit providing less and less thermal protection.

The use of a dry suit requires that the diver adjust the amount of air (gas) that is contained inside the suit. Most sport divers have an additional low pressure (LP) hose routed from the first-stage, that is connected to the primary cylinder, to the inflator mechanism on the suit. However, for more advanced types of diving activities such as that involved in deep diving it may be more prudent, due to

Photo by Steve Persky

Continued evolution in dry suit underwear design has greatly improved diver's comfort in cold water.

131

parameters, to carry a separate cylinder (usually a 13+ cubic foot pony bottle) for the sole purpose of suit inflation. This method allows for the air in the primary cylinder to be used for respiration and BCD inflation, without the added drain of supplying air to the dry suit.

In addition to the use of air for dry suit inflation it is becoming more common for specialized gases such as Argon to be substituted. Due to the fact that Argon is very dense, it is an excellent insulator.

DIVER PROPULSION VEHICLES (DPV's)

Veteran diver Bill Deans with Aqua Zepp DPV.

Photo by Bret Gilliam

Efficient, air-saving maneuverability is a very definite concern for the deep diver. One particular piece of specialized equipment often used by deep divers is a diver propulsion vehicle (DPV), also known as a "scooter". From the state-of-the-art workhorse Aqua Zepp, that is manufactured in Germany and has a working depth in excess of 300 feet, to "beefed-up", altered Tekna and Dacor scooters (they normally have a maximum working depth of approximately 160 fsw/48m, but can be rigged for use in deeper water) deep divers are taking advantage of the benefits of these devices.

DPV's allow the diver to conserve energy and thereby decrease air/gas consumption, which in turn allows for more bottom time. In the case of cave divers, DPV's allow cavers to penetrate further into a cave or cavern system than would normally be permitted if the diver were merely using fins for propulsion. Scooters, primarily the Aqua Zepp due to its larger size, are also utilized as sites of attachment for additional cylinders, lights, cameras, videos, etc.

WEIGHT SYSTEMS

Weight systems used by deep divers vary depending on the type of diving being conducted as well as the type of equipment used. The deeper one ventures into the depths the less weight needed due to the increase in hydraulic pressure (the pressure being exerted upon the diver by the overlying water column). Also, many deep divers who utilize double HP steel cylinders do not wear a weight belt due to the weight of the tanks. Another limiting factor is water temperature (i.e. geographic location). Warm water divers who wear 3mm or less wetsuits and do not require a thicker suit or a dry suit can often avoid the need for a weight belt.

One concern that the reader is advised to be cognizant of is the fact that as the dive progresses and the cylinders are depleted of air/gas, the diver will be somewhat more buoyant due to the loss of the air/gas. This means that even though a weight belt wasn't necessary for the beginning of the dive, it may now become necessary (particularly when decompressing) due to the additional buoyancy. Because of this factor some divers will hang a weight belt with the appropriate amount of weight on the anchor line or the decompression line.

DIVE COMPUTERS (DC's)

The utilization of dive computers as applied to deep diving is a very technical and involved subject. The reader is therefore referred to Chapter 8 for further information about their use.

DEPTH GAUGES

If an individual has elected not to use a dive computer, a depth gauge is necessary. Those gauges constructed of metal (not plastic) are the only acceptable choice for deep diving. Additionally, the gauge should be graduated every 5-10 feet for more accurate reading.

Helium-Filled Depth Gauges:

Aside from the depth gauges incorporated into dive computers, the helium-filled gauges made by SOS Italy are by far the most accurate. These are available in two editions: a 250 ft. model and a 500 ft. model. Long distributed in the U.S. by Scubapro, they are now only available through SOS of Italy. Considered by most experienced deep divers to be the most accurate depth gauge ever built, they are still in wide demand. Many divers still refer to these gauges as the #503 and #507 gauges respectively from Scubapro's catalog.

Back view of deep diver's equipment fully rigged including back-up decompression float and line strapped to left cylinder.

Photo by Bret Gilliam

Front view of a diver fully geared in redundant system for deep diving.

Photo by Bret Gilliam

THE SELF-SUFFICIENT DIVER

In his work entitled *Solo Diving: The Art of Underwater Self-Sufficiency,* von Maier (1991) stated, "For an individual to be completely self-sufficient underwater is certainly the most desirable end result of diver training. Realistically, not all divers are either capable of this (in a complete, definitive sense), or have a desire to achieve it. In fact, for many sport divers, solo diving just doesn't present the same appeal as it does for others. Perhaps they prefer a buddy for personal reasons such as companionship, or they simply feel more comfortable having someone along for the dive. These are reasons that, in this author's opinion, are valid and present no real problems. The problems arise when a buddy is desired to maintain an individual's safety (i.e. to compensate for poor watermanship or inadequate training)."

And so it is with deep diving. Before individuals enter into the deep water realm it is critically important for them to be self-sufficient. It is also imperative that they possess excellent watermanship along with better-than-average skill levels.

If it is important for the normal, everyday recreational diver to be self-sufficient, it is even more important for the deep diver to fit this definition. Aside from the obvious prerequisites – excellent health and watermanship; above-average skill levels; proper training and education - it is necessary for the deep diver to be self-reliant in terms of equipment emergencies as well. This is exactly what equipment redundancy is all about.

EQUIPMENT REDUNDANCY

Proper, quality equipment and deep diving go hand-in-hand. If a diver experiences a second-stage failure at 170 fsw (51.5 m), they'd damn well better have some form of back-up. And the back-up must be a high quality second-stage, not the ubiquitous, inexpensive "octopus" that so many sport divers carry.

The same goes for several other pieces of equipment. Not only does the deep diver need to possess back-up systems (i.e. redundant), but these systems must be of the same high quality and proven performance as the equipment that they are meant to replace.

In Table 7.5 you will find several select pieces of equipment that in the opinions of the authors need to have a redundant counterpart. Again, keep in mind that it is very important for the back-up to be a high quality, reliable piece of gear, not a cheap, inexpensive imitation.

Lamar English exemplifies the well-equipped deep diver as he enters a Florida cave with one of his custom designed high-intensity lights.

Photo by Wes Skils

135

Table 7.5

Equipment Carried in Redundant Form

EQUIPMENT	PURPOSE
Dive Light	For the diver to see at night and in limited visibility, the backup light is carried in case the primary light fails, floods, etc.
Mask	In the case of a lost or damaged primary mask.
Knife (Diver's Tool)	To free a diver from entanglement or to use as a prying tool
Dive Computer (DC)	To be used as a backup if the primary DC fails. *(see Chapter 8)*
Compass	If a compass is necessary for navigation, the backup will replace the primary if lost or damaged.
BCD	Cavers and wreck divers often wear an additional BCD such as Dive Rite's WINGS for emergency use if the primary is damaged.
Depth Gauge	If the diver isn't using a DC, a backup depth gauge is carried in case of primary depth gauge failure.
Bottom Timer	If the diver isn't using a DC, a backup timing device is carried in case the primary bottom timer fails.
Pressure Gauge (SPG)	To be used in case the primary SPG fails or is damaged.
Regulator	To be used as a back-up if the primary regulator malfunctions. Preferably, the back-up regulator should be a Type II Redundant Air Supply.

SUMMARY

Specialized equipment and deep diving go hand-in-hand. Longer exposures and greater depths not only require that the diver be physically and mentally prepared, but that he also possess the proper equipment (as well as the knowledge to utilize the equipment) to safely perform the dive.

Chapter 8

Dive Computers and Deep Diving

"For those of us who love the underwater world, the advent of dive computers has greatly enhanced our recreation. Using computer-assisted multi-level diving techniques will allow divers to spend more time underwater. It is important to remember, however, that dive computers are a tool that must be understood and used properly."

Ken Loyst

DIVE COMPUTERS

To discuss the role of dive computers in deep diving necessitates a preliminary overview of the validity of these devices in standard diving. Like many new evolutions in equipment, dive computers were initially met with skepticism and outright condemnation by some members of the diving community. In retrospect, much of this hostile reception was not deserved. The most vocal critics tended to be the so-called experts who were never fully cognizant of the theory of multi-level diving that was widely applied as far back as the late sixties.

The SOS Decompression Meter was introduced in 1959 but did not gain widespread U.S. distribution until Scubapro gained import rights in 1963. Although not a "computer" by any stretch of the imagination, this relatively simple device provided the first basis of practical underwater calculation of multi-level diving and became popular with professional photojournalists, film makers and divers who were tired of being boxed in to the confines of historical "square profile" table plans. Although many simply dismissed the "decom meter" as invalidated and branded it the "Bend-O-Matic", thousands of divers used it without incident and only grudgingly parted with their well-worn units to make the switch to electronic computers.

DIVE COMPUTER BOOK

Dive Computers: A Consumer's Guide To History, Theory and Performance by Ken Loyst with Karl Huggins and Michael Steidley is specifically designed for any diver that either owns a dive computer or is considering purchasing one. *Dive Computers* is a diver's guide to using dive computers safely and to making an intelligent decision as to which dive computer would best fit your diving needs. Get the straight facts about dive computers currently available. Information includes history of dive computers, historical references of the pioneers in decompression theory, explanations of decompression theory and multi-level diving, and a systematic computer comparison and performance section with 24 dive computers.

Dive Computers: A Consumer's Guide To History, Theory and Performance can be purchased through your local dive retailer or through Watersport Publishing, Inc., P.O. Box 83727, San Diego, CA 92138 • (619) 697-0703.

Obviously, the old "meter" users were comfortable with multi-level profiling and the transition to modern computers was a natural progression. Some early computer models failed to live up to expectations or suffered from design failures that led to flooding, power failures, etc. These initial problems were almost completely eliminated and as we go to press in the fall of 1991, today's diver has over two dozen highly accurate and reliable computers to choose from.

So why use a computer? Quite simply, they are more accurate in measuring depth and time, and virtually every model available incorporates a decompression algorithm more conservative than the standard U.S. Navy tables. Most divers use computers to gain more time underwater safely since the units are "active" devices that compute theoretical tissue/ compartment inert gas loading and outgassing based upon actual depths and times. This provides an obvious benefit to "square profiles" where the diver's uptake and release are modeled on assuming that the entire dive was spent at the deepest depth for the total dive time.

But even if you have a problem accepting the theory of multi-level diving, then modern computers will give you a safety edge based upon their highly accurate depth measuring sensors and timing devices. Using them solely in this application can provide a safety buffer for the strict table user. Some models are significantly more conservative than the Navy tables. For instance, we can all remember that the U.S. Navy tables allow 60 minutes at 60 feet (18.2 m) with no decompression. By comparison, the Dacor Micro Brain Pro Plus computer allows only 44 minutes for the same depth based on its Buhlmann model and program that presumes diving at slight altitude.

The acceptance of diving computers has literally swept through the industry in the nineties. Just a glance around any liveaboard vessel will confirm this, and more and more entry level divers are purchasing computers during or immediately after training.

Although any piece of equipment can fail, modern dive computers are extraordinarily reliable. Additionally, the safety of their decompression models has been proven. In Gilliam's study (1989-90) of 77,680 dives by sport divers, he had zero cases of DCS among computer users (who made up over 50% of the data base).

Recent workshops and symposia have seen respected experts predict such a dominance by computers that dive tables as a primary dive planning protocol may well become obsolete. Although not willing to go on record officially, the majority of professional underwater photographers, resort guides, etct., have already abandoned tables and use computers exclusively. Mount (1991) stated "All my dives since 1983 have been on dive computers. I use two computers in case of a failure. I decompress by the most conservative one. The only time I look at dive tables is when I teach classes, I feel they (tables-Ed.) are ancient history with today's technology."

Selection of a Dive Computer for Deep Diving

Not all computers are suited for deep diving due to their depth limitation. Exceeding a depth barrier or incurring a decompression obligation of more than five minutes was sufficient to put many models into "error" or "out-of-range" modes. In this condition, the diver was locked out by some models and diving could not be resumed for 24 hours.

This book does not have space for an expansive subject treatment of all diving computers and their functions. The authors strongly recommend the text *Dive Computers: A Consumer's Guide to History, Theory and Performance* by Ken Loyst, with Karl Huggins and Mike Steidley (Watersport Books, 1991). Also, it is prudent to consult other experienced deep divers for their input on computer selection.

Deep diver Lynn Hendrickson checks her Dacor Micro Brain Pro Plus dive computer during a decompression stop.

Photo by Bret Gilliam

Computer application should be based on several criteria:

Algorithm

As any diver whom has spent some "hang time" can tell you, there are vastly different decompression models incorporated in the various units. This will involve an informed, educated choice as to what model is most appropriate for your age, water temperature, physical condition, level of deep diving adaptation, etc. Some computers using the Buhlmann algorithm will require substantially more decompression time than others based on more liberal models. Many divers consider this an added safety factor and others consider it a damn nuisance. Take the time to research a computer before buying it and definitely insist on diving a "loaner" before making the investment. Once the unit is selected, conform to its decompression schedule. Never cut "hang times" short.

Depth Range

You can't very well plan a dive to 220 fsw (66.6 m) if your computer isn't designed for that depth. Some very popular and well-designed computers that are appropriate ·for normal sport diving depths are abso-

| Table 8-1 |

DEEP DIVING DIVE COMPUTERS

Dive Computer	Model Type	Dive Timer Range (in minutes)	Full Function Range (in feet)	Depth Gauge Range (in feet)	Decompression Stop Limits (in feet)	Decompression Stop Time (maximum in minutes)
Beuchat Aladin Pro	Buhlmann ZHL-16	199	330'	330'	80'+	99
Dacor Micro Brain Pro Plus	Buhlmann-Hahn P-4	199	270'	330'	98'	90
Parkway Legend	Buhlmann ZHL-16	199	330'	330'	80'+	99
Scubapro DC-11	Buhlmann-Hahn P-5	199	300'	300'	70'	90
Suunto Solution	Nikkola SME	999	325'	325'	140'	99
U.S. Divers Monitor II	Buhlmann ZHL-16	199	330'	330'	80'+	99

lutely ruled out for deep diving. ORCA's workhorse, the Edge, introduced in 1983, was never designed for use beyond 165 fsw (50 m). Likewise, Dacor originally unveiled the 1988 version of the Micro Brain Pro Plus with a depth limitation of 330 fsw (100 m), but in Gilliam's field testing (1989) it was discovered that the unit's case was sufficiently compressed into the internal components so as to render it incapable of true depth registration much below 290 fsw (87.9 m). Dacor modified the depth recommendation to 270 fsw (81.8 m) thereafter. Although not officially sanctioned by the manufacturer, similar experimental dives revealed that the Beuchat Aladin Pro would accurately read out depths well beyond the range in the manual. It is doubtful that the unit is computing gas loading beyond its stated range, but it still offers the benefit of a digital depth gauge. How deep will it read? Gilliam (1990) took one to 467 feet (141.5 m) as indicated in feet of fresh water (ffw) and at least one other has been taken to 480 (145.5 m) as indicated on a mixed gas dive. For the purposes of any reasonable dive exposure, this unit will perform.

Decompression Display

Unless you are comfortable with a computer that tells you a decompression or "ceiling" obligation has been incurred but does not tell you for how long you must remain at that stop, we suggest using a computer that gives decom stops displayed in minutes. This is particularly important for the shallow hangs which can get quite long. Air management is far easier if you know exactly how much time you are obligated to for decompression.

Ascent Rate

Few computers use ascent rates in excess of 60 feet per minute (18.2 m/minute) and most incorporate far slower rates. This is fine for most divers and leads to a more controlled "continuous ascent decompression" within normal sport diving ranges. However, it can be a problem in deep diving where a slow ascent rate can actually contribute to more inert gas loading. The diver is then faced with a difficult decision: increase the ascent rate at least to the 100 fpm (30.3 mpm) level in the deeper segments of the dive (over 100 feet), and then slow down in the shallower segments of the dive, but risk throwing the computer into "error" or confusing it by excessive speed of ascent (at least as far as the computer model is concerned).

DIVE COMPUTER PROFILES

Following is an overview of the six advanced dive computers available in late 1991 which is exerted from *Dive Computers: A Consumers Guide to History, Theory and Performance*. For a quick head-to-head comparison, see Table 8-1 on the proceeding page.

Beuchat's Aladin Pro

Beuchat introduced their most sophisticated dive computer at the January, 1989 DEMA Trade Show. This is the top-of-the-line Aladin. The Aladin Pro is designed with advanced divers in mind and has several addition features that the Sport doesn't, including waiting time prior to flying, total ascent time, decompression stop time, a phosphorescent screen, and an acoustic alarm for ascent rate or decompression violations. This multi-level Swiss Model dive computer uses the newest version of Buhlmann's ZHL-16 Model and is also manufactured in Switzerland by Uwatec. There is less time at depth because of the more conservative approach of these tables *(see Aladin)*. The Aladin Pro uses 6 compartments with half-time ranges from 6 to 320 minutes.

This is the one of the best high altitude dive computers on the market. The Aladin Pro can be used to altitudes of 13,000 feet as either a desaturated dive computer *(after waiting the appropriate time required by the Pro)* or as a repetitive dive computer at altitude which calculates at a higher saturation level. The Aladin Pro is an advanced dive computer with full decompression and high altitude functions.

Note: The Aladin Pro suspends calculations of tissue desaturation while a decompression stop is violated. If violated, the DECOSTOP display will flash accompanied by the acoustic alarm. This means that it is necessary to descend immediately to the decompression stop.

142

Dacor's **Micro Brain Pro Plus**

Distributed by Dacor in the U.S. since early 1989, the Micro Brain Pro Plus, is one of the most sophisticated full decompression computers available with 36 different functions and is a great improvement over the Micro Brain. Made by Divetronic AG, it is a multi-functional dive computer using a Buhlmann/Hahn (P-4) Swiss Model for calculations which makes this computer more conservative than the U.S. Navy Tables and just a shade more conservative than the Uwatec models. The P-4 is an up-dated version of the Swiss Model originating from an abbreviated ZHL-12 Buhlmann Model. The Micro Brain Pro Plus has 6 theoretical compartments using half-times ranging from 6 to 600 minutes which differ from its predecessor the Micro Brain.

The Pro Plus' algorithm is compensated in the same manner as the Micro Brain's for high altitude dives *(and this compensation applies to all dives up to 4,920 feet)* by using a reduced surface atmospheric pressure of 12.7 p.s.i. for its calculations instead of using 14.7 p.s.i. or 1 atmosphere that all other dive computers use. High altitude profiles to 6,560 feet can be accomplished after equilibration to ambient pressure. The Micro Brain Pro Plus functions as a dive timer and altitude compensating depth gauge from 6,560 feet to 14,764 feet, its maximum range.

The Micro Brain Pro Plus was the first dive computer with a built-in simulator that allowed real time simulation of dive profiles. The Pro Plus will handle decompression diving unlike the simpler Micro Brain. Large numbers flash the depth of the first decompression stop and ascent time. Other special features include Logbook Memory, a Dive Recorder and a Dive Planner. The Micro Brain Pro Plus is another advanced dive computer with 36 different functions, yet graphically, one of the simplest units to use.

Parkway's **Legend**

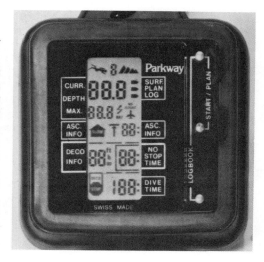

Parkway introduced their new dive computer, the Legend, in 1990. This sophisticated dive computer is similar to the Aladin Pro and is manufactured by Uwatec of Switzerland. Designed with advanced divers in mind, the Legend has all the additional features that the Aladin Pro has incorporated in its new model, including waiting time prior to flying, total ascent time, decompression stop time, and an acoustic alarm for ascent rate or decompression violations.

This multi-level Swiss Model dive computer uses the newest version of Buhlmann's ZHL-16 tables. There is less time at depth because of the more conservative approach of these tables *(see Aladin)*. The Legend uses 6 compartments with half-time ranges from 6 to 320 minutes. The Legend is a bit larger than its cousins the Aladins, but remains a small convenient size, and it easy to read and understand.

The Legend, like the Aladins and Monitors, is part of the group of the best high altitude dive computers on the market. The Legend can be used to altitudes of 13,200 feet as either a desaturated dive computer *(after waiting the appropriate time)* or as a repetitive dive computer at altitude which calculates at a higher saturation level. The Legend is an advanced dive computer with full decompression and high altitude functions.

Scubapro's **DC-11**

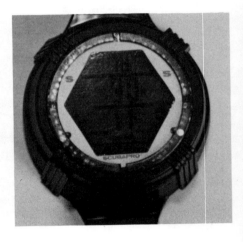

Distributed by Scubapro in Europe since mid 1990, the DC-11, is probably, at this time, one of the most sophisticated full decompression computers available with 45 different functions. This is a very small dive computer, with the screen size about the size of the DataMax Sport. Made by Divetronic AG, it is a multifunctional dive computer using the newest Buhlmann-Hahn (P-5) Swiss Model for calculations. This makes the DC-11 significantly more conservative than the U.S. Navy Tables and, also more conservative than the Uwatec models and the Micro Brains. The P-5 is an up-dated version of the Swiss Model which has been given additional individual saturation allowances that account for bounce diving, rapid ascents, multiple ascents in one day, and repeated dives. The DC-11 has 6 theoretical compartments using half-times ranging from 6 to 600 minutes.

The DC-11's algorithm is compensated in the same manner as the Micro Brains for high altitude dives except its range is to 11,500 feet. The display is programmable by the user for meters and C° or feet and F°. The DC-11 also can freely program safety factors into the model (by selecting high altitude ranges at lower elevations).

The DC-11 will handle full decompression diving. Large numbers indicate the depth of the first decompression stop, decompression time and ascent time. Other special features include a fast time dive planner *(12 times faster)*, Logbook Memory, a Dive Recorder and phosphorescent display lighting.

Suunto's **Solution**

One of the newest developments in dive computers in 1990 was Suunto's Solution. Distributed by SeaQuest in early 1991, this small dive computer has all you could ask for in features. If the success of the SME-ML's is any indication of what the Solution will do, then divers take note. New features include an expanded depth range to 325 feet, altitude range to 8,200 feet, expanded decompression capabilities, variable ascent rate display, audible alarms (for excessive ascent rate, omitted decompression, excessive depth, and excessive decompression), and an expanded memory that allows log book, dive history and dive profiles, plus a 4 time speed simulator.

It is of lighter weight construction than the ML's and the same small size (2.5 inches), but has a larger display screen. The Solution, unlike the SME-ML, is a full decompression dive computer. The Solution's algorithm is the same as the SME-ML's *(see SME-ML in overview).*

U.S. Divers' **Monitor II**

Identical to the Aladin Pro in features, U.S. Divers' Monitor II, was introduced to the U.S. by U.S. Divers in late 1989 *(also made by Uwatec).* This is truly a professional dive computer with all of the bells and whistles (and alarms in this case) like the Aladin Pro. The Monitor II is designed with advanced divers in mind and has several additional features that the Monitor I doesn't have, including waiting time prior to flying, total ascent time, decompression stop time, and an acoustic alarm for ascent rate or decompression violations. This multi-level Swiss Model dive computer uses the newest version of Buhlmann's ZHL-16 tables and is also manufactured in Switzerland by Uwatec. There is less time at depth because of the more conservative approach of these tables *(see Aladin).* The Monitor II uses 6 compartments with half-time ranges from 6 to 320 minutes.

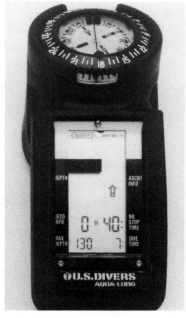

This is the one of the best high altitude dive computers on the market and it can be used to altitudes of 13,200 feet as either a desaturated dive computer or as a repetitive dive computer at altitude which calculates at a higher saturation level *(see Aladin Pro).*

SUMMARY

Dive computers have a valid role in deep diving if used correctly and within their model limitations. The authors advocate redundant computers per diver if tables are not used. During the Ocean Quest experimental studies by Gilliam (1989-90), extensive deep (200+ fsw/60.6+ m) diving was done using the computer models as the sole basis of decompression with no incidence of DCS. These dives were of relatively short duration at depth, however (usually exposures of 30 minutes or less). As divers involved in wreck and cave penetration become involved with more extensive bottom times, the potential of pushing the limits of the decompression model become greater and increase the attendant risk. Custom tables should then take precedence with computers primarily used as digital depth/time instruments and their decompression information used in a back-up role.

Computers have increasingly altered traditional dive planning practices since the diver now has an effective means of calculating deviations from a fixed plan while underwater. We recommend that divers have a working dive plan scenario prior to water entry, but deviation to take advantage of unexpected marine life appearances or dramatic coral formations discovered at deeper depths is reasonable and will not compromise safety. The computer (and back-up) will allow far more flexibility and yet keep track of no-decompression or decompression obligations.

It is good practice for divers to familiarize themselves with the manufacturer's recommendation for computer failure. Each model applies different "Murphy's Law" procedures and are provided in the computer manual. There is a described protocol for at least one computer (ORCA models) so that the diver may re-enter Navy tables. Michael Emmerman authored this suggested procedure and does offer the only viable return to tables scenario.

Computers, like any instrument, can fail but their track record is extremely good in retrospective. Divers must also bring a personal helping of common sense to the table. As it has been pointed out ad nauseam by some critics, it is theoretically possible for a computer to "allow" a potentially hazardous dive profile. However, even a mild grip on reality will suggest that computers be used conservatively much the same as safety buffers have been added to tables (next greater depth or time) for years by divers seeking a cushion. Don't run your computer to the edge (no pun intended) of its decompression model.

Use computers as the valuable tool they can be but don't expect any device to think for you.

Chapter 9

Scientific Applications of Deep Diving

"Like the hard hat divers of the 1950's, scientific divers are really just technicians trying to get to the job site. The role of diving then, is viewed as simply a vehicle to new marine geological strata, species, or resources. How we get there... is really incidental to the project."

Dr. Bob Dill

The scientific community as we know it today has developed into a cooperative body through the worldwide efforts of the Scientific Committee of the Confederation Mondiale des Activites Subaquatiques (CMAS) as well as through the American Academy of Underwater Sciences (AAUS).

It has been able to band together maintaining its independence from outside legislative and governmental interference. This has allowed it to continue self-regulation in all aspects of scientific diving. This includes the subject of 'scientific deep diving.' The reader may find that although deep diving is considered in many ways "taboo" to many divers, scientists consider deep diving a vital necessity to much of their research. This chapter is designed to help the reader understand the past, present and future of scientific diving, particularly the deep diving aspects.

DEPTH CERTIFICATION

The initial Scientific Diving Certificate will authorize the bearer to dive to a depth of 30 feet (9m). All scientific divers who wish to increase their depth certification must be involved in a project that justifies them to dive deeper than the initial certification.

Once justified, certification to 60 fsw (18m), 100 fsw (30m) and 130 fsw (39m) depths may be obtained by successfully fulfilling 12 dives, under supervision, to depths between the diver's current certified depth and to the next greater depth. For example, a diver pursuing an increase in depth certification would log 12 dives between 31 fsw and 60 fsw for a 60 fsw card. The 12 dives should total a minimum time of two hours for the 100 fsw or 130 fsw depth certification. Each time a diver wants to increase his depth certification he must be accompanied by two authorized individuals who are certified to at least the next greater depth. Depth certification will be validated by obtaining signatures of these individuals. Before complete certification is awarded, the diver shall demonstrate competency in the use of the appropriate U.S. Navy decompression tables.

The scientific deep diver who reaches a 130 fsw (39m) depth certification may be certified to depths of 150 fsw (45m) and 190 fsw (57m). This can be achieved by completing four dives near each depth. The individual must demonstrate a working knowledge of special problems associated with deep diving and special safety requirements. All dives must be carefully planned and administered under close supervision of a diver who is certified to this depth.

The depth classification referred to above was derived from Scripps Institution of Oceanography, San Diego, CA. Jim Stewart started diving in the Scripps Submarine Canyon near SIO in 1951. The SIO philosophy of depth certification evolved from Stewart's diving experiences. Initially, SIO authorized a 250 foot (75m) card for scientists. Currently AAUS recommends a maximum depth of 190 feet.

The division of depth classification were based on certain environmental breaks off the San Diego coastline.

    0 - 30 fsw (9m) Inside the kelp bed
    30 - 60 fsw (18m) In the kelp bed
    60 - 100 fsw (30m) Outside the kelp bed to the edge of the canyon
    100 - 130 fsw (39m) Along the edge of the canyon
    130 - 150 fsw (45m) Down along the walls of the canyon
    150 - 200 fsw (61m) Inside the canyon

Bert Kobayashi, a student at SIO in 1960, was certified by Stewart. In a brief period of time, after basic training, Kobayashi received his 200 foot

Scientific diving pioneer Jimmy Stewart, founder of the Scripps Institution of Oceanography (SIO) diving program. Stewart served as Diving Safety Officer at SIO for over 40 years, retiring in 1991.

Photo by Darren Webb

certification. Today he is the Supervisor for Physical Education at the University of California, San Diego (UCSD). Since 1972, Kobayashi has trained over 360 deep divers. The training started at 80 fsw (24m) to 100 fsw (30m), progressing to increments of ten feet, down to 200 fsw (61m). Unfortunately, in 1985 UCSD discontinued the program. During these thirteen years all dives were classified no-decompression dives, and there were no incidences of DCS.

Why did UCSD eliminate the deep diving class? Perhaps it was the liability of training divers below the sport diving limit of 130 fsw. Stewart (1991) notes, "In the old days, there was never a stigma about deep diving. Now you're damned if you do and you're dammed if you don't teach people about deep diving."

EQUIPMENT

The scientific community provides the diver, through modern technology, the proper training to minimize the diver's chances of injury or accident. Yet there will always be risks that accompany all deep dives. With this in mind, scientific programs and research programs have been very successful in terms of safety in scientific deep diving. The deep diving scientist views his equipment differently than of a sport diver. His scuba equipment is simply another tool that allows him to carry out his research. If the diver's research requires him to dive deep, he will simply find the appropriate tools to take him there. In scientific deep diving the emphasis is placed on the diver's work, and not on the depth at which he is working.

DEEP DIVING PROBLEMS

Working at deeper depths may present problems for the diver. His ability to effectively work is controlled by a variety of factors such as nitrogen narcosis, oxygen toxicity and decompression sickness. Although many scientific divers continue to use air as their primary breathing gas, more research projects are taking into account the advantages of mixed gases (see Chapter 11). The problems associated with nitrogen narcosis, oxygen toxicity and decompression sickness may be resolved or at least reduced by the use of NITROX and/or TRIMIX.

ACTUAL ACCOUNTS

NOTE: Following is a brief synopsis of scientific deep diving projects that illustrate some aspects of breathing mixtures, depths, bottom times, problems and equipment associated with deep diving.

Scripps Institution of Oceanography (SIO)

As of 1991, the research diving program of SIO, currently in its fortieth year, has logged approximately 200,000 dives. Only one case of DCS has been documented. This particular incident occurred several years ago at San Clemente Island off the coast of southern California. Six divers were finishing a qualifying dive within the U.S. Navy no-decompression limits. Only one diver decided to carry out a ten foot safety stop. After surfacing, the diver developed DCS. (This example suggests that even though the individual carried out a safety stop, he still got bent. It illustrates the variability between individuals and their physiological make-up; the real dividing line, as opposed to training and education, between who does and who doesn't get bent.) Stewart (1991) asserts, "Decompression sickness is still a crap-shoot."

WEST INDIES MARINE LABORATORY

This facility was opened in St. Croix, U. S. Virgin Islands in 1971 as a branch of Fairleigh Dickinson University. It was designed and implemented as a pure research and teaching marine biology field station complete with extensive laboratory facilities and one of the largest dedicated university diving programs then in existence. From its opening, scientific divers conducted deep diving research excursions in exploring the steep north shore drop-offs. The first diving director, "Clem" Bowman (now a medical doctor), approved and sponsored regular collecting and observation projects in depths between 150 to 300 fsw. In 1977, Dr. Robert Dill, a prominent marine geologist, took over as West Indies Lab Director and

Chief Scientist. Dill, a veteran of numerous deep diving expeditions including Cousteau's first trip to the Great Blue Hole in Belize, sought to substantially broaden the diving program. He persuaded NOAA to relocate the saturation habitat *Hydrolab* from the Bahamas to St. Croix to be administered as a separate project for the lab.

Dill was successful in attracting some of the top scientific and diving staff in the U.S. and the program became NOAA's only on-going saturation system. Dr. William Schane, a retired Air Force hyperbaric specialist, was recruited as the *Hydrolab* medical director and he set up a technically state-of-the-art recompression facility and training program to support the "aquanauts". Dick Rutkowski, then NOAA's deputy director of diving, was frequently brought in from Florida to oversee the continued expansion of the saturation habitat and the hyperbaric facilities.

As in the missions conducted previously in the Bahamas, *Hydrolab* served as a hub for scientific divers from all over the U.S. and the international community. Experimental deep excursion dives were conducted officially (and not so officially at times) by the aquanauts while in saturation at approximately 55 fsw. This allowed dives with little or no decompression to depths of up to 250 fsw.

Hydrolab remained in service from 1977 to 1988 when it was retired to the Smithsonian Institution in Washington D.C. as an exhibit and tribute to the NOAA scientific diving programs. During its career, it played host to literally hundreds of aquanauts and scores of one week saturation missions.

Under Dill's influence and administration, the West Indies lab facility proved to be one of the most extensive university diving programs ever implemented. Uniquely, Dill encouraged diving exploration with little regard to depth limits per se. If the project required diving to as much as 300 fsw to complete the work, then approval was never withheld. His sometimes controversial diving philosophy and often flamboyant managerial style made him a favorite target of critics. But during his Directorship, West Indies Lab enjoyed a perfect safety record and conducted one of the most innovative and exciting scientific diving programs in the U.S.

Dill retired in the early 1980's and the lab was closed in 1989 following a disastrous hurricane that devastated the island of St. Croix.

THE SANTA MONICA PROJECT

Beginning in 1972 and continuing into 1973, Dr. Mendel Petersen conducted a joint exploration project with Dr. Allan Albright of the Caribbean Research Institute set up to locate and excavate historically significant shipwrecks in the Virgin Islands. Petersen was then Curator of

Historical Archaeology at the Smithsonian Institution and had pioneered wreck projects in underwater sites all over the world.

After discovering the sixteenth century wreck of the *Santa Monica* in a southern bay off the island of St. John (near-by the original sites of the *TEKTITE* saturation projects), he funded a systemized excavation project to preserve the wreck from looters and to catalog its cargo. In tracing the original log entries and accounts of the ship's master, he pinpointed its location and reconstructed the circumstances of its sinking. In a running gun battle with a French frigate, the *Santa Monica* struck a seamount some two miles south of the British Virgin Islands in the vicinity of Norman Island. The previously uncharted pinnacle rose abruptly from water several hundred feet deep to within five feet of the surface.

Members of the "Santa Monica Project" with proton magnetometer off St. John, Virgin Islands in 1973. The device registered changes in the earth's natural magnetic field and helped to locate several shipwrecks lost in the area. Left to right: Dr. Mendel Petersen (Smithsonian Institution), George Tyson and Dr. Allan Albright (Caribbean Research Institute), Dave Coston and Bret Gilliam (Ocean Tech).

photo by Bill Willard

The collision with the sea mount, now named Santa Monica Rock, badly holed her bottom and much of her cargo was lost in the area as she dragged over the destructive and hidden reef. In a desperate effort to save the ship and crew, her master jettisoned supplies and various cargo stores including cannon to clear the rock and then limped into the bay south of St. John to sink in shallow water.

Petersen procured an early model proton magnetometer, a device that measures disturbances and interruptions in the earth's magnetic field and set out to locate the dumped cargo of the *Santa Monica* and to search for other wrecks in what was traditionally a haven for pirates and chartered privateers of that era. Petersen towed the device behind his research vessel at varying depths with scuba divers towed on specially designed underwater "sleds" approximately 75 to 100 feet behind the magnetometer array. He monitored the read-outs from his control station at the surface and any suspicious "spikes" prompted him to release the divers on the spot to look closer for telltale signs of wrecks such as ballast stone or cannon.

Typically, he would work areas between 100 to 200 fsw and in many cases far deeper. The divers being towed frequently were surprised by curious barracuda and sharks while hanging on for dear life. Petersen frequently urged the boat captain to cruise at faster than optimal speeds for the towed divers on the sleds. The divers joked that the only way to slow Petersen down and insure their safety was to borrow money from him just prior to the search sweeps.

Using his magnetometer and diver teams, he located several previously "lost" wrecks and was able to place divers on the original site of the *Santa Monica* grounding. A wealth of artifacts, coins, clothing, ceramics and pottery from their cargos was recovered along with numerous cannon. The *Rhone*, an internationally famous shipwreck off Salt Island in the BVI, had a sistership, the *WYE*, lost in the same hurricane of 1867. Petersen's team discovered her remains off St. John.

His work was some of the deepest use of magnetometer and towed diver teams up to that date.

INSTITUTE OF NAUTICAL ARCHEOLOGY (Texas A & M)

In 1984, the Institute of Nautical Archaeology at Texas A & M University started an archaeological diving expedition, led by Dr. George Bass, off the southern coast of Turkey. Every summer for three months the diving archaeologists dived twice a day for six straight days. Each diver spent 45 minutes decompressing (in-water). Surface interval time was five hours between each dive. By 1990, this research project logged a total of 12,542 dives of which 11,340 were between the depths of 100 fsw (30m) and 180 fsw (54m). A total of 3,583 hours were spent at these depths. During this time five incidents of DCS were reported. Three produced pain only. And two were central nervous system (CNS) hits. Throughout the expedition two major concerns were dehydration and over-exertion of the diver. These two factors may have contributed to the onset of DCS.

Several steps were taken to reduce the chances of DCS. In 1986 the use of 100 percent oxygen was incorporated into the divers decompression schedule at 10 fsw (3m) and later in 1989 at 20 fsw (6m). In 1987 the divers switched from the U.S. Navy tables to the more conservative Dick Van tables developed from Duke University.

NATIONAL PARK SERVICE

The Submerged Cultural Resources Unit of the National Park Service (NPS) is involved in deep water archaeology. Under the supervision of Chief Daniel J. Lenihan, the staff of underwater archaeologists are responsible for the mapping, inventorying, and assessing of underwater cultural resources with emphasis on historic shipwrecks in marine and Great Lake parks. The divers also develop plans for management, preservation and recreational use of these resources.

Since 1974 the dives conducted by the National Park Service divers used 100 percent oxygen at their 30 foot or shallower decompression stops. Larry Murphy, the former Diving Safety Officer of Warm Mineral Springs, Florida also used oxygen for in-water decompression. Murphy (1978) relates, "Warm Mineral Springs is a unique prehistoric site in a karst sinkhole on the Gulf Coast of Florida in Sarasota County." It is here from 1974 to 1978 archaeologists dived to 165 fsw (50m) and logged over 1,800 dives (half being repetitive or decompression dives). 175 of these were extreme exposures dives reaching depths of 230 feet (69m). During this project no symptoms of DCS were reported. Murphy contributes this unblemished record to three factors - diver safety training, adherence to the dive program and the use of oxygen while decompressing.

BISHOP MUSEUM DEEP PROJECT, HAWAII

Recent work by Ichthyologist Richard Pyle of Hawaii has shown the benefits of applied deep diving technologies to pure ichthyology research and has enabled him to observe and identify several new species in what he has termed the "twilight zone" of marine biology.

Pyle is working under famed fish researcher Dr. John E. Randall, one of the world's foremost authorities, at the Bishop Museum in Honolulu. The focus of Pyle's work is on coral reef fishes in the 200-450 fsw depth ranges. Since coral reef communities ultimately depend on sunlight to fuel the photosynthetic algae which form a vital component of the food web, it is not surprising that the greatest diversity of reef organisms occurs at depths well above 200 fsw. But in the clear blue waters of typical of tropical oceanic islands, enough sunlight penetrates to sustain a thriving reef community at much greater depths... sometimes well in excess of 400 fsw.

To explore the deeper limits of this coral reef habitat, marine biologists have had to rely on traps, trawls, and deep sea submersibles. But these devices have their limitations. Traps and trawls are not very selective collecting methods, and are generally not effective at collecting the many smaller, more cryptic fishes of a coral reef environment. Submersibles and

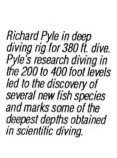

Richard Pyle in deep diving rig for 380 ft. dive. Pyle's research diving in the 200 to 400 foot levels led to the discovery of several new fish species and marks some of the deepest depths obtained in scientific diving.

ROV's can be cumbersome and extremely expensive to operate, especially in the more remote corners of the world's oceans. Most have been designed to penetrate depths of thousands of feet or more, and the uncommon researchers fortunate to obtain funds to utilize them usually concentrate their efforts at depths far greater than 450 fsw. Consequently, the zone of coral reef habitat between depths of about 200-450 fsw (what Pyle refers to as the "twilight zone") remains relatively unexplored.

Pyle's initial work was conducted on air to depths as great as 360 fsw. Together with associate, Chip Boyle of Rarotonga, they discovered six new species and a new genus of coral reef fishes in their first fourteen dives. Utilizing extrapolated decompression tables and pure oxygen for all stops above 30 fsw, they were able to extensively advance their research but quickly realized the advantages of mixed gas not only for safety but for observational and collecting efficiency.

After reading an article by well-known cave diver and mixed gas technician Dr. Bill Stone, Pyle initiated correspondence that resulted in a liaison with custom table expert Randy Bohrer of Undersea Applications. Subsequently armed with special proprietary tables and the tools necessary to conduct his own custom mixed gas blends on-site, Pyle has extended his diving access to 425 fsw. Since making the switch to mix, he reports collecting specimens of a new angelfish species and the discovery and collection of five additional new species of fishes.

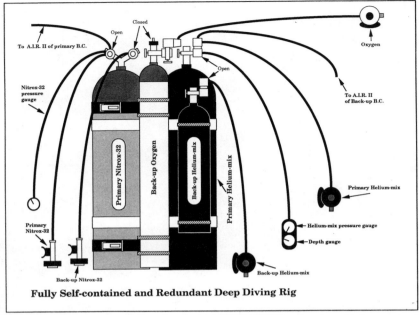

Fully Self-contained and Redundant Deep Diving Rig

Richard Pyle's custom deep diving set employing NITROX, TRIMIX, and oxygen cylinders.

Operationally, Pyle uses standard NOAA NITROX I carried in a 100 cubic foot cylinder as his "travel mix" above 130 fsw and switches to his "bottom mix" of TRIMIX-12/40 also carried in a 100 cubic foot cylinder. Additionally, he carries a cylinder of pure O_2 for shallow decompression and backup cylinders of both TRIMIX and NITROX. (See illustration of equipment package)

Pyle's work is the deepest scientific work by a free-swimming diver currently conducted. In recent correspondence with Gilliam (September 1991) he notes: "My ambition is to use the mixed gas technologies to explore and document the marine organisms that inhabit this 'twilight zone'. My early attempts with air were somewhat limiting, lacking your incredible tolerance of high partial pressures of nitrogen, but provided me with enough incentive to become involved with mix. The Rarotonga trip was a great success, all sorts of new species in just a few dives."

"Unfortunately, most scientific institutions and granting agencies are locked into AAUS and NOAA conservatism for diving, so I've had to fund the deep stuff almost entirely out of my own pocket. My hope is to eventually convince the diving scientific community that these sorts of mixed gas technologies are legitimate, and then maybe I'll be able to obtain funding to get 'deep' into Twilight Zone exploration."

CAVE DIVING

Scientific deep divers have utilized mixed gases designed to increase bottom time, decrease decompression time as well as provide the diver with an unclouded mind. In 1986, diving-gases expert, Dr. R.W. "Bill" Hamilton of Hamilton Research Ltd. , designed special tables for the deep diving expedition known as the Sullivan Connection. Hamilton faced difficulty with the long decompression stops so he adopted a method of using oxygen to shorten the decompression schedule. Dr. Hamilton encountered another problem: the divers would still be in-gassing at the deeper depths. This was resolved by switching over to NITROX, therefore reducing the intake of nitrogen.

The Sullivan Connection led by Parker Turner would be the first long duration dives on mixed gases. Over 50 dives were made without incidence of decompression sickness. The divers penetrated a total of 4,600 feet downstream reaching a depth of 240 feet (72m) for 110 minutes. The success of Sullivan Connection led the way for future scientific expeditions on mixed gases.

In 1986 Dr. John Zumrick passed some survey data along to cave divers Bill Gavin and Parker Turner along with his belief in the "connectability" of Sullivan to Cheryl Sink. Many people believed that this project was impossible due to the great depth and distances involved, Gavin and Turner however did not.

Gavin and Bill Main had already developed a style of cave diving that enabled them to travel farther faster and on less gas than anyone. In fact they were regularly doing dives of over a mile in the upstream section of Sullivan. The trick was to apply these proven techniques to the down-stream which was approximately twice as deep.

Turner believed that a switch to mixed gas was one of the answers and in fact had already been researching the problem for several years. Gavin had previously met Dr. Bill Hamilton at the Navy Experimental Diving Unit and recommended that Parker call Hamilton. After many long conversations Turner became convinced that Hamilton could cut a workable set of tables for the dive.

The choice was made to dive a TRIMIX of 25% He, 18% O_2, balance N_2. This would enable the team to construct the gas without the use of a booster pump which was beyond the projects budget. Hamilton was having trouble reducing the in-water decompression time at the deeper stops due to the rapid ingassing of Helium. He devised a solution of switching to an intermediate mix of 60% O_2, 40% N_2, beginning at 100 ft. By combining the 10 and 20 foot stops the Sullivan divers were able to spend almost half their decompression in one place. This led to the technique of placing a cattle trough upside on the cave ceiling to allow the divers an air space. This provided warmth and a convenient place to drink fluids and eat. It also relieved the terrible tedium of in-water decompression allowing the divers to carry on conversation between breaths of 100% O_2.

Although it greatly increased the logistics it soon became obvious that gas was by far safer both from the standpoint of narcosis and that of decompression. Concerned over the thermal characteristics of helium the decision was made to inject argon in their dry suits. This proved to be quite effective and soon became the rage amongst cold and deep water divers.

In the meantime Gavin had customized the Tekna DV3-X to go deep by pressurizing it with N_2. These innovations enabled the team of Gavin, Main, Turner and Lamar English to connect Sullivan to Cheryl establishing a new World's Record for the Longest Underwater Cave. One dive during the connection sent Gavin, Main, and Turner 4700 feet downstream at a depth of 240 feet! The bottom time was 100 minutes resulting in a 288 minute decompression.

Later based on the successful man dives at Sullivan, Bill Stone unhappy, with the impossibly long schedules developed by Dr. Ed Thalman for the Wakulla Project, contracted Hamilton who developed similar tables for the Project which also proved successful.

After the Connection the need for mixed gas and standards was driven home for a final time by the tragic death of cave explorer and brilliant cartographer Bill McFaden. Although mixed gas was available, McFaden chose air for a 220 foot deep project. The resulting narcosis probably set of a chain reaction of problems which eventually overwhelmed Bill just 50 ft. short of the exit. This resulted in Turner drawing up an operations manual at the request of the U.S. Forest Service which called for a mandatory use of mixed gas past 190 feet while diving in the Leon Sinks Area.

Finally in 1987 Gavin, Main, Turner and Lamar English traveled from Sullivan to Cheryl in an 8440 ft., 240 ft. deep trip breaking the records for the World's Longest Traverse and World's Deepest Traverse.

Soon afterward Turner was contacted by Steve Omeroid and then Jim King and Billy Dean who wanted to apply the same techniques to deep wreck diving. Both John Crea and Randy Boher asked Turner for a copy of the now·proven Sullivan Tables and tweaked Buhlmann's algorithm until it produced similar results and began to produce custom tables for mixed gas dives.

Based on the successes of these later projects mixed gas has found its way into Florida States Academic diving program. The ground breaking Warm Mineral Springs Archaeological Research Project employs the same techniques for their research dives. FSU's Underwater Speleology Unit recently completed a mapping project at 217 ft. in Warm Mineral Spring, thus breaking the 190 ft. barrier erected previously by University Programs.

Today Gavin and Turner still actively dive deep under the auspices of the National Speleological Society. They have been joined by divers Steve Irving and Sherwood Schile who by applying the same techniques have recently completed several mile long penetrations at 240 ft.

All dives are evaluated by FSU's Doppler detector. This has led to an emphasis on controlling factors that increase decompression obligation and employing techniques that decrease the latter. One of the most effective was exercising during decompression. Turner believes that this has enabled him to maintain low Doppler scores despite his advancing age.

Gavin is the program manager for the Navy's EX19 Mixed Gas Rebreather Project. Turner serves as the Cave Diving Coordinator for FSU and the project Director of the NSS Woodville Karst Plain Project. The Leon Sinks Cave System at 48,754 ft. is still the longest underwater cave in the world and the southern end is still going, headed straight for Wakulla. The challenge of this awesome cave continues to provide inspiration for new technologies and techniques as well as a crucible in which they and the men who employ them are tested.

WAKULLA SPRINGS PROJECT

Between October and December of 1987 the United States Deep Caving Team begun a series of dives into the Wakulla Springs located in Florida. This expedition brought together over 20 scientists and cave explorers. Using Hamilton's tables, the divers reached a depth of 380 feet. They mapped an aggregate total of 10,858 feet into various caverns. A total of 126 dives were made on air and 36 dives were made on gas. Decompression times of seven hours were not uncommon. An expedition of this degree required an assortment of high-tech equipment. Skiles (1990) conveys, "Many of the tanks we'd take down were the fiber-composite type, and were filled to pressures exceeding 5,000 psi to give us the volumes needed." As stated by Parker Turner, "...the Sullivan Connection and the dives made by the U.S. Deep Caving Team at Wakulla Springs were considered very heavy dives for their time." Four years later, they are still considered as such.

SUMMARY

The scientific diving community has, for many years, successfully conducted deep diving projects as well as instituted various guidelines for deep divers. Through the combined efforts of many individuals and the experience gained from countless thousands of dives, the deep diving community has greatly benefited from scientific divers and their acquired knowledge of a subject still in its infancy.

Chapter 10

NITROX

"Mother Nature provided the planet Earth with a NITROX atmosphere known as air. She never said that air was the best breathing medium for divers. Here, as in many other fields of endeavor, human beings have used their knowledge of natural laws to go one step beyond what Nature has provided for them."

J. Morgan Wells, Ph.D.

NITROX, although having been in widespread use for over thirty years, still remains largely a mystery to divers outside the commercial or scientific communities. One popular misconception is that NITROX is a specialized deep diving gas, when, in fact, it is rarely used below 130 fsw. Strictly speaking, some might argue that NITROX has no place in a deep diving text but upon closer examination we shall see its various applications.

WHAT IS NITROX ?

Technically, the term NITROX can be used to describe any combination of nitrogen-oxygen (N_2-O_2). The air around us is NITROX. Your first dive on compressed air was a NITROX dive. Standard, compressed air is a 79/21 mixture (79% N_2/21% O_2). This is referred to as a normoxic nitrox mixture (the term normoxic referring to normal oxygen pressure).

A NITROX mixture with less than 79% nitrogen and greater than 21% oxygen is called Enriched Air Nitrox (EAN), and due to the decreased amount of nitrogen can offer significant advantages (see below).

The National Oceanic and Atmospheric Administration (NOAA) currently recognizes two standard NITROX mixes: NOAA NITROX I (68% N_2/32% O_2) and NOAA NITROX II (64% N_2/36% O_2). NOAA NITROX I has a depth limit of approximately 130 fsw (39.4 m) and is the most commonly used mixture, whereas NOAA NITROX II, which is currently being evaluated, has a depth limit of approximately 100 fsw (30m) or less. (See Chapter 5 for FO_2 depth limits for various mixes.)

WHY NITROX ?

The use of NITROX by the sport diving community is a relatively new concept. However, commercial divers and the U.S. Navy have been using it successfully for decades. In fact, in the 1979 edition of the NOAA Diving Manual tables and procedures for the use of NITROX were published.

In addition to the Navy and commercial diving industry, the scientific/research community as well as select segments of the advanced sport diving community (technical or high-tech divers) have begun to take advantage of the benefits of Nitrox such as increased bottom times, shorter surface intervals and reduced inert gas narcosis (nitrogen narcosis).

Currently, interest in the use of NITROX has widened in the traditional sport diving community. If we were to accept the national scuba training agencies' recommendations for less experienced divers to be 130 fsw, then NITROX would really be the obvious choice. ANDI (American NITROX Divers Inc.) has developed a certification program for both users of NITROX and instructors to teach this emerging sport diving program. To avoid the stigma of mixed gas jargon and any tinge of "high tech" confusion, ANDI is promoting NITROX in this market as SAFEAIR. They have aimed the program directly at entry level divers and encourage the use of the gas in conjunction with standard air tables or air diving computers. With the elevated O_2 percentage and subsequent decreased N_2

percentage, the mathematical probability of decompression sickness has been significantly reduced. It is hoped that the use of the SAFEAIR program will broaden the sport diver's knowledge and experience with NITROX and make the sport safer.

As stated in the NITROX MANUAL (1990) by Dick Rutkowski, "Air has been used as a breathing gas by divers since the beginning of diving. Its principal advantage is that it is readily available and inexpensive to compress into cylinders or use directly from compressors with surface supplied equipment. It is not the 'ideal' breathing mixture because of the decompression liability which it imposes." The decompression liability referred to here is a definite limiting factor of compressed air. A simple review of the U.S. Navy No-Decompression Tables (No-Stop tables) will show that at a depth of 60 fsw (18m) the no-stop limit is 60 minutes. On the other hand, the no-stop limit for 60 fsw with NOAA NITROX I is 100 minutes. Conversely, according to the U.S. Navy Air Decompression Tables a dive to 60 fsw for 100 minutes would result in the diver being required to make an obligatory decompression stop at 10 fsw (3m) for 14 minutes. The benefits in this particular example are obvious: more bottom time, less decompression obligations. (Also, see Table 10-1 for further review.)

Another factor to consider in the use of NITROX involves not only an extension of the no-stop limits and a reduction of decompression time if the limits are exceeded, but due to the fact that the nitrogen (an inert gas) content is reduced by diluting it with oxygen (a gas that can be metabolized

Table 10-1

NITROX I No-Decompression Limits

Depth (fsw)	No-decompression limits	A	B	C	D	E	F	G	H	I	J	K	L	M	N	O
20		35	70	110	160	225	350									
25		25	50	75	100	135	180	240	325							
30		20	35	55	75	100	125	160	195	245	315					
40		15	30	45	60	75	95	120	145	170	205	250	310			
45	310	5	15	25	40	50	60	80	100	120	140	160	190	220	270	310
50	200	5	15	25	30	40	50	70	80	100	110	130	150	170	200	
60	100		10	15	25	30	40	50	60	70	80	90	100			
70	60		10	15	20	25	30	40	50	55	60					
80	50		5	10	15	20	30	35	40	45	50					
90	40		5	10	15	20	25	30	35	40						
100	30		5	10	12	15	20	25	30							
110	25		5	7	10	15	20	22	25							
120	25		5	7	10	15	20	22	25							
130	20			5	10	13	15	20								
140	15			5	10	12	15									
150	10			5	8	10										

by the body) a diver will be slightly less affected by inert gas narcosis (nitrogen narcosis) and will be at a lesser risk of incurring a DCS hit. Also, because of the decreased nitrogen content and the subsequent reduction in nitrogen uptake (ingassing), there will be a reduction of residual nitrogen in the body following a dive.

In addition to the use of NITROX as a primary gas, it is also utilized in various mixes and combinations for stage decompression diving and in recompression chamber environments. See the section OTHER USES FOR NITROX below for more information.

EQUIVALENT AIR DEPTH (EAD)

The specific decompression procedure that must be followed when diving NITROX is based on the concept of "equivalent air depth" (EAD). This is a procedure that equates the inspired nitrogen pressure of a NITROX mixture at one depth to that of standard air at another depth, the EAD. This is a procedure that has been used extensively by the military and commercial diving industry for over 30 years with both semi-closed and closed-circuit mixed-gas underwater breathing systems. It is highly recommended to use a pre-calculated EAD table and several are widely available.

By using the following formula, any combination of nitrogen-oxygen mixtures can be applied to the standard U.S. Navy Air Decompression tables:

$$EAD = \left[\frac{(1.0 - FO_2)}{.79} (D + 33) \right] - 33$$

$1.0 =$ **Fraction of the total gases at 1 ATA**
$FO_2 =$ **Decimal equivalent of percent of O_2 in mix**
$.79 =$ **Inert gas content of air**
$D =$ **Depth in feet of salt water (fsw)**

Sample Problem: A diver wishes to make a 120 fsw (36.4m) dive on NOAA NITROX I but does not have the NOAA NITROX I tables with him. What EAD can he use to relate into the USN Air Decompression tables ?

Solution: EAD = $\frac{[.68 \times 153]}{.79}$ - 33

Answer: EAD = 98.7 fsw or 100/25 (USN Air Decompression table)

Divers wishing to simplify this process can use the NITROX SAFEAIR EAD conversion multiplier Tables (See below). These were developed by ANDI and are easy to use. The diver simply selects the FO_2 in his NITROX mix and a conversion decimal number is listed.

EQUIVALENT AIR DEPTH (EAD) CONVERSION FACTORS

fO_2	fN_2	CONVERSION FACTOR
.22	.78	.98734
.23	.77	.97468
.24	.76	.96202
.25	.75	.94936
.26	.74	.93670
.27	.73	.92405
.28	.72	.91139
.29	.71	.89873
.30	.70	.88607
.31	.69	.87341
.32	.68	.86075
.33	.67	.84810
.34	.66	.83544
.35	.65	.82278
.36	.64	.81012
.37	.63	.79746
.38	.62	.78481
.39	.61	.77215
.40	.60	.75949
.41	.59	.74683
.42	.58	.73417
.43	.57	.72151
.44	.56	.70886
.45	.55	.69620
.46	.54	.68354
.47	.53	.67088
.48	.52	.65822
.49	.51	.64556
.50	.50	.63291

©Copyright American Nitrox Divers Inc. 1991. All Rights Reserved.

SAFETY CONSIDERATIONS

One concern that some divers have is whether or not specialized equipment is required with NITROX. The best answer is: standard equipment is OK but it must be cleaned prior to use with NITROX. There is a lot of confusion about using "straight from the manufacturer, out of the box" scuba gear. The authors recommend that divers contemplating using various enriched air mixtures take a proper course in NITROX usage as a prerequisite.

NITROX can be obtained by several mixing or blending methods. The preferred method is via the Continuous NITROX Mixer in conjunction with an oil-free compressor. In this system, the scuba tank and regulator are never subjected to the hazards of high pressure oxygen. If all NITROX filling systems were using this blending method, then it would be acceptable for regular scuba gear to be used without special handling as long as the O_2 percentage did not exceed 40% ($FO_2 = .4$ maximum). NOAA's policy limits the FO_2 to .4 but other professionals have argued that an FO_2 of .5 is allowable. When even the experts cannot agree, it's time for the user to carefully consider the implications of improper cleaning.

The most common mixing method is still by the Partial Pressure Method. This involves transfilling pure O_2 into the scuba cylinder first to a certain pressure, and then topping off the cylinder with air. This is potentially extremely hazardous and should never be attempted by untrained users! Since partial pressure mixing does exist, we recommend (and so does ANDI) that all equipment be oxygen cleaned prior to NITROX service.

It would be beneficial to discuss at this time the following terms:

Oxygen Clean
Oxygen Compatible
Oxygen Service

These terms are unclear and misunderstood by the majority of divers. **Oxygen clean** refers to the absence of contaminates. Contaminates are varied but the most serious are hydrocarbons such as: machine oils and thread lubricants, cleaning solvents, paint or marking crayons, oily fingerprints or grease, airborne dust or soot, metal scale or burrs, metal filings and some metal oxides, rust dust, lint from cloths used to remove any of the above, pipe thread sealants and soapy water used for leak checking.

Scuba equipment shipped from the factory is never rated oxygen clean; however, equipment may be rendered so by means of a variety of cleaning processes. Such services can be obtained through a professional scuba facility such as those listed in our Reference Section or through an ANDI affiliate. The diver has the option of having his original equipment cleaned or purchasing pre-cleaned and labeled NITROX (or O_2) regulators and cylinders.

Oxygen compatibility involves both combustibility and ease of ignition. Materials that burn in air will burn violently in pure oxygen and

NITROX cylinder showing color band and labeling. The top portion (or cylinder neck) is "oxygen green", and the cylinder body is yellow. Note the DIN fitting valve and clip harness for attachment to diver or stage line.

Photo by Bret Gilliam

explosively in pressurized systems. Also, many materials that do not burn in air will do so in pressurized systems. In oxygen systems, the selection of materials is of paramount importance. Some common materials used in scuba equipment that are not compatible with pure oxygen are teflon seats, buna-N o-rings, silicone grease and neoprene diaphragms to name a few.

Briefly stated, compatibility means that all the materials that are in contact with the gas are compatible with the gas at the working pressure of the system.

Oxygen service refers to a product's or component's suitability for use in conjunction with oxygen. Oxygen service requires **BOTH** oxygen clean **AND** oxygen compatible components.

From the above explanation we can see that a component may be oxygen compatible but contaminated (not oxygen clean). Likewise, we could have an oxygen clean component that is not oxygen compatible (pressure rated). This may be a bit confusing at first, but you're in good company. Even most diving instructors have little working knowledge of these terms.

Ed Betts, president of American NITROX Divers, Inc. (ANDI) with NITROX filling station and gas analyzer.

When utilizing oxygen enriched mixtures it is recommended that all components are first oxygen cleaned before entering service. As long as the percentage of O_2 does not exceed 50%, most conventional scuba equipment is considered compatible (after cleaning). Recommended service intervals must be strictly adhered to when using NITROX (SAFEAIR) mixtures.

All NITROX should be properly analyzed before and after filling. Also, prior to use the mix should be analyzed, particularly if the cylinder has been stored for any length of time.

CODING AND LABELING

Each piece of equipment must now be dedicated to NITROX service and labeled accordingly. This includes the regulator system. Tags are available to identify such gear as NITROX equipment. If the regulator system is put back into conventional air service it is no longer considered oxygen clean and the process must be repeated.

Cylinders shall be marked as per the Compressed Gas Association (CGA) recommendations for cylinder coding. As such, a scuba cylinder in NITROX service should be color coded (yellow body with a four inch oxygen-green band at the upper portion; some NITROX tanks are coded with the entire neck portion of the cylinder painted oxygen-green instead of a band; either coding is acceptable).

Further, each cylinder should be tagged with a NITROX identification tag that lists its pressure, FO_2, FN_2, date filled and the name of the filler/analyzer. No NITROX mixture should ever be used by a diver without analyzing it immediately prior to use! If a cylinder is returned to air service be sure to remove the NITROX coding.

Dick Rutkowski, president of International Association of NITROX Divers (IAND).

Photo by Bret Gilliam

Another important consideration is special training and education in the use of EAN. Several excellent training facilities are currently in operation in the continental United States with perhaps the most well-known of these operations being Dick Rutkowski's Hyperbarics International, Inc. in Key Largo, Florida and Ed Betts' American NITROX Divers, Inc. in Freeport, New York. (Also, see Reference Materials for a listing of additional training facilities.)

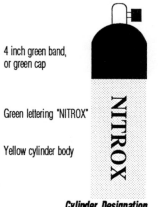

4 inch green band, or green cap

Green lettering "NITROX"

Yellow cylinder body

Cylinder Designation

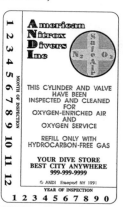

1 2 3 4 5 6 7 8 9 10 11 12
MONTH OF INSPECTION

American Nitrox Divers Inc

Safe Air N₂ O₂

THIS CYLINDER AND VALVE HAVE BEEN INSPECTED AND CLEANED FOR OXYGEN-ENRICHED AIR AND OXYGEN SERVICE

REFILL ONLY WITH HYDROCARBON-FREE GAS

YOUR DIVE STORE BEST CITY ANYWHERE 999-999-9999

© ANDI Freeport NY 1991

YEAR OF INSPECTION
1 2 3 4 5 6 7 8 9 0

ANDI Visual Inspection decal

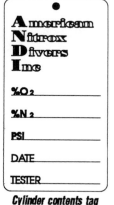

American Nitrox Divers Inc

%O₂ _____

%N₂ _____

PSI _____

DATE _____

TESTER _____

Cylinder contents tag

Founded in 1985 by Dick Rutkowski, former Deputy Diving Coordinator for NOAA and the Founder and Director of the NOAA Diving/Hyperbaric Training and Diver Treatment Facility from 1973 to 1985, Hyperbarics International specializes in NITROX instruction using the standards and procedures set forth by American NITROX Divers, Inc. (ANDI). The International Association of NITROX Divers (IAND) and American NITROX Divers Inc. (ANDI) course is designed to train qualified divers in the safe use of Nitrogen-Oxygen mixtures. Subjects covered include: (but are not limited to) history, physics, physiology, equipment, analysis, safety precautions, advantages, disadvantages, potential consequences of misuse, dive table procedures, gas mixing, repetitive dives, and heavy emphasis on oxygen toxicity. Students who successfully complete the course are awarded IAND or ANDI certification.

OTHER USES OF NITROX

50/50 NITROX is a popular decompression gas that is used as a safety buffer instead of standard air as a "wash-out" mix due to its elevated oxygen percentage. 50/50 and 60/40 mixes are also utilized in recompression chamber environments when the patient and tenders must be subjected to treatment depths in excess of 60 fsw (18.2 m). This effectively limits the inert gas loading on chamber occupants and still allows proper oxygen balance for the best gradient across the tissue-bubble interface.

The benefits of NITROX can clearly be seen in the case of a patient/tender at 165 feet (50 m) on the U.S. Navy Treatment Table 6A. On standard air, the no-decompression time is very limited, but on 50/50 NITROX a tender is subjected to an EAD of only 92 feet (28 m) allowing him 25 minutes without decompression. This allows him to "lock-out" before his no-decompression time and before another tender replaces him. It also markedly lessens the risk of "bending" the tenders on deep treatment or saturation tables.

EQUIVALENT AIR DEPTHS (EAD) BASED ON AIR DEPTHS

SafeAir® 68% NITROX 32% OXYGEN			SafeAir® 64% NITROX 36% OXYGEN		
ACTUAL DEPTH	EAD	PO$_2$	ACTUAL DEPTH	EAD	PO$_2$
5	0	0.38	7	0	0.45
16	10	0.48	20	10	0.58
28	20	0.60	32	20	0.72
40	30	0.71	44	30	0.85
46	35	0.77	50	35	0.92
51	40	0.82	57	40	0.99
63	50	0.94	69	50	1.12
75	60	1.05	81	60	1.26
86	70	1.16	94	70	1.39
98	80	1.27	106	80	1.53
109	90	1.39	113	85	1.60
121	100	1.50	118	90	1.66*
132	109	1.60	131	100	1.80*
133	110	1.61*	143	110	1.93*
144	120	1.72*	155	120	2.07**
156	130	1.84*	168	130	2.20**
167	140	1.95*	180	140	2.33**
179	150	2.06**	192	150	2.47**

* EXCEEDES NORMAL OXYGEN PARTIAL PRESSURE LIMIT OF 1.6 ATA

** EXCEEDES EXCEPTIONAL OXYGEN PARTIAL PRESSURE LIMITS OF 2.0 ATA

BEST MIX FOR SHALLOWEST EQUIVALENT AIR DEPTH (EAD)

FSW	ATA	fO$_2$	PO$_2$	EAD
70	3.1212	.51262	1.6	30.544
75	3.2727	.48888	1.6	36.873
80	3.4242	.46725	1.6	43.202
85	3.5757	.44745	1.6	49.531
90	3.7272	.42926	1.6	55.860
95	3.8787	.41250	1.6	62.189
100	4.0303	.39699	1.6	68.518
105	4.1818	.38260	1.6	74.848
110	4.3333	.36923	1.6	81.177
115	4.4848	.35675	1.6	87.506
120	4.6363	.34509	1.6	93.835
125	4.7878	.33417	1.6	100.16
130	4.9393	.32392	1.6	106.49
135	5.0909	.31428	1.6	112.82
140	5.2424	.30520	1.6	119.15
145	5.3939	.29662	1.6	125.48
150	5.5454	.28852	1.6	131.81
155	5.6969	.28085	1.6	138.13
160	5.8484	.27357	1.6	144346
165	6.0000	.26666	1.6	150.79
170	6.1515	.26009	1.6	157.12
175	6.3030	.25384	1.6	163.45
180	6.4545	.24788	1.6	169.78
185	6.6060	.24220	1.6	176.11
190	6.7575	.23677	1.6	182.44
195	6.9090	.23157	1.6	188.77
200	7.0606	.22660	1.6	195.10

©Copyright American Nitrox Divers Inc. 1991. All Rights Reserved.

Equivalant air depth (EAD) based on NITROX mixtures at depth
NOAA NITROX I 68% NITROGEN 32% OXYGEN

DEPTH FSW	EAD FSW	AIR TABLE FSW	OXYGEN PARTIAL PRESSURE ATA	MAXIMUM NORMAL O₂ EXPOSURE (CHART 2-4)
15	8.32	-	0.47	-
20	12.62	-	0.51	-
25	16.92	-	0.56	-
30	21.23	-	0.61	720
35	25.53	-	0.66	570
40	29.84	-	0.71	570
45	34.14	-	0.76	450
50	38.44	40	0.80	450
60	47.05	50	0.90	360
70	55.66	60	1.00	300
80	64.27	70	1.10	240
90	72.87	80	1.19	210
100	81.48	90	1.29	180
110	90.09	100	1.39	150
120	98.70	100	1.48	120
130	107.30	110	1.58	45
140	115.91	120	1.66	-
150	124.52	130	1.77	-

©Copyright American Nitrox Divers Inc. 1991. All Rights Reserved.

Equivalant air depth (EAD) based on NITROX mixtures at depth

NOAA NITROX II 64% NITROGEN 36% OXYGEN

DEPTH FSW	EAD FSW	AIR TABLE FSW	OXYGEN PARTIAL PRESSURE ATA	MAXIMUM NORMAL O_2 EXPOSURE (CHART 2-4)
25	13.98	-	0.63	570
30	18.04	-	0.69	570
35	22.09	-	0.74	450
40	26.14	-	0.79	450
45	30.19	40	0.85	360
50	34.24	40	0.90	360
60	42.34	50	1.01	300
70	50.44	60	1.12	210
80	58.54	60	1.23	180
90	66.64	70	1.34	150
100	74.75	80	1.45	120
110	82.85	90	1.56	45
120	90.94	100	1.67	-

Chapter 11

An Overview To Mixed Gas

"Our original investigation into mixed gas protocol and operational physiology left me firmly convinced of one thing, at least... there has to be a better way of doing this."

Hannes Keller

Editor's note: *This is a highly technical chapter and it involves a number of esoteric terms and principles. It has been included as an aid to those who desire a brief, albeit advanced, overview to mixed gas.*

The primary thrust of this text is aimed at divers using compressed air, but as we have already discussed, air divers involved in lengthy decompression schedules routinely utilize other gases to make decompression more efficient and faster. The use of NITROX and oxygen in these applications usually lays the groundwork for most divers' introduction to the complexities of mixed gas and its emerging wider use among the high-tech community.

As with NITROX, the diver needs special training in order to be a safe "user" of the gases selected. Under no circumstances should divers attempt any mixed gas diving without proper training. This training is becoming readily available and the reader is urged to consult with one of the training facilities listed in our reference section. Divers should not be intimidated by the science of mixed gas diving; if you have been comfortable with the subject materials presented thus far in this text you should be able to make a smooth transition to mixed gas under the responsible supervision of one these experts.

This chapter is concerned with the elements involved in the choice of breathing mixtures for diving. Two aspects are obligatory from the beginning: a diver's breathing gas must be supplied under pressure approximately equal to that of the diver's lungs, and all mixtures must contain appropriate amounts of oxygen.

Beyond this the trade offs begin, and the ideal choice of a gas mixture is a compromise of several factors. These factors, oxygen toxicity, metabolic requirements, inert gas narcosis, HPNS, density, voice, thermal properties, decompression, fire safety, cost and logistics... are covered in the second part of this chapter.

A summary of the various factors involved in the choice of a diving gas as they relate to certain gases is given in Table 11-1.

Current diving modes require the selection of optimal breathing mixtures for each of several operational situations. These include scuba, closed and semi-closed breathing systems, surface supplied gas, and the atmosphere of both submersible and deck chambers. In addition to the equipment used, the particular diving situation affects the choice of the gas mixture. Physiologic factors also are involved. These include duration of exposure, ambient water temperature, work load and whether the diver is immersed in a gas mixture or breathing it by mask or mouthpiece. We will discuss the typical gas mixes such as HELIOX and various TRIMIX blends and take a look at some experimental mixes currently under evaluation.

The immediate future promises an affordable closed circuit rebreather with fully redundant safe-guards offering up to 12 hours bottom time regardless of depth. Dr. Bill Stone of CIS-LUNAR Development Laboratories has gone beyond working prototypes with his Mark 2R unit and the implications of such a system for expanding the "envelope" in deep diving has veterans dizzy in expectation. Stone noted in 1990, "Metabolically, enough O_2 (if used with 100% efficiency) could be carried in one standard 2200 liter cylinder for a diver to remain underwater for more than 2 days at a depth of 95 meters!"

PROPERTIES OF GASES

The properties of the various gases are intimately involved in the choice of the best ones to use for diving. The pertinent gas properties are summarized in table 11-1. Detailed listings of properties of the gases and gas mixtures traditionally used in diving, as well as details of gas mixing and the use of breathing apparatus, are contained in the *U.S. Navy Diving Manual, Volume II*.

TRIMIX diver, Michael Menduno, prepares to dive the 260 fsw wreck of the Wilkes Barre off Key West, Florida. The Navy cruiser was deliberately sunk and has become a favorite deep wreck site for advanced "high tech" divers.

Photo by Bret Gilliam

OXYGEN: Metabolic needs and toxicity

The fundamental requirement in a breathing gas is for oxygen to meet the metabolic needs of the body. These needs are met by supplying a breathing mixture containing an adequate partial pressure of oxygen.

The partial pressure of oxygen (PO_2) considered "normoxic" and to which man is adapted is 0.21 atmospheres inspired. A healthy person can maintain normal blood oxygenation at an inspired oxygen partial pressure of about 0.16 atmospheres; below this point a relative hypoxia (mistakenly called "anoxia" by some) will prevail. There was concern for a time early in the development of deep diving techniques that extremely dense mixtures (e.g., 80 atm of He-O_2, or 12 times the density of air at sea-level) would cause a diffusion limitation in the lung ("The Chouteau effect," Chouteau et al., 1967) and that this could render a PO_2 of 0.21 atm inadequate. Subsequent experiments, however, involving densities twice this great showed no evidence of this limitation (Strauss, et al. 1972).

The upper limit for oxygen breathing is discussed in great detail in section C of this chapter. In practical terms, oxygen limits can be set for in-water work, for chambers, and for habitats. Where decompression is to follow, it appears that an advantage lies in maintaining the highest possible PO_2 during the pressure exposure. For a lone diver in deep water and working hard, a limit of 1.2 to a maximum of 1.4 atm is a reasonable compromise between toxicity and optimal decompression. Under less strenuous conditions up to 2.0 atm may be tolerable. These are practical limits which

TABLE 11-1

PHYSICAL PROPERTIES OF GASES

	Hydrogen	Helium	Neon	Nitrogen	Oxygen	Argon
Molecular weight	2.016	4.003	20.83	28.016	32.000	39.944
Density at 0° C, 1 atm (gm/liter)	0.0056 (lb./ft.3)	0.1784	0.9004	1.251	1.429	1.784
Viscosity at 0° C, 1 atm micropoise	89.2 (28.1° C)	194.1	311.1	175.0 (19.1° C)	201.8	221.7
Thermal conductivity at 0°C, 1 atm, cal/°C-cm²-sec	39.7×10^{-5}	34.0×10^{-5}	11.0×10^{-5}	5.66×10^{-5}	5.83×10^{-5}	3.92×10^{-5}
Specific Volume, 70°F, 1 atm, cu..ft./lb.	192	96.7	19.2	13.8	12.08	9.67
Specific Heat C_p cal/mole degree	3.39	4.968	4.968	6.95	6.97	4.968
Solubility in water at 38°C cc/1000gm	168.6	9.7	13	28.9 (25° C)	26	
Solubility in oil at 38°C cc/1000gm	50 (40° C)	15	19	61	120 (40° C)	140

consider such features as mixing variations and analytical errors. In-water work at higher PO_2 than this may be risky. Some experienced diving operators avoid the use of pure oxygen in the water at all. However, others embrace the utilization of pure oxygen in water during decompression.

For a habitat the same lower limits (0.16 atm) should prevail; 0.25 to 0.5 atm seem to be an optimal operational level for indefinite periods, while pressures up to 1.0 atm may be maintained safely for only a few hours. During treatment for decompression sickness using the U.S. Navy Oxygen Treatment Tables a diver is exposed to 2.8 ATA for several 20-minute periods. This has been found to be tolerable to most divers and hence operationally suitable, but a certain risk of convulsion is never the less present.

Another aspect of the oxygen requirement of a diver, in addition to a suitable partial pressure range, is the amount of oxygen needed to supply metabolic needs. In the diving situation where oxygen is usually supplied at tensions near the upper limit of tolerance and where CO_2 elimination is usually the predominant factor controlling breathing, metabolic needs are easily met. Semi-closed breathing rigs and conventional helmets, as well as all closed chambers, must be supplied with oxygen in accordance with the physiological demands of the diver. The oxygen actually consumed by the body varies from about 0.5 liter per minute at rest to about 1.0 liter per minute for moderate work to 3.0 or more liters per minute for very heavy work. The requirements for supplying the various types of gas with the appropriate oxygen flow are given in detail in the U.S. Navy Manual.

INERT GAS NARCOSIS

The cause of the narcotic effect of nitrogen seen during the course of dives performed using air at depths in excess of 100 fsw has remained obscure for more than a century. In the older literature dealing with caisson operations, the usual mood of workers in a compressed-air atmosphere was euphoria. In scuba diving the expansive feeling at pressure depths is euphemistically referred to as "rapture of the depths."

Damant (1930) and Hill (1932) observed that deep-sea divers at depths of 270 to 300 fsw (9 - 10 ATA) had difficulty in assimilating instructions and making decisions. Severe emotional disturbances, as well as loss of consciousness, were reported. In the Harvard pressure chamber at 4 ATA, it was apparent that even at this relatively low pressure, individuals experienced varying degrees of euphoria with tendency to fixation of ideas accompanied by some impairment of fine manipulative procedures. Behnke et al. (1935), in reporting reactions under seemingly favorable environmental conditions, attributed them to the narcotic effect of nitrogen in accord with the Myer-Overton hypothesis that inhaled gases, generally with high lipid-to-water solubility ratios, were narcotic/anesthetic in varying degrees.

The term, narcosis, designates general depressant phenomena produced by drugs and gases. Anesthesia is a special instance of the general phenomenon characterized by loss of consciousness, altered cortical electrical activity, loss of pain sensation, and other signs familiar to the medical practitioner. Narcosis is an apt term to denote many psychic reactions, including stupefaction and neuromuscular impairment associated with inhalation of inert gases under pressure, which may or may not be followed by loss of consciousness.

The gas of primary concern to the deep scuba diver is nitrogen, or in particular, air. There is no established upper limit for the safe breathing of nitrogen; a partial pressure of 15 atmospheres has been shown to cause severe narcosis and possibly nausea but is not incompatible with survival (Adolfson 1967; Hamilton 1972).

It is generally considered safe to dive to about 200 fsw breathing air, primarily due to the tolerable degree of impairment seen at these depths. However, dive conditions can vary this "safe depth." Cave diving and wreck penetrations can be assumed to mandate a greater degree of alertness than a comparable open water dive. Increasing hazards will thus set the acceptable depth limits to shallower depths. Dives utilizing air in these depths ranges produce a noticeable narcosis on the first exposure, but a great deal of accommodation is seen on the next few dives to the same depth if they follow no later than a day or two. A diver living in an undersea habitat acquires a resistance to narcosis related to the partial pressure of nitrogen in the habitat.

Nitrogen is believed to "interact" with high levels of both oxygen and carbon dioxide; these gases apparently increase the susceptibility of the diver to the narcotic effect of nitrogen. Thus, consideration must be made as to the performance of the breathing apparatus as it relates to carbon dioxide levels at depth. The leading cause of elevated carbon dioxide levels during scuba dives is the inability of many regulators to deliver adequate fresh gas flows to meet the physiologic requirements of the diver (maximum fresh gas flows delivered to the diver, and the work of inhalation and exhalation all can contribute to this problem).

Helium and neon are non-narcotic. Hydrogen apparently causes a narcosis at very high pressures that is balanced by the hydrostatic pressure effect. All other gases are more narcotic than nitrogen; this category theoretically includes oxygen, but the narcotic properties of oxygen are not manifest until well beyond the usual CNS toxicity limits. Argon has been used in diving; however, it is about twice as narcotic as nitrogen and its solubility presents severe problems in decompression.

HPNS AND HYPERBARIC ARTHRALGIA

The high pressure nervous syndrome (HPNS) is an increasingly important consideration as depths exceed about 600 fsw. It is invoked by gases with low lipid solubility, hence its early designation "helium tremors." Helium, and to a slightly lesser extent neon, is associated with HPNS because they allow high hydrostatic pressure to be applied without a compensating narcotic effect. In situations where HPNS is a problem, its effects may be counteracted by including in the breathing mixture a gas with sufficient lipid solubility to counterbalance the compression effect (presumably in the lipid component of cell membranes). The optimal "doses" are not yet established, but it has been shown that rapid compression to 1000 fsw cause far less tremor and other manifestations of the syndrome when 12-25% nitrogen is included in the inert component of the breathing mixture. Lessor percentages of gases which have higher anesthetic potency might also be used with the effect on decompression being the deciding factor.

Another direct pressure effect is hyperbaric arthralgia. The mechanism of this phenomenon is likely to be different from that of HPNS – perhaps due to osmosis – and the mitigation effect of narcotic gases has not been demonstrated. Slow rates of compression seem to be the best procedure for managing this problem, or for short jobs the opposite approach of a rapid compression and faster decompression. In any case, until hyperbaric arthralgia is better understood the choice of gas will most generally be determined by other operational considerations.

DENSITY AND VISCOSITY

As a diver's depth increases, the density of his breathing gas increases as an almost linear function of his absolute pressure. High gas densities act to limit the diver's ability to ventilate his lungs and to increase the work required; this effects acts on both the diver and his equipment. The viscosity of a gas, however, does not change appreciably with depth, and the viscosities of most respiratory gases are similar (Lamphier, 1969). Breathing a mixture of dense gases at sea-level has been shown experimentally to be essentially identical to breathing a lighter gas at increased pressure, provided the densities are equivalent (Maio and Fhori, 1967).

The salient facts are that during laminar flow the pressure required to cause gas to flow is a linear function of viscosity, but that during turbulent flow, pressure must increase approximately with the square of the flow. Turbulent versus laminar flow has an important role in both the breathing equipment and in the pulmonary system. Fittings and/or connectors that cause gases to make sharp changes in direction increase the degree of turbulence seen in breathing equipment. All efforts should be made to eliminate the inclusion of these types of fittings in regulators used at depth. Normal breathing at rest involves some turbulent flow and consequently the work of breathing is increased when denser gases are breathed. This effect is exaggerated during exercise, when respiratory flow rates are increased.

In diving the physiological effect of a limitation in breathing capability is slightly different from that at sea-level, in that oxygen partial pressures are usually more than adequate to meet the metabolic needs. Restrictions on lung ventilation, therefore, cause only a build-up in CO_2. The rate of removal of CO_2 is entirely a function of ventilation volume flow (VE) whereas adequate oxygen can be delivered at very low rates of ventilation.

Another important factor in respiratory mechanics is the concept of airway collapse. In a forced expiration there is a maximum possible rate of gas flow beyond which extra effort will not provide extra flow, but instead will force temporary constriction of the airways (intra-thoracic airways). This situation is reached more easily with denser gases (with denser gases a higher intra-thoracic pressure is required for the same flow rate), and although a person does not require these high flow rates under normal circumstances, at high densities the maximum flow capability and minimum ventilatory requirement tend to converge. The result is that a limit will be encountered at increasing pressures of the amount of work which a diver can do. Artificial respiratory assistance is not likely to be very helpful other than to do the extra work of overcoming the resistance of the breathing apparatus.

Gas densities as great as 25 times that of sea-level air have been breathed experimentally (Lambertsen, 1972); it was found that work was restricted to less than 3/4 the sea-level maximum for the individual, but that this amount of work could be accomplished at densities up to about 18 times normal. These experiments were conducted with equipment having low resistance and low dead space; with standard diving gear, problems will be encountered.

The same gas properties prevail in breathing equipment as in man, and both density and viscosity of the gases to be used must be considered in engineering design. It is worth mentioning that equipment must be designed to provide the maximum peak flow during a breathing cycle, rather than just the average minute volume.

Ordinarily, breathing gas density is not a limitation in the use of air or nitrogen-oxygen mixtures (or argon) since narcosis becomes a definite problem before density becomes limiting. This may not be the case where deeper depths can be tolerated as a result of adaptation to nitrogen in a hyperbaric habitat. Also, the density of air at 200-300 fsw is enough to be difficult to breathe through inadequate equipment or at inadequate supply pressures. One other difficulty with air is that with any CO_2 accumulation which might occur it can interact unfavorably with the effects of both the nitrogen and the oxygen of air.

One of the most desirable characteristics of helium is its low density and the consequent ease with which it is breathed. The same applies to hydrogen. Experiments at the University of Pennsylvania have shown that density equivalent to that of a helium-oxygen mixture at 5000 fsw can be tolerated at light work levels (Lambertsen, 1972). Because narcosis does not limit the depth at which it can be used, neon mixtures can pose density limitations to both equipment and man. A good practical depth limit for Neon 75 (75% neon, 25% helium) using current equipment is 650 fsw.

VOICE

Voice distortion is encountered when light gases (e.g., helium and hydrogen) are breathed, and the distortion increases in severity with increasing depth. This is due to an increase in the speed of sound in the gas, and the effect of this increase in the phonetic properties of the resonant cavities used in speech (Sergeant, 1969). (Some distortion occurs when air is breathed at depth, but this is a minor problem at the depths man is limited to due to narcosis.) Helium speech involves a linear increase in the frequency of important formants (the frequency bands which make up the phonetic quality of vowel sounds) by a factor of about 2.25 (Gertsman et al., 1966). Electronic devices (helium speech unscramblers) which restore these formants to their original frequency will restore the intelligibility of helium speech, although quality must necessarily be sacrificed if this is to be done in "real time." A practical aspect of the frequency shift is that many formants are shifted out of the range of ordinary communications gear, so that a really useful system requires suitable microphones and preamplifiers as well as an unscrambler.

Hydrogen causes slightly greater distortion than helium – but in one experiment at 200 fsw no greater loss in intelligibility than seen with helium at the same depth (Sergeant, 1972) – but is reasonably well translated by a good helium speech un-scrambler. Neon causes much less distortion than helium, preserving a high level of intelligibility throughout the depth range of up to 600 fsw. Many diving operators add 10 or 15% nitrogen to a helium-oxygen mixture in order to improve voice intelligibility (as well as to help keep the diver warm). The addition of small amounts of very dense gases such as SF6 or CF4 have also been suggested.

THERMAL PROPERTIES

Another gas property which has a prominent effect on the success of a gas used for deep diving is the way it influences the loss of heat from a diver's body. Divers lose heat by two routes, the skin and the respiratory

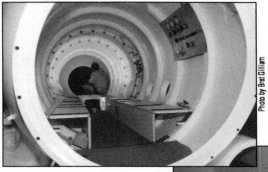

Interior of SEAVIEW submersible showing diver staging/travel compartment and lock-out hatch in rear.

Photo by Bret Gilliam

This deep diving submersible is equipped to handle up to ten divers and three crew with a depth rating of 800 fsw. Divers breathing mixed gas can "lock-out" of the after chamber of the sub and enter the open water for exploration or research and return to complete decompression aboard. Such technology is available to all divers; limitations are strictly budgetary.

Photo by Bret Gilliam

tract. An unprotected diver in shallow water has most of his heat loss to the water through his skin, but even here the tremendous heat exchange capabilities of the lungs are significant. At greater pressures, especially where helium is used, the proportion of heat lost through the breathing system increases with the increase in density of the breathing gas, until at 20 atmospheres this may equal the metabolic heat production of the body (Webb and Annis, 1966). Exercise at depth to produce more heat is no help because respiratory gas exchange increases almost linearly with increased metabolism. Most deep diving experience is based on helium and it has been found that respiratory heat losses where helium-based mixtures are used as breathing gas is a considerable problem. It is practically impossible to carry out prolonged deep dives (beyond one hour) in cold water without heating the breathing gas (Webb, 1973). This problem is complicated by the pressure effect on insulation. Virtually all thermal insulation relies on vacuum or "dead" gas space; at pressure, conventional insulations are compressed to a fraction of their original dimensions and to make matters worse the little remaining space may become filled with a thermally conductive gas (e.g., helium). Insulation containing tiny non-compressible spheres is effective, or a new gas space can be created by addition of pressured gas as depth (but helium is not much help here; air, nitrogen, argon, freon, or carbon dioxide are more effective insulators).

As in the case of voice improvement, small proportions of a denser (hence less thermally conductive) gas added to a helium-oxygen breathing mixture may reduce heat loss enough to be worth the added density and decompression complications. Neon has been used in large proportions (up to 75%), and subjectively appears to help.

Another important situation concerning heat loss to a gaseous medium is that of the transfer bell of a SDC (submersible decompression chamber). The bell is a particularly difficult problem since a diver may be required to decompress in the bell for several hours after leaving the water, already in a chilled condition and without a chance to rewarm.

Heat loss is an important aspect of undersea habitats and saturation chambers. Divers in helium atmospheres are comfortable at about 30°C. Though they feel comfortable, there is an extra energy burden which may approach 2000 kcal per day in helium habitat dwellers (Webb, 1973).

DECOMPRESSION CONSIDERATIONS AND COUNTER-DIFFUSION

A discussion on the relative merits of the different inert gases with regard to their effect on decompression will, if it sticks to experience with human divers, be almost entirely concerned with the relative merits of helium versus nitrogen. The properties which presumably govern the decompression characteristics of a gas are solubility in water, solubility in fat, diffusivity, thermodynamic properties and derived factors such as oil/water solubility ratio.

Helium was first suggested as a diving gas on the basis of its low solubility with regard to its low density and high diffusibility. In small animals the advantages of helium are substantial, resulting a reduction of safe decompression time as compared with nitrogen. These advantages prevail in humans, but to a lesser extent. Because it is taken up much faster than nitrogen (2.65 times as fast in diffusion limited compartments), there are situations where this advantage is lost (usually seen in dives of less than approximately 100 minutes).

A convenient way of comparing the decompression properties of these two gases is to look at the limiting half-times that are 2 to 3 times as long as those of helium.

It has been suggested, on the basis of the "independent" partial pressures of gases in a mixture, that a "porridge" of gases could be prepared which would permit immediate decompression. If seven different inert gases were used, each giving a partial pressure of one atmosphere, then a dive to 200 fsw would involve no more than one atmosphere of each gas, hence no super-saturation for any one gas. In practice this does not work; partial pressures are additive with respect to tendency to form a gas phase (Graves et al., 1972).

Whether or not all gases in solution act independently, there is evidence that changing the gases being breathed during decompression can substantially influence the decompression (Workman, 1969; Buhlmann, 1969, 1983, 1987). Standard practice in deep commercial helium-oxygen ("mixed gas") diving involves a shift to air as the breathing mixture during the later stages of decompression, with a final shift to 100% oxygen at the final stages.

Other gases which are considered here from a decompression point of view are oxygen, neon and hydrogen. Argon is appreciably more soluble than even nitrogen, and because of this must in any event be used sparingly. Neon has a low solubility in the same order as helium, both in fat and water, but resembles nitrogen more in diffusion. How each of these factors affects whether one gas is "better" than another depends on how each gas is used and in what manner a comparison is made. For example, though helium is "unloaded" about 3 times as fast as nitrogen (if diffusion only is considered), certain deep, short dive profiles result in a shorter decompression time with nitrogen than with helium (Workman, 1969).

The metabolic gases CO_2 and oxygen also play a role in decompression. Oxygen displaces inert gas, and if time is allowed for it to be consumed in the tissue it will not likely be involved in bubble formation; however, oxygen acts as a vasoconstrictor at high pressures and as such no doubt influences gas transport. On the other hand, carbon dioxide acts as a vasodilator, and likewise will affect gas transport. In tunnel work a high level of CO_2 has been observed to be associated with an increased bends incidence (End, 1938; Kindwall, 1973).

Different theorists in decompression computation treat the matter of different gases in different ways. The basic "Haldanean" approach was used for the development of the U.S. Navy Helium Tables. Here a 2.15:1 ratio was used, with the longest half-time 75 minutes; by contrast, the exceptional exposure air tables used a longest half-time of 240 minutes and a 2:1 ratio (Workman, 1969).

The same approach, essentially, is used by Buhlmann in a slightly different way; he sums the nitrogen and helium partial pressures in equivalent compartments (240 minutes for helium and 635 minutes for nitrogen) and uses a Haldane ratio which varies for the two gases (and is averaged based on the percentage of each inert gas present) and is reduced as a function of total pressure. Buhlmann basically considers that gas movement and transport is perfusion-limited (Buhlmann, 1969, 1983,

1987). Schreiner (1971) uses a further pragmatic yet physiologic modification of this method in which the half-times are determined for any gas on the basis of the oil-water solubility ratio and blood perfusion assumptions; all gases are summed in each compartment, and ascent is controlled via a matrix of M-values (Workman, 1965) which reflect total depth. Hempleman's single-tissue concept considers helium's properties, since it is based on the rate of linear diffusion into a "slab" of tissue. Hill's (1969) thermodynamic model regards gas transport as diffusion-limited, and consequently considers the diffusion properties of the gas in question.

Under certain conditions it is possible to evoke many aspects of the syndrome associated with decompression sickness without a change in pressure. This phenomenon, known as counter-diffusion, results when a diver is loaded with and immersed in one gas (e.g., helium) and breathes a denser, more slowly diffusing gas (e.g., nitrogen). The most apparent effect is intense itching of the exposed skin (skin covered with foil or blanketed in the gas being breathed does not itch), but symptoms similar to vestibular decompression sickness have been seen (Blenkarn et al., 1973; Idicula et al., 1972). For the helium-nitrogen system a "soak" of at least two hours in helium is needed at a pressure of at least several atmospheres before breathing the nitrogen; symptoms then appear in about 20 minutes. Lesions seen in animals are clearly bubbles of gas. An in-vitro model system has been devised with demonstrates that supersaturation can occur when two gases of different diffusivities (and perhaps solubilities) are diffusing in opposite direction through a lipid layer (Graves, et al., 1972).

The most obvious relevance of this phenomenon to diving is in the laboratory, where such exposures have taken place and where a new tool is now available for the study of gas transport. The severity of the symptoms seen makes intentional human exposure not advisable. Whether the effects will appear when a diver immersed in nitrogen breathes helium is not apparent; even if skin lesions are not seen, disorders in the ear, for example, are possible. A diver saturated in a nitrogen habitat who wishes to make a deep excursion breathing helium-oxygen may be more susceptible to decompression sickness than he otherwise would be.

FIRE SAFETY

Fire safety is mainly of concern in habitats. The choice of a breathing gas mixture has significant effect on fire safety if it results in a chamber having an oxygen level which will support combustion readily. It is the percentage of oxygen more than the partial pressure which determines its flame propagating character, mixtures with less than 6% oxygen being safe. It is more difficult to heat materials to the ignition temperature in a helium-oxygen atmosphere than in an equivalent one with nitrogen, but once ignited things burn better.

Effects of other possible diving gases on flame propagation have not been determined, with the exception of hydrogen. Here, of course, the fire safety situation is of a different order of magnitude. Mixtures of hydrogen with less than 5 or 6% hydrogen will neither burn nor support combustion, but safely making these mixtures and coping with other general handling problems with hydrogen are formidable tasks (Edel, 1972).

COST AND LOGISTICS

This section is concerned with the question of obtaining, storing and delivering to a dive site the various gases. Air is, of course, the least expensive gas available, requiring only a clean compressor (with proper filtering) provided a pollution-free atmosphere is available. The components of air, nitrogen and oxygen, are likewise inexpensive, and handling, mixing, analyzing, storing, etc., makes up the bulk of the cost of using nitrogen-oxygen mixtures. These costs apply to some extent to any gas used except air.

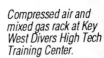
Compressed air and mixed gas rack at Key West Divers High Tech Training Center.

Photo by Bret Gilliam

Nitrogen-oxygen mixtures may have roles in diving which are as yet unexploited, in their use in habitats from which excursions are made to deeper work sites (Hamilton, et al., 1973). The narcosis which limits safe use of air or N_2-O_2 mixtures can be tolerated at greater depths on excursions from saturation than in bounce dives from the surface (Schmidt, et al., 1973). By using the normal oxygen consumption of the divers to "breathe down" the oxygen in a habitat to a tolerable range, such operations can be conducted entirely by means of compressors and gas available at the site.

The term "mixed gas" in its broadest interpretation as applied to diving refers to any gas being used for diving except air (and perhaps the rarely used pure oxygen case). In its general usage, however, the term refers specifically to helium-oxygen mixtures, which may or may not contain a little nitrogen.

Helium, although abundant in the universe, has been found in commercial quantities in only certain places on earth. It is usually found with natural gas in practical percentages of from 1 to as much as 8%. Until recent years the only helium production was in the U.S., but sources have now been found in Canada, Poland, and the Soviet Union. The U.S. has had laws controlling export and requiring conservation of helium — these were relaxed in 1969; helium stockpiling by the Bureau of Mines was also discontinued and the Helium Research Unit at Amarillo was closed.

In the U.S. helium is not particularly expensive, a typical bulk price (in 1972 dollars) being about $0.06 per cubic foot. This cost can appreciate by a factor of 2x to 4x the base cost per cubic foot for gas delivered to a North Sea diver on the sea floor. The expense of using helium in diving operations in remote locations is dictated by the cost of handling, which includes mixing, shipping and storing. The basic container is the conventional gas cylinder, varieties of which hold 200 to 300 standard cubic feet of gas at pressures of 2000 to 3000 psi. The empty weight may be 150-200 pounds. For easier shipboard handling these are often manifolded into "quads" of four or six cylinders. Larger quantities of gas are handled in trailers holding 10,000 to 150,000 cubic feet.

Much mixed-gas diving is done using gas mixtures prepared on shore and shipped to the dive site as mixtures. In addition to the bulk shipping problem, this practice involves other inefficiencies. Depth of use (hence optimum oxygen percentage in the mixture) must be anticipated well in advance of need, and not only must the "steel" be shipped back, but in deep diving operations a considerable amount of gas remains unusable in the quads when its pressure falls below the appropriate delivery pressure. However, this system has certain advantages, in that large initial capital investments can be replaced by distributed shipping costs, and there is less dependence on highly trained technicians at the dive site.

With the addition of compression, storage and analytical equipment, gases can be mixed to order, invoking the obvious advantages. Still another method of preparing diving gas mixtures is by means of on-line mixing devices. Using a system of appropriate regulators and flow-meters, mixtures can be "dialed" as needed from bulk storage of the pure component (Gilardi, 1972).

As the final step in mixed gas logistics it is relevant to consider the methods of gas conservation, recovery and reuse. The basic breathing apparatus is an open-circuit demand system, whereby each inspiration is taken from a compressed source and each expiration is lost "overboard." Some breathing systems use partial or total recirculation of the breathing gas, removing the accumulated CO_2 with a chemical absorber. A "push-pull" hookah system returns expired gas from the diver to the bell atmosphere, where it is scrubbed and recirculated to the diver. On decompression the gas from the bell can be used to pressurize the deck chamber, with the divers transferring after equalization has taken place. Simple buffering, scrubbing and recompression systems can be assembled to permit reuse of a large fraction of the mixture used in a deep dive (Schmidt, et al., 1973). More sophisticated systems have been developed which actually re-refine helium, separating pure helium from all other components and contaminants in a mixture. These systems are complex, expensive and require a supply of liquid nitrogen, but where usage is great and supply lines long they can be cost-effective (Slack, 1973).

Along with the development of devices and procedures for conserving helium there has been a continual push to develop alternatives to the use of helium for mixed-gas diving. This effort has been to circumvent the physiological, economical and operational disadvantages of helium as well as to avoid dependence on a politically-sensitive commodity. The two gases considered as serious alternatives to helium are neon and hydrogen.

Neon is a product of the distillation of atmospheric air, being present at about 18 parts per million (air also contains 5 ppm of helium). Purified neon is too expensive to consider for ordinary diving operations, but mixtures of neon and helium that are produced as by-products of air distillation (commercial production of oxygen is via air distillation) are usable (Schreiner, et al., 1972). From the uncondensed fraction in an air distillation column (normally discarded) a mixture of neon and helium can be obtained, in the proportion of 72-78% neon, 22-28% helium. It is called "first run" neon or Neon 75. This mixture is relatively inexpensive; it could be available at $0.10 -$0.20 per cubic foot if bought in large quantities. The significant fact about neon is that as a product of the atmosphere it is available anywhere there is sufficient industrialization to require an air reduction plant.

Neon has another logistic advantage; because of its thermo-dynamic properties it is the diving gas most easily transported and stored as a liquid.

Hydrogen is available by electrolysis of water, and as such rivals air in its worldwide availability and low cost. Hydrogen's high flammability and diffusivity add to its cost — perhaps substantially — by increasing the difficulty of handling and mixing it safely (Edel, 1972). Increasing interest in the use of hydrogen as a low pollution fuel should result in future improvements in handling methods and equivalents.

CONVENTIONAL BREATHING MIXTURES

This section considers the various breathing mixtures in general use, their history, uses and advantages and disadvantages.

AIR AND NITROGEN-OXYGEN MIXTURES

Until the introduction of helium to diving in the late 1930's the history of diving was the history of air diving. Although most early diving exploits were breath-holding or snorkel dives, Alexander the Great is reported to have descended in an air-filled bell, and a compressed-air bell was designed in 1690 by Edmund Halley (of comet fame). Preminet first used a bellows to pump air down to a diver in the 1770's, but diving as we know it began in 1819 with the invention of the diving suit by August Siebe (Larson, 1959). This suit, supplied with compressed air, had all the essential features of the classical diving gear still in use today (Goodman, 1962).

Air, because of its availability and suitability for shallow diving, is the gas of choice for nearly all diving to about 150 fsw. Beyond this depth narcosis becomes a factor which will limit safe and effective diving to divers adapted to nitrogen and well trained for the job at hand. If suitable support (e.g., a diving partner, life lines, air supply, communications), is available the safe depth can be extended to 250, perhaps 300 fsw for short times (less than 0.5 hours). For short dives (usually 1.0 hour bottom times or less) in the deeper air range decompression is actually easier with air than with helium-oxygen mixtures.

Air is the gas of choice for undersea habitats to a depth of at least 70 fsw – at some depth beyond this, oxygen toxicity may cause lung discomfort after a few days – an appropriate depth-duration trade-off for this limit has not yet been established (however, it is known that by keeping the inspired oxygen partial pressures less than 0.5 atm, unlimited durations are possible with no toxicity).

Nitrogen-oxygen mixtures (NITROX) having a greater oxygen fraction than air are being used with more frequency in the last few years. The added oxygen being for the purpose of displacing inert gas and hence of reducing decompression. Nitrox is not an answer to diving deeper, but allows longer bottom times at appropriate depth with less decompression than required with a comparable dive utilizing air.

The U.S. Navy Mark XV mixed gas (Heliox) rebreather diving system with back cover shroud removed showing internal components including oxygen and diluent helium gas cylinders.

Photo AquaCorps Journal

Michael Menduno wearing Mark XV rebreather. System is lightweight and provides up to six hours dive time.

Photo by Bret Gilliam

HELIUM ("Mixed Gas Diving")

The record shows that C.J. Cooke applied in 1919 for a patent on the use of helium-oxygen mixtures to be supplied to men under pressure, but apparently never tried it (Edel, 1939). Credit for development of helium should go to the eminent chemist Dr. Joel H. Hildebrand, who with R. R. Sayers and W. P. Yant of the U.S. Bureau of Mines, tried helium decompressions with small animals (Sayers, Hildebrand & Yant, 1925). It was on the basis of its low solubility that these investigators proposed helium, and they reasoned correctly that this property would improve decompression time in comparison with nitrogen. It was not until End tried breathing helium, and, with Nohl actually tried helium on a 420 fsw dive (End, 1937; End, 1938) that the real advantage of helium was noted — its lack of narcotic properties. Shortly thereafter Momsen, with Behnke and Yarborough, at the U.S. Naval Experimental Diving Unit explored the use of helium to the pressure equivalent of 500 fsw (Ellsberg, 1939) and in 1941 it was successfully used in dives to 440 fsw (Behnke, 1942). The salvage of the submarine *Squalus* could not have been accomplished safely without helium.

The use of helium in diving has exceeded the expectations of its early proponents, with the 1000 fsw mark surpassed at sea and depths twice that deep reached in the laboratory. These dives have not been without problems, however. Serious HPNS symptoms may result if compression is rapid, and long exposure to hyperbaric arthralgia and extended decompression are consequences of slow compression rates. Helium is presently the diluent gas of choice for virtually all commercial and military diving beyond 150 fsw. Where immediate decompression is to follow, oxygen is kept as high as possible in the mixture, so as to produce a bottom gas oxygen partial pressure of 1.2 - 2.0 atmospheres; the higher the oxygen in the breathing mixture the lower will be the exposure to inert gas during the dive. For saturation, oxygen is kept between 0.2 and 0.6 atm, but it should be raised during decompression.

Nitrogen is sometimes added to helium-oxygen mixtures for the purpose of improving voice communication and mitigating slightly the chilling effect. The range used for this purpose is 5-15%; higher doses might be used, but even 15% is enough to have a detrimental effect on decompression. Another purpose for adding nitrogen is to counteract the effects of the HPNS. Here 12-25% might be used; with the exact concentration required still to be precisely determined. Use of larger percentages of nitrogen of diving in the 200-300 (as used in the "Sullivan Connection" dives in 1988) fsw range has been suggested, where conservation of helium (and economy) is more important than hasty decompression.

To summarize the properties of helium as they affect its use as a diving gas: Helium is light and very easy to breathe; it has a low solubility and high diffusivity, which properties cause it to be easy to eliminate during most decompressions. The same low solubility gives it no narcotic properties (as predicted by the Myer-Overton hypothesis of narcosis), but allows the HPNS to become manifest in rapid compressions. Although not expensive, helium can only be obtained in certain locations. When kept under pressure helium has a high leak rate, and it can leak into devices stored in it, such as a TV tube or a diver's watch. And one of the most disturbing factors about helium is its sonic velocity, which when helium is being breathed makes speech difficult to understand.

NITROGEN-HELIUM-OXYGEN MIXTURES (TRIMIX)

Recently, the use of helium-nitrogen-oxygen mixtures (TRIMIX) has received widespread publicity in the cave diving community, with the utilization of TRIMIX during the Sullivan Connection expedition demonstrating the feasibility of TRIMIX in the exploration of deep cave systems.

TRIMIX was also utilized to some degree during the Wakulla Project, and has been used with great success during the recent re-exploration and mapping of Eagles Nest Sink in Hernando County, Florida (King, 1990). TRIMIX has two advantages for the deep scuba diver over the use of HELIOX.

1) TRIMIX can be significantly less expensive in both gas and equipment when compared to a comparable heliox dive.

2) TRIMIX can also offer significant decompression saving when compared to a comparable heliox dive, especially when you consider the usual bottom times most of the high tech diving community are encountering.

Utilizing the same decompression calculation model, for short bottom times the order of total decompression required is:

Air < TRIMIX < HELIOX

This relationship holds true for bottom times less than 90 minutes, with total decompression times converging at approximately 125 minutes bottom. After that point, the order reverses with:

HELIOX < TRIMIX < Air.

OXYGEN

With the advent of fully-closed mixed gas rebreathing systems which produce no bubbles and allow a long bottom time on a single charge of gas, the incentive to use pure oxygen underwater has disappeared. The main use of pure-oxygen rebreathing systems was for clandestine operations where the presence of bubbles is unacceptable. The Italian Navy used closed-circuit oxygen re-breathing early in WWII, and the LARU (Lambertsen Amphibious Respiration Unit) was introduced in the U.S. Navy shortly there-after (Larson, 1959).

Because of the possibility of CNS toxicity (convulsions) the use of such units is restricted to a maximum depth of about 25 fsw (partial pressures of 1.6 or less in the working diver are allowed).

EXPERIMENTAL BREATHING MIXTURES

This section deals with the more unusual diving gas mixtures – those which are not in routine use but on which some experience has been accumulated. A qualitative approach is used in this discussion, with attention directed primarily at the components of a mixture, not the proportions.

HYDROGEN

Although highly explosive when mixed with air in the proper proportions, hydrogen can be used in diving because at increased pressures enough oxygen to meet physiologic needs can be added and the mixture can still remain below the lower flammability limits (Dorr & Schreiner, 1969). Physiologically it appears to be inert.

Hydrogen was used in experimental dives with animals as far back as 1914, before helium had been discovered in enough abundance to merit consideration of its use in diving (Gaertner, 1920). More recently Zetterstrom made successful dives with hydrogen-oxygen mixtures, but unfortunately died in a diving accident (Zetterstrom, 1948; Bjurstedt & Severin, 1948). His death, although unrelated to the use of hydrogen, had the effect of setting back work with this gas.

In addition to its low cost and ready availability – advantages partially offset by its explosive properties – hydrogen has a physiological advantage which might make it the gas of choice for deep diving; the narcotic properties of hydrogen apparently counteract the neurological disturbances due to high hydrostatic pressures (Brauer & Wav, 1970). Hydrogen is about one-fourth as potent as nitrogen in causing narcosis. Further, its low density makes hydrogen mixtures the easiest ones to breathe at great depths.

The thermal properties of hydrogen seem comparable to those of helium, and it causes a voice distortion of equal proportions. Helium unscramblers, however, seem to work with hydrogen too.

Short diving exposures to hydrogen conducted by Edel have revealed no contradictory indications against the eventual use of hydrogen in diving (Edel et al., 1972). Decompression times appear to be generally comparable to helium, perhaps slower. Hydrogen offers an intriguing possibility for exploring the question of whether perfusion or diffusion plays the limiting role in decompression; it has a diffusion comparable to helium and oil/water solubility ratio like nitrogen. In practice, hydrogen appears to fall between helium and nitrogen in its decompression efficiency.

Not all reports on the use of hydrogen are favorable. Experiments conducted with rabbits at pressure of 280M (917 fsw) showed reduction in peculiar thermal susceptibility (LeBoucher, 1970).

Currently most of the work being done with hydrogen is being done in France by COMEX. They have reported successful manned dives (in the laboratory) to approximately 2000 fsw

NEON

The high cost of neon has limited the study to this gas for use in diving. Numerous experiments with animals and other biological models have shown no detrimental effects (Schreiner et al., 1962; Miller et al., 1967; Hamilton et al, 1972); human exposures have verified this and also have shown that neon has virtually no tendency to produce narcosis to at least 1200 fsw (Hamilton, 1972).

Because of the expense of pure neon, most experiments have concentrated on the use of a mixture of neon and helium, Neon 75, which is obtained by distillation of air. Neon, therefore has worldwide availability in this form.

Experiments designed to evaluate neon as a diving gas in side-by-side comparison with nitrogen and helium (Schreiner et al., 1972) have shown it to be equivalent to helium in its effects on mental and psychomotor processes, and that it presents no particular problems in decompression. Voice is less distorted by neon than by helium or hydrogen, and the lower thermal conductivity of neon might prove to be advantageous when diving in cold water. Divers who have used neon at sea report some subjective reduction in heat loss but definitive measurements of this factor remain to be made.

It appears that the optimal use of neon will be in the range 150-600 fsw. Deeper depths result in enough of an increase in gas density that Neon 75 mixtures may be hard to breathe by a diver doing heavy work and who is limited by breathing equipment designed for helium.

ARGON
The properties of argon are not beneficial with respect to its use as a diving gas. It has a high lipid solubility and is consequently narcotic and a problem in decompression. Further, its density makes it difficult to breathe at pressures, but it does allow effective voice communications and also acts as a fair insulator against heat loss.

Argon has been used as a decompression gas, with the purpose of reducing the inspired partial pressures of both helium and nitrogen (Keller and Buhlmann, 1965; Keller, 1967). The real benefits of argon in this situation have not been systematically explored, but its use seems to be effective (Schreiner, 1969).

Argon is about twice as narcotic as nitrogen, causing an equivalent decrement in performance test at about half as much pressure (Ackles & Fowler, 1971).

OTHER GASES
Few other biologically inert gases exist which seem to be practical as the major component of a diving gas mixture, and scant data exists on the ones that do exist. Heavier gases exhibit the same deficiencies as argon,

The future of high-tech diving includes Dr. Bill Stone's MK-2R fully redundant mixed gas rebreather currently in development. The unit shown is configured for cave diving and includes a separate ARGON cylinder for suit inflator and a 105 cubic foot composite- fiber bail-out cylinder mounted on the backpack shell. The design includes two independent 9-hour range closed circuit systems and three separate open-circuit contingency systems. Weight is only 92 pounds, less than most advanced deep diving open circuit sets now in use. Stone's company, CIS-LUNAR Development Laboratories, hopes to produce an affordable (approximately $10,000) unit in the near future.

having high lipid solubilities which result in both narcosis and difficult decompression, and high densities which cause increased breathing resistance.

Of the light gases, deuterium is not available in sufficient quantities to be considered; it should have properties similar to hydrogen and helium, and offers no particular advantage. Methane is sufficiently inert and lighter than most other gases, but its lipid solubility should make it reasonably narcotic. Like hydrogen it is not flammable if the oxygen percentage is kept low (below about 4%).

Certain gases have some value when added as only a small fraction of a breathing mixture. Gases known to be narcotic may reduce symptoms of HPNS. A heavy gas having a relatively low solubility may improve voice communication; such a gas is CF4, tetrafluoromethane (Airco; patent No. 3,676,563; July 11, 1972). Other fluorinated hydrocarbons (freons) are used as fire extinguishing agents. These freons are apparently not completely "inert," in that they exhibit certain toxic characteristics (see Freon references).

One additional use of gases in diving is to simulate other conditions in the laboratory. Examples are the use of nitrous oxide to cause narcosis similar to that of hyperbaric nitrogen (Brauer & Way, 1971; Hamilton, 1973). Nitrous oxide is 30 to 40 times more narcotic than nitrogen. Sulfur

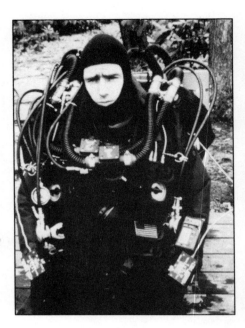

Diver wearing the MK-2R.

hexafluoride has a molecular weight of 146, making it about 5 times as dense as air. This property has been used to study breathing resistance as a function of density (Uhl et al., 1972; Antoneisen et al., 1971).

CONCLUSION

Only a few short years ago, a discussion of non-commercial divers using mixed gas technology would have been preposterous to many industry professionals content within the confines of traditional scuba. To suggest the use of affordable, safely engineered closed-circuit units would be as foreign as "man on the moon" predictions in the 1950's. But here we are, none the less, and poised on new technological breakthroughs every day.

Diving evolved historically from military applications and systems that were adopted by commercial interests and ultimately by sport divers. If you were to plot a line graph for the three segments an interesting shift would occur in the mid-seventies when commercial companies broke away from naval influences and began to chart their own course in innovative table research, saturation systems and specialized equipment. In the nineties, it appears that private sector development springing from the high-tech diving community may well provide the impetus and leadership in a bold new technology reaching for the twenty-first century.

Chapter 12

Dive Tables

"The reliability of a decompression table or procedure is not determined by any mathematical process, but by what works in practice. What works... is what works!"

John Crea III

"Any passive decompression device can only inform the diver of his or her decompression status. How that information is used is the responsibility of the diver."

Karl Huggins

DIVE TABLE EVOLUTION

The first research work in decompression physiology was not directed at scuba divers. It was noticed that people working at elevated pressures in either caissons (a caisson is a water-tight box inside which men can do construction work underwater), or construction tunnels beneath rivers would succumb to symptoms of pain and paralysis. These symptoms were first witnessed in 1841 and by the 1880's were popularly called "the bends" because of the positions the workers took to alleviate the pain. Soon this high pressure disease was referred to as caisson disease. Later, in cases from hard hat divers, decompression sickness was termed "diver's palsy".

The DCS research conducted in the 1800's eventually gave rise to a series of principles as well as a set of decompression tables that were published in 1908 by Boycott, Damant and Haldane. The principles eventually came to be known as Haldane's Principles of Decompression and, in combination with the decompression tables, formed the basis for current decompression theory including the development of the original U.S Navy Decompression Tables.

For all practical purposes, there are four principles involved:

1) "The progress of saturation follows in general the line of a logarithmic curve... The curve of desaturation after decompression is the same as that of saturation, provided no bubbles have formed."

2) "The time in which an animal or man exposed to compressed air becomes saturated with nitrogen varies in different parts of the body from a few minutes to several hours."

3) "In decompressing men or animals from high pressure the first part should consist in rapidly halving the absolute pressure: subsequently, the rate of decompression must become slower and slower so that the nitrogen pressure in no part of the body ever becomes more than twice that of air."

4) "Decompression is not safe if the pressure of nitrogen inside the body becomes much more than twice that of the atmospheric pressure."

The reader should note that although these four principles provided the earliest basis for decompression table theory, the latter two principles have been proven flawed and have since been extensively modified.

DIVE TABLES: A COMPARISON

Most divers accept the U.S. Navy diving tables as gospel and rarely question the validation of the model. Some interesting facts need to be considered, however, when we apply those tables in sport diving applications. Such as: the Navy tables were designed originally for single dives only. Further, the divers using them were to be closely supervised by a Navy divemaster who dictated their dive profiles and controlled their decompression, if any, by in-water stages. Most diving operations were supported by on-site recompression chambers and access to a diving medical officer. Even then, an incidence rate of decompression sickness around 3 to 5% was considered acceptable (facilities being available for treatment).

Now consider that the Navy made a grand total of approximately 120 test dives (!!!) with human subjects before accepting the repetitive dive tables for use. These tables still enjoy the widest use by sport divers, in spite of their apparent drawbacks when considered in the perspective of the average diver's age and physical condition.

None the less, these tables have proved to be valid and with some forty years of field use and perhaps millions of dives on them by sport divers, their worth must be accepted. Recently though, a plethora of new tables have undergone research and testing with an eye to producing tables more appropriate for actual sport diving needs.

In 1908, Haldane conducted extensive studies of decompression on goats while formulating his original "decompression model". Based on his work with goats in various hyperbaric chambers he derived what he concluded to be logical extrapolations to human physiological responses to pressure and subsequent decompression schedules. Some of his assumptions, of course, were later proved to be not entirely correct. But given the tools of research for his era and the primitive monitoring equipment at his disposal, his pioneering experiments and recommendations would provide the "seed" from which the "oak tree" of decompression science and diving tables would grow.

Originally, he felt that his animal studies had confirmed his hypothesis that if no symptoms of DCS where present post-decompression, then no bubbles were formed in the blood systems. Obviously, with the benefit of today's technology and Doppler monitors, we know that bubbles do occur in a statistically large percentage of dives made that were previously thought to be "safe" from such development. In assessing the saturation exposure for goats, he applied a time factor of three hours to assume full inert gas loading and later postulated that humans would reach saturation in five hours.

In designating his half-times for his five "tissue" groups (now generally referred to as "compartments"), he selected his slowest group to be the 75 minute tissue. This was selected since it would be 95% saturated after five hours in keeping with his hypothesis on maximum time for humans to reach theoretical saturation loading. Certainly he was on the right track, but most table model experts now allow as much as 24 hours for such saturation to fully take place and current custom table models employ slow "compartments" rated up to 1200 minutes!

Haldane produced three table schedules for air diving:
Schedule One: for all dives requiring less than 30 minutes of decompression time.

Schedule Two: for all dives requiring more than 30 minutes of decompression time.

Schedule Three: for deep air diving to 330 fsw using oxygen decompression.

These schedules were typified by a relatively rapid ascent from depth to the initial decompression stop depths, then followed by markedly slower ascents to the surface. The British Royal Navy adopted these in 1908 and continued to use them with revisions well into the late 1950's. It should be noted that it was discovered that Schedule One proved to be too conservative for practical use and Schedule Two proved to be too "liberal" with the percentage of DCS hits unacceptable. In 1915, the first tables for the U.S. Navy were produced called the C and R tables (Bureau of Construction and Repair); these were used with success in the salvage operation on the submarine F-4 at a depth of 306 fsw.

In 1912, Sir Leonard Hill offered his "Critical Pressure Hypothesis" wherein he questioned Haldane's theory of staged decompression. Hill advocated the use of continuous uniform decompression and offered both experimental and theoretical evidence to support his position. Although the validity of his decompression schedules were not substantively disputed, the widespread use of staged decom stops remained in practice.

Other development included the works of Hawkins, Shilling and Hansen in the early 1930's in which they determined that the allowable supersaturation ratio was a function of the tissue half-time and depth and duration of the dive. Yarborough expanded on their work by recomputing a set of tables for the U.S. Navy based only on the 20, 40 and 75 minute half-time groups. These were adopted by the Navy in 1937 and used until the modified U.S. Navy Standard Air Decompression Tables came into use in 1957. These tables remain in widespread use today although continued research is being conducted by the Naval Experimental Diving Unit (NEDU) including recent work with the Navy E-L Algorithm which assumes that nitrogen is absorbed by tissues at an exponential rate (as in other Haldanean models) but is discharged or "out-gassed" at a slower linear rate. This predicts slower elimination during surface intervals and resultant higher residual nitrogen levels on repetitive dives.

The British Navy branched off slightly in 1958 to follow the theories of U.K. physiologist Hempleman. "He had observed that over a particular depth range, the first symptom of DCS to appear was usually pain at or near a joint... and assumed that the tissue involved (e.g. tendon) was, therefore, the tissue with the greatest overpressure of nitrogen for that depth range, and that gas elimination from that tissue must control the decompression. He pictured the body as a single tissue and believed that the quantity of gas absorbed in the body could be calculated by a simple formula which related depth and time. Unlike Haldane, who believed that gas uptake and elimination took identical times, Hempleman assumed that gas elimination was one and a half times slower than uptake. Utilizing the theory that the tissues could tolerate an overpressure of 30 fsw, (he) constructed a new set of decompression schedules... that are the current Royal Navy schedules." (Deeper Into Diving, Lippman 1990)

Workman, in 1965, introduced the concept of "delta P" for gas partial pressures which was easier to handle than ratios and fitted the data better. He introduced the concept of "M values": that each "tissue" or theoretical compartment would have a maximum nitrogen tension that can be safely tolerated at the surface without bubble formation. M is short for maximum and the M-value is the maximum allowable tissue tension at a specific depth.

Attempting to improve the safety of his original tables, Hempleman revised them in 1968 to include using a variable ratio of tissue nitrogen tension to ambient pressure to predict safe decompression. However, the Navy was not happy with the newly restrictive results and refused to implement them. Following more trials and revisions with Hempleman more closely attentive to the Navy's suggestions for practical work needs, the tables were modified, reproduced metrically, and adopted in 1972.

Schreiner changed the accounting from "per gas" to "per compartment" in 1971, thus making it possible to handle different gases and gas mixtures. Table computation then is largely "bookkeeping": keeping track of the gases in the compartments and comparing them with the "matrix" of M-values. Diving practitioners speak of "half-times" and "M-values" as if they were real entities, but it must not be forgotten that this is only a mathematical model. In fact, it is not really a "model" as that term is normally used, but rather a computational method.

In summation, we note that Haldane's calculations are inadequate:
1. Long, deep dives require more decompression than originally provided.
2. Fixing these tables messes up the short, shallow dives which are working fine.
3. Various tricks can be used to make the tables match the data using Haldanean calculations.
4. Other ways to calculate tables have been proposed and any model will work if there are enough variables to adjust and a data base in making the adjustments.

Currently, divers are faced with a diversity of tables and decompression models incorporated into diving computers. Some are simple reconfigurations of the basic U.S. Navy tables and others are distinctly different in their approach to decompression management. For the purposes of advanced deep diving, the tables available through the national scuba training agencies will prove excessively limiting to most readers of this book due their tendency to end around 140 fsw and to offer only minimal decompression information.

New developments in bubble detection equipment prompted Dr. Merril Spencer to suggest re-evaluation of recommended no-decompression limits with the goal of minimizing bubble development after a dive. His 1976 revisions where extensively tested by Dr. Andrew Pilmanis and Dr. Bruce Bassett and found to significantly decrease detectable bubble formation. In 1981, Karl Huggins, an assistant in Research at the University of Michigan generated a new set of decompression tables based on Spencer's recommendations. These became known variously as the "Huggins tables", "Huggins/Spencer tables", "Michigan Sea Grant tables", etc., and were to be the basic algorithm used in the diving industry's first practical electronic dive computer produced by Orca Industries and known as the Edge.

Significantly, the Defence and Civil Institute of Environmental Medicine (DCIEM) in Canada has continued on-going revision to their tables based on ultra-sonic Doppler studies. These tables have gained wide popularity due their unique criteria for development geared to minimal bubble formation. John Crea, a professional consultant in custom table generation and a practicing anesthesiologist, specifically recommends the DCIEM tables for deep divers if a "stock" table reference is acceptable.

Other models include the conservative Buhlmann Swiss tables based on the work of Dr. Albert Buhlmann of the Laboratory of Hyperbaric Physiology of the University of Zurich. His algorithms have been extensively integrated into popular diving computers such as Dacor's Micro Brain Pro Plus and Beuchat'S Aladdin Pro as well as use in the form of custom tables.

A group of researchers at the University of Hawaii have come to be known as the "Tiny Bubble Group" after their theory of physical properties of bubble nucleation in aqueous media. Their Varying-Permeability Model indicates that cavication nuclei, that are thought to "seed" bubble formation are "spherical gas phases that are small enough to remain in solution yet strong enough to resist collapse, their stability being provided by elastic skins or membranes consisting of surface-active molecules"

(Hoffman 1985). In comparison of table models, Huggins observes (1987), "the ascent criteria for this model is based on the volume of bubbles that are formed upon decompression. Growth in size and number of gas bubbles is computer based on the physical properties of the 'skins' and the surrounding environment. If the total volume of gas in the bubbles is less than a 'critical volume', then the diver is within the safe limits of the model". Although tables have been produced based on this model, not enough actual human testing has been conducted to be considered statistically relevant. On square profile comparisons with the U.S. Navy tables, the "Tiny Bubble" model is more conservative down to the 140 fsw level.

Further projects in table models include the Maximum Likelihood Statistical Method developed by the Naval Medical Research Institute (NMRI). In consideration of a diver's exposure to depth/time "doses", they have produced a statistical model that reflects probabilities of DCS occurrence and are expressed as 1% and 5% tables. The diving supervisor would have the option of selecting his risk factor based upon the priority of work to be accomplished.

What tables, then should deep divers use? It's really too broad a question to pin down to a single answer as to "this table is the best". Many experienced deep diving professionals prefer to work with custom or proprietary tables specifically designed for their application (see next section of this chapter). Crea (1991) makes this observation:

"Computations can compare different tables or practices, but cannot determine what is best. As stated before, what works... is what works. Good tables are at the current state of knowledge empirical. The algorithms are good, however, to use yesterday's experience to predict tomorrow's dive."

In the process of table development and validation, several basic and separate steps are employed with feedback on field use:

1. Concept or "algorithm" for a table, usually based on some experience. Laboratory trials, with feedback and revision as needed. Move to provisional operational use at some point. Provisional use "at sea". Acceptance as "operational". Results fed back, revisions as necessary.
2. Judgement needed as to when to take the next step; this should be a responsible body of the developing organization; this body decides how many trial dives under what conditions, etc.
3. This process, laid out in a workshop by the Undersea and Hyperbaric Society, is more or less what is currently practiced, but there is no set protocol for making the formal judgements.

Photo by Bret Gilliam

Dr. R. W. "Bill" Hamilton, the industry's decompression and custom table expert.

Divers on particularly strenuous or cold dives should modify their plan to make more conservative allowances in dive table planning.

The following table will contrast nine of the current models for the reader's comparison. Extrapolated depth/times are available for deeper exposures.

Comparison of No-Decompression Limits

DEPTH (fsw)	NO-DECOMPRESSION LIMITS (in minutes)								
	U.S. Navy	Buhlman*	Spencer	Navy E-L**	British *	DCIEM	Tiny Bubble	NMRI 1%	NMRI 5%
30	None	300	225	296	232	380	323	170	240
40	200	120	135	142	137	175	108	100	170
50	100	75	75	81	72	75	63	70	120
60	60	53	50	57	46	50	39	40	80
70	50	35	40	44	38	35	30	25	80
80	40	25	30	37	27	25	23	15	60
90	30	22	25	31	23	20	18	10	50
100	25	20	20	27	18	15	15	8	50
110	20	17	15	24	16	12	12	7	40
120	15	15	10	20	12	10	11	5	40
130	10	12	5	17	11	8	10	5	30

Metric conversion to next greater depth   **Approximate calculations from Thalmann, 1984**

For a more detailed history of tables and model evolutions the authors recommend reading "Development of Dive Tables" by Karl Huggins as contained in *Microprocessor Applications to Multi-level Air Decompression Problems* (Michigan Sea Grant publication 1987) and *Deeper Into Diving* by John Lippman (Aqua Quest Publications 1990)

CUSTOM OR PROPRIETARY TABLES

It is common practice in the international commercial diving industry to modify or build from "scratch" proprietary tables for use within their private companies. Historically, these tables have been religiously guarded and controlled for the company's own use for two reasons: 1. They are expensive to produce and validate. 2. Fear of potential liability if injury should occur if used by others.

Proprietary tables came into being in hopes of improving on the U.S. Navy Tables and making the working commercial diver safer and more efficient. Pioneering work in such tables was done by individuals like Bill Hamilton of Hamilton Research Ltd. (see Reference Materials) who consulted with various diving contractors and even foreign navies such as Japan, Sweden and Finland to create air and mixed gas tables for bounce diving, saturation work and treatment schedules.

Although the diving contractors still remain competitive with each other, much of the secretive nature of proprietary tables was relaxed in the late 1980's to reflect a more open exchange of information for safety purposes. And, realistically, the security of private tables was shaky at best. If a diver switched employers and had been happy with the set of tables generated by his old contractors, they had a mysterious habit of accompanying him to his new workplace.

The business of custom tables has seen new growth not only in the commercial industry but in the scientific and emerging high-tech sport diver communities. Our section entitled Reference Materials cites several sources for custom table production, but Hamilton remains preeminent among this small and esoteric professional group. His capable expertise has been applied to computer technology to design a program that allows the field user to produce custom tables essentially on his own. Hamilton's program is called DCAP and DCAP Plus (Decompression Computation and Analysis Program) and has been the basis for much of the field custom table generation.

In correspondence with Gilliam (1991), Hamilton notes, "About the matter of preparation of custom tables, this is somewhat of a sensitive issue and one about which I have mixed feelings. I think it would be worthwhile to discuss it a bit. One issue relates to whether professional diving physiologists should support the extreme environment diving that some folks want to do. Another is whether a 'calculated' table will be reliable enough to keep the user out of trouble. When I started in this business, 'they' told me what they were going to do. And it appeared that they would make up the tables themselves if I did not provide them. Thus blackmailed, and lacking humility enough to realize that some of the more experienced high-tech divers could easily construct a special table as well as I could, I went ahead with it. With some trepidation, I might add. It has worked out well, and because of the excellent feedback and sufficient repetition of the process, I am now relatively comfortable with it."

Hamilton is particularly concerned with the validation of the special tables and encourages precise record keeping of his tables in field use. He assigns a specific "Base case" identification to each set and provides up to 20 pages of generic instructions in their use with additional guidelines for special applications. He prohibits the re-sale of his tables as they are intended for the specialty end-user only.

John Crea of Submariner Research and Randy Bohrer of Underwater Applications (see Reference Section) will also generate a set of custom tables for specific diving needs upon demand. The cost is not cheap; figure between $300 and $500 to set up a basic custom table. And, like Hamilton, they will probably extensively interview the applicant to insure his proper experience, equipment, training and reasons for the dive. Hamilton estimates in May of 1991 that 10-15% of his business was devoted to exceptional exposure applications.

Crea, an anesthesiologist, enjoys an exalted reputation in the high-tech circle since he is an active cave diver who actually dives his own tables. This is the ultimate in validation confidence. His program is called DECOM and is currently in its 9th generation.

The cave diving community is a prime example of a group benefiting from custom tables. Since cavers are faced with extremely long and deep penetrations (now approaching 400 fsw/121.2 m threshold) that require extensive penetration into the cave system, they pose a unique scenario in mixed gas table models. Modification to shorten their extreme decompression obligations with use of 100% O_2 is common and a new practice of constructing dry underwater "stages" is gaining favor. Likewise, extreme exposure tables for air can be generated as Bohrer did for Gilliam's 1990 assault on the depth record.

GILLIAM'S PROPRIETARY TABLES

FIRST EDITION: Randy Bohrer to Bret Gilliam's specifications to 500 fsw. Produced in 1989.

Notes: Descent rate can be up to 100 fpm; descent time plus time at depth is equal to ten minutes. For example, the 500 fsw table is calculated for 100 fpm or five minute descent time, then five minutes at 500 fsw. This ten minutes ends upon beginning ascent. This technique adds a bit of conservatism, gives credit for the descent time, but does not bind Gilliam to a particular descent rate. Ascent rate is 60 fpm for the first 100 ft., then 30 fpm thereafter. Ascent rate between stops is instantaneous, so the stop should be left at a time such that the decompression time for that stop expires just as the next stop is reached. Diving gas is air, but if oxygen is used in any combination of the 30 through 10 ft. stops, each minute of breathing O_2 can be considered to two minutes breathing air.

Depth (fsw)	Decompression Stop (ft. / min.)											
	120	110	100	90	80	70	60	50	40	30	20	10	Total
300								1	3	4	8	13	29
350							1	3	4	7	10	20	45
400						2	3	3	7	8	14	29	66
450					2	3	3	6	7	11	19	42	93
500			1	2	3	3	6	5	10	15	26	57	128

SECOND EDITION: Modified to assume entire 10 minutes was spent at depth (no credit for descent time), 30 fpm ascent rate.

Depth (fsw)	Decompression Stop (ft. / min.)											
	120	110	100	90	80	70	60	50	40	30	20	10	Total
300							1	3	4	7	10	21	46
350						2	3	4	7	8	16	32	72
400			1	2	3	5	6	8	12	23	47	107
450		2	2	3	5	5	8	10	17	32	68	152
500	1	2	3	3	5	5	7	9	16	23	42	98	214

Note: Bret Gilliam significantly further modified the table before his record dive to 452 fsw on Feb.14, 1990; this table is presented as an exemplar of custom tables and under no circumstances should be used by other divers.

Saturation habitats similar to Hydrolab may be used in the future for Cave and wreck exploration within the "technical diver" community.

Photo by Bret Gilliam

THE FUTURE

Hamilton is pursuing grant funding to develop a variety of "generic" custom tables to address several typical models to accommodate current requested profiles. Undoubtedly, we will see a continuing trend away from the "old standard" U.S. Navy Tables as technology pushes forward and as increasing data shows that Navy tables do not have an acceptable DCS rate with deeper/longer dives (Thalman 1985).

Perhaps we will begin to see the efficacy of shallow water saturation habitats emerge for special projects. Early scientific habitats such as NOAA's *Hydrolab* and *TEKTITE* proved the worth of sat diving in research and observation studies. *Hydrolab*, now enshrined in the Smithsonian, would be considered primitive by today's standards. Little larger than the interior of a recreational vehicle, it was able to support four aquanauts in saturation for a week or more and allowed deeper "excursions" from "storage depth" to 200 fsw (60.6 m) for up to two hours with only minor stage stops back to the habitat.

The high-tech community might consider *Hydrolab* or something similar a luxury for extended exploration of deep shipwrecks or extensive cave systems. By going to NITROX (any N_2/O_2 mixture other than air; the FO_2 may be reduced) as the chamber breathing gas instead of standard air, and relocating deeper to 80 fsw (24.2 m), an entire new galaxy of excursion dives opens up. Imagine two-hour bottom times at 300 fsw (90.9 m) on rebreathers or short excursions to 500 fsw (151.5 m) and beyond. It's all possible and the technology is available to implement such systems.

It's a quantum leap to saturation dives from a habitat for "sport divers" when only forty years ago we did not have repetitive diving tables for our

Navy divers, but here we are staring down the face of the 21st century limited still only by our imaginations.

CONCLUSION

Much debate still centers on what is the "best" table to use, and there clearly is no pat answer to that question. The authors opinion is that the best possible scenario for safe deep diving would include the use of a custom table matched to the individual and the dive application but obviously many divers will not utilize this level of technical support. But we urge our readers to make an informed choice in table selection. Don't just grab the first thing that's handy and expect it to suit a myriad of dive situations. And in all cases, do not push a model to the edge of its limits.

Another area of continuing controversy is the question of multi-day repetitive diving. Until 1991, many experts have suggested limiting dives to no more than two a day and then taking a day off following the fourth day of diving. This was postulated to allow a safety edge and to lessen the chance of DCS. The recommendation actually had little basis in documented sport diving statistics upon close examination. Grossly, it would appear that some sport diver DCS incidence rates could be linked to multi-day repetitive diving but with a finer eye toward the "broad" view it seems that the real culprit is poor diving technique. Less experienced divers are the primary victim of DCS and this is due to a variety factors.

At the 1991 American Academy of Underwater Sciences Workshop on Multi-day Repetitive Diving held at Duke University, the recommendation for the "mid-week lay-off" was dropped from the guidelines basically because there was no lab or field data to justify the practice. Gilliam was a speaker at that program and presented data obtained from a one year study of intensive four day repetitive diving by sport divers from age 7 to 72. In 77,680 dives during that period, he recorded only 7 DCS hits; all on relatively inexperienced divers. Interestingly, 5 of the 7 hits were within table limits and reflected diving averaging two dives a day usually to depths less than 100 fsw.

The more experienced diver population that made far more aggressive dive profiles typified by as many as five dives per day for up to four straight days had no cases of DCS. Gilliam's conclusions as to DCS occurrence centered more on the divers' watermanship than on their dive profiles. The more experienced group dived more and dived deeper than the less experienced group but they also were far more observant of ascent rates, hydration, safety and/or decompression stops, and displayed far better dive planning disciplines either through the use of tables or dive

Controversy still divides experts on the intensive diving from liveaboards. Although in limited use in the early 1970's, liveaboards have shown unrestrained growth in the 1980's and into the 1990's. This photo taken in 1976 aboard the Virgin Diver shows Bill Walker, Geri Murphy, Paul Tzimoulis and Bret Gilliam preparing for their sixth dive of the day; earlier dives had typically been as deep as 200 fsw with progressively shallower dives. Tzimoulis, then editor of Skin Diver magazine, was one of the earliest supporters of liveaboards and exotic dive travel.

Photo by Lois Leonard

computers. It would seem that attention to these good diving skills played a far greater role in their safety than frequency of diving or depths. More research and particularly, more field data of actual diving practices needs to be accumulated to accurately make recommendations.

It is common practice on liveaboard dive vessels for guests to make from 4 to 6 dives per day. It is not uncommon for the serious photographers and "hard core" divers to do many more dives. Veteran dive travel specialist Carl Roessler of Sea & See Travel in San Francisco regularly did as many as 12 dives per day dating back to the early 1970's; his dives were "controlled" by the SOS/Scubapro decom meter popular during that era and still in use today. In 1976, Paul Tzimoulis, then editor of Skin Diver Magazine, averaged 6-8 dives per day with several Caribbean liveaboards. Many of his dives were repetitive 200+ fsw exposures and all were governed by the SOS meter. Gilliam, Mount, Gentile, Gleason, Tzimoulis, Roessler and a wide variety of other diving professionals have engaged in deep repetitive diving dating back to the 1960's and have progressed through profile planning dictated by Tables, the SOS meter and now modern dive computers. The point to be made is that aggressive repetitive diving even in deeper depths may not specifically suggest a statistically higher incidence of DCS; there are simply too many divers following such plans without any problems and the practice has been going on for decades.

In all cases, caution and prudence are recommended but the overly conservative "prohibitions" still offered by some academicians may not necessarily be proven in the field.

As has been noted several times in this chapter, "what works is what works". Tables and determination of "safe" dive profiles are very much an experimental science. Hopefully, we shall see more substantive objective research and data sampling emerge.

Chapter 13

Decompression Sickness, Theory, and Treatment

"Bends is a statistical inevitability..."
Bret Gilliam

"Decompression accidents are unique in that, with few exceptions, it is the layman who is responsible for patient assessment, diagnosis, early therapeutic intervention and, in some cases, even definitive care."
Dick Clarke

DECOMPRESSION SICKNESS

That's right folks, if you get bent on a dive trip the chances of having immediate medical help are slim to none. It is vital that divers, especially those involved in deep diving activities, have a clear and thorough understanding of decompression sickness (DCS) symptoms and predisposing conditions. Early recognition of DCS signs and symptoms and appropriate first responder care are key to the stricken diver's successful recovery. DCS is a statistical inevitability and must be accepted as an assumed risk by divers. You can do everything exactly by the book and still get bent; hopefully, this is not news to anyone. In Gilliam's study (1989-90) of sport divers covering the customers of a large liveaboard dive/cruise ship, 71.4% of DCS cases he treated in the vessel's recompression chamber were diving within the limits of their diving tables. There is no guarantee that any table or computer is infallible.

CAUSES OF DCS

In a nutshell, improper decompression resulting in occlusive inert gas bubble formation is probably our major culprit in decompression sickness. Although some would argue to the contrary, most experts generally agree that ALL dives are decompression dives. Even ones without stage decompression obligations have ascent rates factored into their model as a means of decompression. Hopefully divers are now routinely practicing slow ascents in the last two atmospheres, 66 fsw (20 m) to the surface in conjunction with a recommended 5 minute "safety stop" around the 10-15 fsw (3.03-4.5 m) level.

CONTRIBUTORY FACTORS TO DCS

Primary Direct Effects of Physics: Depth, time, rate of release (dive profile).

Secondary Effects, Inherent: Physical fitness and overall health condition, age, body fat level (obesity or extreme lean condition), height, muscular makeup, old injuries that may affect circulation, etc., theories of male versus female susceptibility.

Secondary Effects, External: Thermal conditions (cold water or excessively hot conditions), physical exertion during and after dive (elevated pCO_2 levels), constrictive equipment factors (tight wetsuit, over-weighting, binding straps, etc.), improper hydration, smoking, alcohol use, drugs (including over-the-counter drugs).

Equipment factors: Breathing regulators with excessive resistance, inaccuracies of depth gauges or watch, failure of dive computers.

Decompression Models: Use of unvalidated tables, improper manipulation of tables for averaging or extrapolation, etc., failure to compute repetitive dives correctly, improper decompression stops, compromised model or table through improper ascent rates, high altitude diving, use of extreme exposure tables, flying after diving.

Stress: Time pressure and task-loading.

There are many excellent reference texts cited in our bibliography that can provide a detailed subject treatment of the patho-physiology of decompression sickness and so only a brief review is offered in this section. We are more concerned with divers being able to recognize symptomotology effectively and react accordingly. Divers with a desire to delve deeper into the mechanisms of DCS are encouraged to access these separate materials.

At the surface we are basically saturated with nitrogen at one atmosphere. As we descend, pressure increases and the inert gas (nitrogen) is dissolved and absorbed by the body's tissues and blood. The deeper we go, the more inert gas is "loaded". Theoretically, after a period of time (based upon the longest half-time utilized in the model) at any given depth, be it 60 fsw (18.2 m) or 600 fsw (181.8 m), we are saturated with all the inert gas we can hold and no further decompression obligation would be incurred no matter how long we stayed down. This is the basis of "saturation diving" theory where aquanauts are placed underwater in a bell or habitat to work for as much as a week or more and then decompressed when brought back to the surface.

As untethered free swimming-divers we do not have the luxury of saturation support equipment and we must come back to the surface. Herein lies the problem with the inert gas we have absorbed (in-gassed or loaded) during our brief, by comparison, sojourn into the deep.

Remembering our diving history, we will recall that Haldane originally postulated his theory that our body could tolerate inert gas pressure up to twice that found normally at the surface. This 2:1 ratio became the basis of the earliest dive tables and accounted for the presumption that we could have unlimited bottom times at 33 fsw (10 m). However, as more research study was accomplished it became evident that his ratio theory was flawed and has since been modified to be expressed as approximately 1.58:1, a significant difference. In fact, authenticated DCS cases have been observed in divers at 18 fsw (5.5 m) after extended time periods.

Haldane offered other valuable principles of decompression that included the theory of exponential inert gas uptake that provided the basis of tissue half-times and compartment M values. We are now overwhelmed with new decompression models or algorithms that stem from Haldane's early work and go considerably farther in scope. Navy tables were developed assuming a 120 minute tissue/compartment as the slowest; we now see use of models that incorporate compartments with 689 minute half-times in dive computers and far longer in custom tables!

But all this was to serve the purpose of preventing bubble formation in the blood as pressure was decreased upon ascent. Haldane and other pioneers in DCS originally thought that no bubbles would form if their decompression models were followed. Through the use of modern Doppler devices it is now known that bubbles may exist on every dive. Such scanning is frequently employed to monitor divers during test criteria for new table development and as a benchmark of decompression stress. "Bubble trouble" as a term was first popularized by Rutkowski as a convenient catch-all for DCS and embolism manifestations. In our discussion, we are concerned with inert gas bubbles, of course, not air bubbles as would be the problem in lung over-expansion accidents typical of breath holding ascents.

Where these bubbles are located and their size will dictate the presentation of DCS symptoms.

SIGNS AND SYMPTOMS

Many texts distinguish DCS symptomotology into type I (pain only) or type II (serious symptoms, central nervous system involvement). To the layman or diver in the field, this distinction is not of great importance and requires special training in many instances to classify presentations. Most importantly we want our readers to be able to recognize any symptoms or signs of DCS and leave diagnosis and treatment selection to trained chamber staff or medical consultants. But what you do for the patient and the observations you can record and pass along to treatment personnel will be of significant aid to his ultimate hope of recovery.

Type I (pain only, mild symptoms):
- "Skin bends"- skin blotching or mottling of the skin producing a red or purplish-blue tinge.
- Itching similar to fiberglass irritation.
- Fatigue
- Indifference, personality or mood swings, irritable behavior, diver unaware of surroundings.
- Pain usually associated in or near a joint such as shoulder or knee. Onset may be gradual and may be transient (niggle).

Type II (CNS involvement, etc.):
- CNS spinal and cranial abnormalities usually gradual in onset with initial subtle symptoms often masked by pain distractions.
- Cardiopulmonary symptoms are typically manifested by "chokes", a dry persistent non-productive cough. Cerebral symptoms may follow; all effects in this group should be considered life-threatening.

- Unusual fatigue
- Dizziness or "staggers", vertigo
- Numbness, paralysis, progressive loss of feeling in skin patches.
- Shortness of breath
- Unconsciousness, collapse, syncope
- Loss of bladder and bowel control, inability to urinate.
- Muscular weakness, poor grip, poor resistance to restraint of motion.
- Visual disturbances, inability to hear fingers rubbed close to ears etc.
- Headache
- Abdominal encircling pain or lower back pain precursor of overt spinal symptoms. Frequently this presentation is misdiagnosed as less serious Type I DCS.
- Convulsions
- Any symptoms developing while still underwater.

The alert diver will recognize that many of these symptoms are nearly identical to those of embolic event presentations. Since treatment and first aid are essentially the same, don't worry about the distinction. This table illustrates symptoms as categorized by Type I and Type II but consider all symptoms serious in the field.

One of the most frustrating aspects of sport divers and DCS is their stubborn denial of symptoms and failure to accept early treatment. This has historically led to the majority of sport diver accidents being unnecessarily delayed for treatment. Even divers that knew beyond a doubt that they were at risk from their profile and were presenting early symptoms have refused oxygen when readily available due to some perceived ego threat or for fear that fellow divers would think less of them. Others refuse to accept the possibility that DCS could be involved since "I can't be bent, I was within the limits of the tables".

Early recognition, reporting and treatment of DCS problems dramatically improves patient resolution prognosis. Bends can happen to anyone, it is no one's fault and should involve no "loss of face". Indeed, the prudent diver and his dive group should overtly encourage prompt relation of any ailment that even remotely resembles the symptoms list. Many divers may mistake DCS symptoms as muscle strains or limb numbness due to sitting on it, etc. ALWAYS ERR ON THE SIDE OF CAUTION. If you are suffering from DCS it is only going to get worse as symptoms are progressive. A diver should not wait to seek qualified help!

FIRST AID IN THE FIELD

Immediately give the patient oxygen for surface breathing. Many divers do not realize the importance of 100% O_2 administration and this can only be accomplished via a system incorporating a demand valve/mask (or by use of an oxygen-clean scuba system regulator connected to an oxygen cylinder). This seal should be tight fitting to insure the maximum level of O_2 delivered to the patient. Air leaks around the mask will dilute the percentage of O_2 (FO_2) inspired. Care must be taken to insure the integrity of the mask seal especially in male patients with beards or mustaches or any patient with facial wrinkles, etc. As a rule of thumb, you want the mask seal to be good enough for the patient to breathe on his back underwater. Free flow oxygen systems, although still widely in use, are not recommended. Most free flow devices usually will not deliver 100% O_2 and are extremely wasteful of the gas.

Oxygen is administered primarily to help eliminate inert gas and reduce bubble size to some extent. By breathing pure O_2 at the surface, the blood's oxygen partial pressure is elevated dramatically. This provides a breathing media totally absent of the harmful inert gas, and establishes a steeper gradient across the tissue-bubble interface. This allows more efficient out-gassing of the occlusive nitrogen and also contributes to better oxygenation of the tissues where the bubble insult has occurred. Key to the outcome of this therapy is sufficient pO_2 (best accomplished by a 100% O_2 demand valve system) and adequate flow for delivery.

Many patients will relieve of symptoms simply by proper and immediate oxygen first aid techniques. Davis was a leading advocate of O_2's role in field resolution and Gilliam's experience (1989-90) recorded 12 cases of symptomatic DCS that were completely relieved by 100% O_2 administration during transit of the patient to his chamber facility.

Training is available widely in oxygen administration (see Appendix). One of the first programs implemented was developed by EMT/dive instructor Jim Corry for NAUI and recently the Diver's Alert Network (DAN) has offered a similar course. Both programs are excellent and require between six and eight hours of hands on training in equipment, patient scenarios and theory. Most diving conferences and trade shows will usually offer such courses as a seminar and the benefits to divers are invaluable.

Until recently patient management included positioning the diver in either Trendelenberg (head down, legs bent at knees, left side tilted down) or Scoltetus (head down, legs straight). Recommendations from DAN in 1990 have modified this traditional advice to suggest use of simple supine

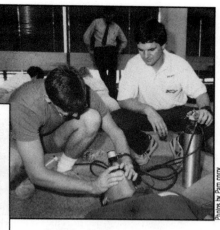

EMT/dive instructor Jim Corry (on right) developed one of the first training programs in oxygen administration. Derivatives of his original course are now taught all over the U.S.

positioning (patient lays flat on his back). Trendelenberg proved to be of little benefit except in the first 10-15 minutes of surfacing primarily in arterial gas embolism (AGE) cases, and the difficulty of maintaining this posture was not felt to be significantly beneficial.

Removal of the diver's wetsuit, etc. is desirable but insure that he is kept warm and comfortable. Cover with blankets, towels or dry clothing. Observe for any "skin bends" symptoms. Continue administration of oxygen until delivered to medical care or supply is exhausted.

Oral fluids should be given if the patient is conscious. Regular drinking water or unsweetened apple juice in amounts of 12 to 16 ounces every 30 minutes will help keep the patient properly hydrated. This amount may require urination if transit is prolonged. This is a good sign and should be accommodated in the supine position. Inability to urinate may indicate more serious Type II manifestation. Such urinary retention will ultimately become quite painful. If the patient is unable to pass water within a reasonable time period, back off on continued administration of fluids.

Do not administer pain drugs other than two aspirin initially (aspirin has been shown to effect a decrease in platelet aggregation in the blood). Pain killers may mask other symptom development.

Be prepared to initiate CPR and rescue breathing if patient condition deteriorates. Deep diving should automatically infer that the dive team as

219

well as the surface support crew is well trained and well experienced in CPR techniques.

TRANSPORTATION

If you are shore diving, insure initial patient care and make sure victim is attended at all times. Hopefully, a properly planned dive will include a contingency list of medical professionals and the nearest recompression chamber facility. Call the chamber or hospital and advise them of the incoming patient. If they direct you to wait for an ambulance team, do so. Otherwise transport patient to the facility they designate and by their proscribed method, either vehicle or aircraft.

If at sea, call the Coast Guard via VHF radio or cellular phone. It may be necessary to relay messages through another vessel if sufficiently offshore that your radio cannot reach the mainland. Make certain that the Coast Guard knows that this emergency involves a diving accident victim and requires transportation to a recompression facility. At this point, they may direct you to proceed with your vessel to a designated port where assistance can meet you or they may decide to send an evacuation helicopter to intercept your vessel and extract the diver for faster transport (see Table 13.2).

It is incumbent upon divers to know what facilities are available to them in an emergency. This becomes particularly important if your trip is remotely located or out of the United States. Prior to leaving on that long-awaited dive vacation to the South Pacific or Caribbean inquire as to the availability of medical staff, chamber locations and medivac flights if required. You should also determine if the resort or liveaboard has 100% demand mask O_2 available on their boats; insist on it. If enough divers demand proper equipment it will finally be made standard practice.

Call DAN to confirm chamber locations and readiness with listings of local addresses and phone numbers. Now is an excellent time to join a diving insurance program such as DAN or DSI which can cover your costs if treatment or medivac "life flight" is required. Costs of air ambulance, chamber time and medical staff can easily exceed $30,000 from a remote location. Dive insurance is an inexpensive hedge against such a financial burden.

RECOMPRESSION CHAMBERS

Many divers have seen a chamber either in photographs or in real life, but very few have ever had occasion to be in one unless they were being treated. As a result a certain "mystique" has developed about chambers and many divers regard them as hostile and menacing environments. Briefly, we would like to acquaint our readers with the realities of these important devices.

Generally, chambers are divided into two categories: **recompression chambers** (used for the treatment of diving related injuries and other ailments) and **decompression chambers** (used for surface or deck decompression facilities so the working diver can be removed from the water and complete decom obligation in a dry and controlled situation).

Both of these units are also properly referred to as "hyperbaric chambers", meaning that the pressure inside will be higher than normal atmospheric pressure. These elevated pressures are usually expressed in feet of seawater (fsw) just as if we were diving in the ocean. Air pressure is introduced to the chamber to raise its internal pressure and begin the "dive". We can then use these chambers to treat DCS or AGE cases, conduct "dry" surface decompression schedules, or simulate dives for research purposes.

In hospital situations, the role of hyperbaric medicine has been recognized as a speciality wherein victims of such injuries as crush wounds, burns, skin grafts, gangrene and carbon monoxide poisoning are treated with oxygen in large climate-controlled chambers. These typically are able to accommodate as many as 18 patients at once, have hatches shaped and sized like conventional doors, are equipped with air conditioning and humidity controls and even piped in music.

In the field, things are just a little bit different. Forget the creature comforts and get prepared for close quarters. Although a well set up field chamber can provide the same therapeutic benefits to a stricken diver, they are substantially smaller in most cases.

Field chambers range in size typically from 48 inches in diameter to 72 inches and are usually made of steel. In the past, monoplace chambers were in common use in commercial diving theatres and were designed to pressurize one patient in a single cylinder. This did not allow an inside tender to attend the patient and therefore he was pretty much on his own once treatment was initiated. Rarely will these chambers be encountered today. Most will be variations on the multi-place (more than one patient or tender) multi-lock (two or more pressure compartments with sealing hatches). These allow several divers to be treated at once with an inside tender to monitor their condition. Medical equipment or relief staff can be "locked" into or out of the chamber by use of the outer lock which can be pressurized to equal the treatment inner lock and subsequently depressurized to travel back to the surface pressure.

From the outside of the chamber, the supervisor can control the depth of the dive or treatment schedule and choose what gases will be supplied to the occupants. Pressurization is accomplished with standard air but most modern treatments call for oxygen therapy beginning at 60 fsw (18.2 m and 2.8 ATA). NITROX mixes of 50/50 (N_2/O_2) or 60/40 (N_2/O_2) are commonly used deeper than 60 fsw instead of air to lessen narcosis and safely keep the O_2 partial pressures within tolerance ranges. Both O_2 and NITROX therapy gases are delivered to the patient or tender via BIBS (built-in-breathing-system) masks similar to aviator oxygen masks.

The chamber supervisor monitors his gauges that are calibrated to

Our Lady of the Lake Hyperbaric facility is typical of large hospital-based treatment chambers. Note the "door" style entrance hatch and remote control operator panel to regulate pressure and gases within the chamber. Located in Baton Rouge, LA.

Photo by Rock Palermo

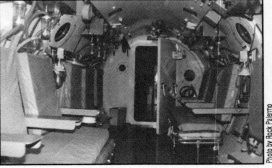

Interior of Our Lady of the Lake chamber showing spacious main treatment lock capable of handling up to a dozen patients comfortably.

Photo by Rock Palermo

display pressure in fsw graduations. He also has an oxygen analyzer plumbed into the chamber to monitor the inside environment's O_2 percentage. Due to fire hazards, this percentage of O_2 (FO_2) will not be allowed to exceed 25%. Most BIBS are set up with "overboard dumps" that exhaust the expired oxygen outside the chamber to prevent the rapid rise of the FO_2. However, it is common to have some leakage of masks due to improper fit, etc., and O_2 will be leaking into the chamber from this source. As the supervisor sees the FO_2 approach the 25% level he will institute a chamber "vent" where the inner lock is flushed with air by inputting pressure and simultaneously exhausting the incoming air from an outflow

TABLE 13.2

HELICOPTER PROCEDURES

Photo by Ken Loyst

1. Post lookout to watch for chopper's arrival on scene.
2. Attempt to establish radio communication via VHF channel 16
3. Maintain vessel speed at 10 to 15 knots if possible. Pilot will count on your constant speed for his approach. Do not slow down or stop.
4. Assume a course that places your vessel with the prevailing wind approximately 20 degrees on port bow. If wind is calm or insignificant, maintain course to shore.
5. Lower antennas, masts, flag staffs, etc., that could interfere with chopper's deployment of uplifting device.
6. Secure all loose objects and equipment on decks. Prop wash from rotor blades can be severe.
7. Do not touch the lift device or cable until it has touched the deck of your vessel and grounded. Electric shock can result otherwise.
8. Have patient wear life jacket. If available, also give him smoke flare for day or night flare if dark. This will help find the patient if he falls out of the basket or if it is dropped. Have lookout watch patient until secure inside chopper. If patient goes into sea, follow man-overboard drill immediately. Have crew member ready to go overboard to rescue patient and establish buoyancy. Swift action and anticipation of contingencies are vital to insure patient's survival.
9. Secure patient in basket (stretcher) via provided harness or tie in with seizing line; ideally with quick release knots that patient can access if necessary.
10. If patient cannot communicate or is unconscious, fasten (duct tape, safety pin, etc.) as much information about his condition, dive profile, name, age, address, next of kin, emergency phone numbers, etc., as possible. If he was diving on a computer send it with him. Make note of tables utilized to acquire profile, etc.
11. Advise or reconfirm that patient is diving victim and requires evacuation to recompression facility.
12. If patient dies while chopper is en route, inform flight crew or Coast Guard operator. This may prevent a needless heroic effort at rescue by the flight crew if bad weather was a factor.

valve. This scrubs the chamber of excess O_2 and also cools and refreshes the atmosphere.

The supervisor is assisted by an outside operator and a record/time keeper who logs all stages of the treatment. They can communicate with the inner occupants via a low voltage radio or sound-powered phone handset to discuss patient status or to confer on treatment procedures.

Inside the chamber, the patient will either lie in a supine position or sit up with the legs outstretched while leaning back against the chamber wall.

Dick Rutkowski's Hyperbarics International field chamber in Key Largo, FL used for training medical and diving staff in recompression protocols.

Photo by Bret Gilliam

A fire retardant mattress is usually provided or bunks may be hung from the chamber sides. Medical equipment, or fluids, etc., may be passed inside via a medical lock (small hatch door compartment usually about 12 inches in diameter) or through the same outer lock that accommodates staff transfers.

A patient is cleaned of all oils such as sun tan lotions or chap sticks and he is given fire retardant clothing to wear. This further reduces the chance of fire.

CHAMBER DIVES

As the chamber is pressurized with air, the occupants will immediately sense the pressure change in their ears and equalization techniques will be necessary. Usually the outside operator will observe signals from the inside tender that all occupants are clearing comfortably. If problems occur and someone is slow to clear, descent is stopped until rectified. Remember that our patient needs to get down to 60 fsw as quickly as possible to begin treatment so in many cases the dive is conducted as fast as the occupants can equalize. In cases where severe DCS symptoms are present and the patient cannot clear, the ear drum may be punctured by the inside tender to allow the dive to continue (a ruptured ear drum will heal, DCS may not).

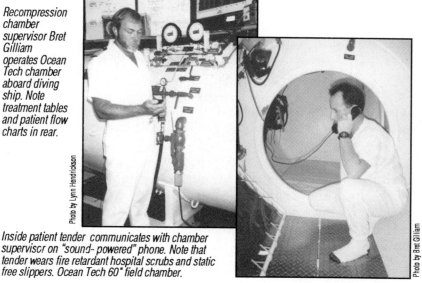

Recompression chamber supervisor Bret Gilliam operates Ocean Tech chamber aboard diving ship. Note treatment tables and patient flow charts in rear.

Photo by Lynn Hendrickson

Inside patient tender communicates with chamber supervisor on "sound-powered" phone. Note that tender wears fire retardant hospital scrubs and static free slippers. Ocean Tech 60" field chamber.

Photo by Bret Gilliam

During the dive it gets quite noisy inside as air pressure is introduced and protective ear muffs are provided for occupants. It also gets hot! Compression of the air atmosphere rapidly raises the temperature inside the inner lock to nearly 100 plus degrees F in tropical locations. Newcomers will be surprised to notice the high pitched speech caused by the increased air density. This becomes more pronounced and distracting as depth increases. In deep treatments, as in Table 6A at 165 fsw, speech even between staff members is discouraged if the chamber environment is air. The altered voice effects can stimulate narcosis in less experienced tenders or ones with less adaptive time at chamber depths. Once reaching treatment depth the chamber will be aggressively vented to flush out the stale, hot, humid air and replace it with fresh air. The patient will be breathing O_2 via BIBS mask in 20 minute intervals with five minute "air breaks" where the mask is removed and chamber air is breathed.

Air breaks are provided for the patient's comfort and to allow him recovery time from breathing pure oxygen for prolonged periods. At any time during treatment if symptoms of chronic or CNS O_2 toxicity are noted, the tender will suspend BIBS mask breathing and provide a 15 minute air break. This time is not counted as part of the treatment table. After this rest, the schedule is resumed on BIBS O_2. Standard treatment Table 5 is two hours and 15 minutes long and Table 6 is four hours and 45 minutes long. Extensions may be added to tables at the supervisor's discretion.

Table 5 is reserved for the less serious, pain-only bends while Table 6 is used for more serious DCS involvement and pain-only bends that is not relieved in the first ten minutes of O_2 breathing at 60 fsw. Most chamber supervisors will now go directly to Table 6 in treating sport divers. This is due to the fact that upon close neurological examination of patients it has been found that pain only symptoms frequently masked or distracted from the more severe but less compelling (in the patient's mind) Type II symptoms of numbness, etc.

The more immediate treatment is instituted, the better the chances of complete recovery.

During treatment, the ascent phases will be marked by the chamber dramatically cooling as the pressure is reduced. In many instances, the air will become so humid that a dense mist is formed, almost like being in a cloud. The mist can be irritating to the throat if inhaled and cause coughing or choking so breathing is always done through the nose. If coughing, etc., develops, the ascent will be stopped to avoid the hazard of embolism.

Training is available in chamber operations and medical support from several sources (see Appendix). Some facilities offer seminars designed for sport divers to learn more about chambers and afford the opportunities to make actual chamber dives. The Catalina chamber sponsors such programs and Gilliam (1989-90) developed a PADI/NAUI certification program in Accident Management/Recompression Chambers that included patient handling and first aid, O_2 administration, symptom recognition and two chamber dives. Almost two thousand sport divers went through this training during that period aboard the dive/cruise ship *Ocean Spirit*. Similar programs will be offered in new dive ship operations.

QUALIFICATION OF DCS

When a patient is presented to a chamber facility, the diver medical technician (DMT) or chamber supervisor will want to perform a gross physical and neurological examination to list the diver victim's symptoms. There is a protocol for rapid neurological exams that can be done in four minutes. In severe cases, the exam will be done in the chamber if the patient's condition precludes further delay. The DMT will note the patient's deficits and observe that many of them may fall in our symptom list. However, that alone does not qualify our patient as a confirmed DCS case.

Confirmation or qualification of DCS is accomplished by a Test of Pressure. The patient is recompressed to a depth of 60 fsw (2.8 ATA) and put on O_2 via BIBS mask for a twenty minute breathing period. If pain,

TABLE 6—MINIMAL RECOMPRESSION, OXYGEN BREATHING METHOD FOR TREATMENT OF DECOMPRESSION SICKNESS AND GAS EMBOLISM

1. Use—treatment of decompression sickness when oxygen can be used and symptoms are not relieved within 10 minutes at 60 feet. Patient breathes oxygen from the surface.
2. Descent rate—25 ft/min.
3. Ascent rate—1 ft/min. Do not compensate for slower ascent rates. Compensate for faster rates by halting the ascent.
4. Time at 60 feet—begins on arrival at 60 feet.
5. If oxygen breathing must be interrupted, allow 15 minutes after the reaction has entirely subsided and resume schedule at point of interruption.
6. Tender breathes air throughout. If treatment is a repetitive dive for the tender or tables are lengthened, tender should breathe oxygen during the last 30 minutes of ascent to the surface.

Depth (feet)	Time (minutes)	Breathing Media	Total Elapsed Time (minutes)
60	20	Oxygen	20
60	5	Air	25
60	20	Oxygen	45
60	5	Air	50
60	20	Oxygen	70
60	5	Air	75
60 to 30	30	Oxygen	105
30	15	Air	120
30	60	Oxygen	180
30	15	Air	195
30	60	Oxygen	255
30 to 0	30	Oxygen	285

TABLE 6 DEPTH/TIME PROFILE

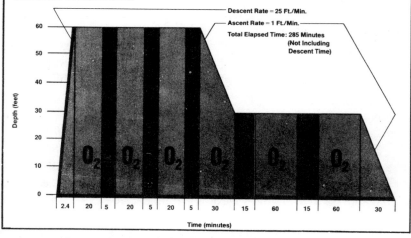

Descent Rate = 25 Ft./Min.
Ascent Rate = 1 Ft./Min.
Total Elapsed Time: 285 Minutes (Not Including Descent Time)

Table 5 is reproduced graphically below for information only.

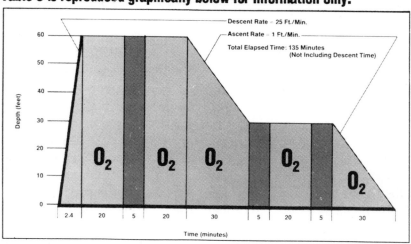

Descent Rate = 25 Ft./Min.
Ascent Rate = 1 Ft./Min.
Total Elapsed Time: 135 Minutes (Not Including Descent Time)

paralysis, weakness, etc., is relieved or improved during this test of pressure breathing period it is presumed that DCS exists and is the source of the patient's problems. Similarly, if no relief is noted then DCS is not considered a factor in the patient's ailment

This distinction is important since divers can manifest symptoms that would be very similar to DCS from other problems including muscle strains from lifting gear or an idiosyncratic reaction to medication. This test of pressure confirms whether further recompression therapy would benefit the patient. Applying this test has proven to be nearly 100% reliable.

During the period of the test of pressure a determination will be made as to what appropriate Treatment Table applies. This is determined by the time factor involved for the relief of symptoms and the seriousness of symptom presentation. Patients resolving in ten minutes or less have historically been treated on Table 5. If resolution takes longer or if any Type II symptoms were initially presented, a Table 6 is chosen. This is a judgement call and the current trend is more towards committing to a Table 6 regardless of time factor resolution. Experienced field chamber supervisors such as Rutkowski, Gilliam and Mount (1991) all suggest application of Table 6 if DCS diagnosis is made.

You may then ask: what about the patient who manifests symptoms, reports promptly and relieves after O_2 administration during transit? Opinion is divided on this issue. If the patient is unsymptomatic and a test of pressure does not confirm DCS at that time, can they be considered a bends case?

Unquestionably, patients have had DCS and been relieved by O_2 breathing. This only confirms the importance and validity of aggressive O_2 use in first aid. If transportation from a remote site involving significant financial cost is a consideration, we recommend close observation and suspension of diving activities. However, if a field chamber is readily available and the diver's profile would seem to have put them at risk, we recommend treatment to be administered at least to the extent of Table 5. It can't hurt the patient, and may provide a safety net for recurrent symptoms.

An interesting observation is offered here for the reader's consideration. Can you get bent free-diving (breath hold diving)? Most divers would answer no. But there is no requirement that you breathe compressed air from a scuba tank to manifest DCS. The malady is dependent on time and depth primarily and therefore expert breath hold divers can, in exceptional diving circumstances, place themselves within a window of vulnerability.

Competitive spearfishermen, South Pacific native working free-divers and Japanese Ama divers are most at risk. Typically, these divers can attain relatively deep depths (80 to 130 fsw) for up to three minutes bottom time. Their profiles reflect an average to rapid descent followed by a "working" period at depth. Ascents are rapid, sometimes assisted by buoyant apparatus. Considerable exertion may be expended on the dive if the diver must struggle to land a large fish or to swim objects off the bottom.

Originally, little serious consideration was given to the prospects of free-divers falling victim to bends hits, but with Bob Croft's dramatic 240 fsw breath hold dive in 1968 some discussions were prompted. Dives exceeding four minutes had already been recorded and anecdotal accounts of longer breath hold dives were in circulation. A 1962 National Geographic article recounts the diving style of a South Pacific diver: "A man from the Tuamotos who at 59 years old went to 100 feet as many as 50 times a day summed up his attitude toward this skill, 'It is nothing... I have big lungs and a strong body. It is my work.' Two minutes, three, four... a long time if you are holding your breath, but what if you are trying to follow a fish?"

Surprisingly, no correlation between deep breath hold dives and symptomatic DCS was made in many cases. In National Geographic's 1980 book *Exploring the Deep Frontier* the authors relate rather naively," "Oxygen deprivation much longer (than four minutes)... can be damaging or fatal. In the Tuamotos, those who make successive, lengthy dives to great depths, risk a condition they call taravana, a sickness that includes vertigo, nausea, partial or complete paralysis, and unconsciousness." Don't these symptoms have something of a familiar ring to them? A quick glance through the DCS symptom list should provide some easy match-ups.

Competitive free-diving spearfishermen in the Virgin Islands in the early seventies experimented with wearing the old Scubapro/SOS decom meter during prolonged diving days with interesting results.

Many were able to advance the analog needle almost into the "red zone", indicating required decompression, while diving in 100+ fsw depths. During this same era, in St. Croix commercial lobster diver Sam Espinosa presented himself to Bret Gilliam for evaluation after suffering from numbness, exceptional fatigue and joint stiffness following his diving day. "I did a neurological examination on him and confirmed that his symptoms were progressively worsening. I was convinced he was bent. He told me that he had been diving since sun rise between 90 and 110 feet deep and stopped just before dark. It was only after I started to record his actual dive profiles and surface intervals, that I realized he was free-diving!" Espinosa responded well to a thirty minute breathing period on pure oxygen from a demand regulator and declined recompression treatment. When questioned further by Gilliam, he said several of his fellow lobster divers had similar episodes.

Admittedly, it takes an exceptional diver to get bent holding his breath but it obviously does happen. Readers are cautioned about deep breath hold diving following aggressive scuba diving activities. Dive instructor Scott Valerga of Virgin Gorda had made repetitive scuba dives in 1978 while taking tourist divers on scuba tours. When he was unable to free his anchor following the last dive, he made several dives to 90 feet holding his breath to break out the anchor. Within minutes after getting back on board, he was symptomatic of DCS. His previous diving schedule was within the limits of the Navy tables but with little safety margin. He was treated in the St. Croix recompression chamber operated by NOAA's *Hydrolab* facility with full recovery.

PORTABLE CHAMBERS

Recent advances in light weight low pressure designs have resulted in a practical portable field chamber that can actually be transported in two hand carried cases easily stowed in a van or dive vessel. Weighing around 160 pounds for the pressure tube and control panel, this unique package allows for a patient to be placed under pressure immediately in the field, blown down to 60 fsw with a patient O_2 BIBS mask including overboard dump, and then the entire unit evacuated to a full size field chamber of hospital based unit. Procedure for patient transfer without decompression is simple: put the portable chamber inside the treatment chamber and remove the patient after pressures are equalized.

This unit was first introduced in 1989 by SOS Ltd. of England and is called the Hyperlite. The chamber is constructed of a remarkable seamless, flexible tube of Kevlar encapsulated in a silicone rubber matrix. Dimensions are 7 feet long, 23 inches wide and weighs 88 pounds, approximately. Obviously, it was designed for one occupant but its value as a method of patient stabilization during transport is unquestionable.

End panels are placed in the tube with control pressure hoses equipped with non-return valves in the patient's foot end. Pressurization is accomplished by scuba tanks while O_2 is supplied from an included oxygen cylinder. Options include a portable O_2 analyzer and CO_2 monitor. Working chamber depth is slightly in excess of 60 fsw so it is compatible with standard Treatment Table depths.

If a formal treatment facility is accessible, the unit can be transported via land conveyance or by boat, or even winched aboard a helicopter. If in a remote site, the Hyperlitecan effectively conduct a full Treatment Table 6 on its own assuming enough O_2 is on hand for therapy gas and enough scuba tanks are available for pressurization and venting.

This innovative product would seem to be an affordable option for remote diving in exotic locations or carried for a diving emergency aboard a liveaboard dive vessel. Dive clubs or expedition groups should contact the manufacturer at the address below; price in mid-1991 was approximately $28,000. SOS Ltd., Box 328, London NW7 3JS, England (phone: 081-959-4517)

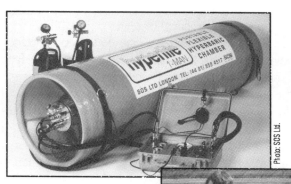

The SOS Hyperlite Portable field chamber showing control panel in case and scuba tank/oxygen cylinders for pressurization and therapy gas respectively.

The SOS Hyperlite chamber can be easily carried by four persons and used n the remotest site conditions. It can be winched aboard a helicopter for patient evacuation or can conduct an entire treatment in the field.

IN WATER RECOMPRESSION

Now we enter an area of major controversy. Ask any hyperbaric expert or chamber supervisor their feelings on in-the-water recompression and you will get an almost universal recommendation against such a practice. The logistics of attempting to manage equipment for sufficient gas supply, thermal protection for the patient, marine life considerations, etc, not to mention the hazards of patient management all basically add up to a grim scenario. Most divers will not be equipped to handle even the compressed air requirements for an Air Treatment Table which can last over six hours. And air is the least effective recompression gas; in fact such efforts could lead to worsening the patient's condition by loading him up further with nitrogen and subjecting him to debilitating cold even in tropical conditions.

A shade of gray is introduced if the dive team has access to surface supplied oxygen in adequate quantity. Rutkowski (1991) recommends that oxygen not be used deeper than 45 fsw (13.6 m) and only then in an extreme emergency. He would prefer a long "soak" at 30 fsw (9.1 m) on O_2 in 20 minute cycles with 5 minute air breaks. Ideally O_2 should be delivered via a full face mask. The authors emphasize that this is not a blueprint for divers to follow but represents a discussion of worst case scenarios where evacuation is not a practical or realistic possibility.

There are protocols for in-water recompression therapy in existence primarily with tables developed by the Australians. Missionary EMT Jack Thompson had surprisingly good results with custom in-water therapy tables in Roatan before a chamber was available and both Mount and Gilliam have successfully conducted in-water proprietary oxygen tables on patients with full resolution.

The decision must, of course, ultimately be made based upon personal circumstances and training. However, when faced with no alternative such extreme practices may present a choice. We do not sanction or endorse in-water techniques and they are presented here for discussion purposes only. Table 13-3 outlines the procedures for in-water decompression following the Australian method.

AUSTRALIAN IN-WATER TREATMENT TABLES

(from *Diving and Subaquatic Medicine*)

Note: This technique may be useful in treating cases of decompression sickness in localities remote from recompression facilities. It may also be of use while suitable transport to such a center is being arranged. In planning, it should be realized that the therapy may take up to 3 hours. The risks of cold, immersion and other environmental factors should be balanced against the beneficial effects. The diver must be accompanied by an attendant.

EQUIPMENT

1. Full face mask with demand valve and surface supply system OR helmet with free flow.

2. Adequate supply of 100% oxygen for the patient and air for the attendant.

3. Wet suit or dry suit for thermal protection.

4. Shot with at least 10 meters of rope (a seat or harness may be rigged to the shot.

5. Some form of communication system between patient, attendant and surface.

METHOD

1. The patient is lowered on the shot rope to 9 meters breathing 100% oxygen.

2. Ascent is commenced after 30 minutes in mild cases, 60 minutes in severe cases, if improvement has occurred. These times may be extended to 60 minutes and 90 minutes respectively if there is no improvement.

3. Ascent is at the rate of 1 meter every 12 minutes.

4. If symptoms recur, remain at depth an additional 30 minutes before continuing ascent.

5. If oxygen supply is exhausted, return to the surface rather than have the patient breathe air.

6. After surfacing, the patient should be given one hour on oxygen, one hour off, for a further 12 hours.

SHORT OXYGEN TABLE

DEPTH (meters)	ELAPSED TIME in Min.	
	Mild	Serious
9	030-060	060-090
8	042-072	072-102
7	054-084	084-114
6	066-096	096-126
5	078-108	108-138
4	090-120	120-150
3	102-132	132-162
2	114-144	144-174
1	126-156	156-186

Rate of ascent is 12 minutes per meter.
Total Table time is 126 minutes to 156 minutes for mild cases and 156 minutes to 186 minutes for serious cases.

SUMMARY

With good diving practices and some luck you may never need to see the inside of a recompression chamber. But it is more than likely that you will encounter a DCS incident during your career for another diver.

Remember, prompt treatment is vital. Administer oxygen by demand valve mask, if conscious provide oral fluids, do not give pain killing drugs and transport victim by fastest available method to a recompression chamber facility. **We strongly encourage signing up for a dive insurance program as well.**

Help promote recognition of DCS symptoms and prompt reporting. Denial of DCS problems is not macho, it is foolish. As elaborated in previous chapters, proper training and education are vital factors in any dive planning. A conscious effort by all divers, not just those who push the envelope, will ultimately improve our sport and help to lay the foundation of greater adventures for future generations.

U. S. Navy Standard Air Decompression Tables to 270 fsw

Depth (feet)	Bottom time (min)	Time to first stop (min:sec)	90	80	70	60	50	40	30	20	10	Total ascent (min:sec)	Repetitive group
150	5										0	2:30	C
	10	2:20									1	3:30	E
	15	2:20									3	5:30	G
	20	2:10								2	7	11:30	H
	25	2:10								4	17	23:30	K
	30	2:10								8	24	34:30	L
	40	2:00							5	19	33	59:30	N
	50	2:00							12	23	51	88:30	O
	60	1:50						3	19	26	62	112:30	Z
	70	1:50						11	19	39	75	146:30	Z
	80	1:40					1	17	19	50	84	173:30	Z
160	5										0	2:40	D
	10	2:30									1	3:40	F
	15	2:20								1	4	7:40	H
	20	2:20								3	11	16:40	J
	25	2:20								7	20	29:40	K
	30	2:10							2	11	25	40:40	M
	40	2:10							7	23	39	71:40	N
	50	2:00						2	16	23	55	98:40	Z
	60	2:00						9	19	33	69	132:40	Z
	70	1:50					1	17	22	44	80	166:40	Z

Depth (feet)	Bottom time (min)	Time to first stop (min:sec)	110	100	90	80	70	60	50	40	30	20	10	Total ascent (min:sec)	Repetitive group
170	5												0	2:50	D
	10	2:40											2	4:50	F
	15	2:30										2	5	9:50	H
	20	2:30										4	15	21:50	J
	25	2:20									2	7	23	34:50	L
	30	2:20									4	13	26	45:50	M
	40	2:10								1	10	23	45	81:50	O
	50	2:10								5	18	23	61	109:50	Z
	60	2:00							2	15	22	37	74	152:50	Z
	70	2:00							8	17	19	51	86	183:50	Z
	90	1:50						12	12	14	34	52	120	248:50	**
	120	1:30				2	10	12	18	32	42	82	156	356:50	**
	180	1:20			4	10	22	28	34	50	78	120	187	535:50	**
	240	1:20			18	24	30	42	50	70	116	142	187	681:50	**
	360	1:10		22	34	40	52	60	98	114	122	142	187	873:50	**
	480	1:00	14	40	42	56	91	97	100	114	122	142	187	1007:50	**
180	5												0	3:00	D
	10	2:50											3	6:00	F
	15	2:40										3	8	12:00	I
	20	2:30									1	5	17	28:00	K
	25	2:30									3	10	24	40:00	L
	30	2:30									6	17	27	53:00	N
	40	2:20								3	14	23	50	93:00	O
	50	2:10							2	9	19	30	65	128:00	Z
	60	2:10							5	19	19	44	81	168:00	Z

* See No Decompression Table for repetitive groups
**Repetitive dives may not follow exceptional exposure dives

U.S. NAVY STANDARD AIR DECOMPRESSION TABLE

Depth (feet)	Bottom time (min)	Time to first stop (min:sec)	110	100	90	80	70	60	50	40	30	20	10	Total ascent (min:sec)	Repetitive group
190	5												0	3:10	D
	10	2:50										1	3	7:10	G
	15	2:50										4	7	14:10	I
	20	2:40									2	6	20	31:10	K
	25	2:40									5	11	25	44:10	M
	30	2:30								1	8	19	43	63:10	N
	40	2:30								8	14	23	55	103:10	O
	50	2:20							4	13	22	33	72	147:10	Z
	60	2:20							10	17	19	50	84	183:10	Z

Depth (feet)	Bottom time (min)	Time to first stop (min:sec)	130	120	110	100	90	80	70	60	50	40	30	20	10	Total ascent (min:sec)
200	5	3:10													1	4:20
	10	3:00												1	4	8:20
	15	2:50											1	4	10	18:20
	20	2:50											3	7	27	40:20
	25	2:50											7	14	25	49:20
	30	2:40										2	9	22	37	73:20
	40	2:30									2	8	17	23	59	112:20
	50	2:30									6	16	22	39	75	161:20
	60	2:20								2	13	17	24	51	89	199:20
	90	1:50				1	10	10	10	12	12	30	38	74	134	324:20
	120	1:40				6	10	10	10	24	28	40	64	98	180	473:20
	180	1:20		1	10	10	18	24	24	42	48	70	106	142	187	685:20
	240	1:20		6	20	24	24	36	42	54	68	114	122	142	187	842:20
	360	1:10	12	22	36	40	44	56	82	98	100	114	122	142	187	1058:20
210	5	3:20													1	4:30
	10	3:10												2	4	9:30
	15	3:00											1	5	13	22:30
	20	3:00											4	10	23	40:30
	25	2:50										2	7	17	27	56:30
	30	2:50										4	9	24	41	81:30
	40	2:40									4	9	19	26	63	124:30
	50	2:30								1	9	17	19	45	80	174:30
220	5	3:30													2	5:40
	10	3:20												2	5	10:40
	15	3:10											2	5	16	26:40
	20	3:00											3	11	24	42:40
	25	3:00										3	8	19	33	66:40
	30	2:50									1	7	10	23	47	91:40
	40	2:50									6	12	22	29	68	140:40
	50	2:40								3	12	17	18	51	86	190:40
230	5	3:40													2	5:50
	10	3:20											1	2	6	12:50
	15	3:20											3	6	18	30:50
	20	3:10										2	5	12	26	48:50
	25	3:10										4	8	22	37	74:50
	30	3:00									2	8	12	23	51	99:50
	40	2:50								1	7	15	22	34	74	156:50
	50	2:50								5	14	16	24	51	89	202:50
240	5	3:50													2	6:00
	10	3:30											1	3	6	14:00
	15	3:30											4	6	21	35:00
	20	3:20										3	6	15	25	53:00
	25	3:10									1	4	9	24	40	82:00
	30	3:10									4	8	15	22	56	109:00
	40	3:00								3	7	17	22	39	75	167:00
	50	2:50							1	8	15	16	29	51	94	218:00
250	5	3:50												1	2	7:10
	10	3:40											1	4	7	16:10
	15	3:30										1	4	7	22	38:10
	20	3:30										4	7	17	27	59:10
	25	3:20									2	7	10	24	45	92:10
	30	3:20									6	7	17	23	59	116:10
	40	3:10								5	9	17	19	45	79	178:10
	60	2:40					4	10	10	10	12	22	36	64	126	298:10
	90	2:10		8	10	10	10	10	10	28	28	44	68	98	186	514:10
260	5	4:00												1	2	7:20
	10	3:50											2	4	9	19:20
	15	3:40											4	10	22	42:20
	20	3:30									1	4	7	20	31	67:20
	25	3:30									3	8	11	23	50	99:20
	30	3:20								2	6	8	19	26	61	126:20
	40	3:10							1	6	11	16	19	49	84	190:20
270	5	4:10												1	3	8:30
	10	4:00											2	5	11	22:30
	15	3:50										3	4	11	24	46:30
	20	3:40									2	3	9	21	35	74:30
	25	3:30								2	3	8	13	23	53	106:30
	30	3:30								3	6	12	22	27	64	138:30
	40	3:20							5	6	11	17	22	51	88	204:30

Glossary

A

AAUS
American Academy of Underwater Sciences

ABSOLUTE PRESSURE
Also referred to as "atmospheres absolute", absolute pressure is a measure of the pressure exerted on an object from all sources; includes water pressure and atmospheric pressure.

ACUTE CNS OXYGEN TOXICITY
The effects of breathing high-pressure O_2 (i.e. greater than 2.8 ATA/60 fsw/18.2 m), also known as the Paul Bert effect. An extremely dangerous manifestation which can include convulsions and collapse.

ADAPTATION THEORY
Theory supported by subjective reporting that cumulative experience in the deep diving environment will lesson and/or retard the onset and severity of inert gas narcosis. Recent work would also seem to apply this theory to DCS susceptibility and to the effects of oxygen toxicity.

AIR CONSUMPTION RATE
See SURFACE AIR CONSUMPTION RATE (SAC RATE)

AIR EMBOLISM
See ARTERIAL GAS EMBOLISM (AGE)

ALVEOLI
Plural of alveolus. It is the alveoli that rupture when a lung overexpansion injury occurs. (See ALVEOLUS)

ALVEOLUS
Small air cells in the lungs.

ALVEOLAR EXCHANGE
The exchange of oxygen for carbon dioxide; occurs in the alveoli.

AMBIENT PRESSURE
The sum of air and water pressure at depth expressed in terms of absolute pressure.

ANDI
American NITROX Divers, Inc. (See Reference Materials)

ANOXIA
Deficiency of oxygen.

APNEA
The cessation of breathing for short intervals of time.

ARCHIMEDES PRINCIPLE
"Any object wholly or partially immersed in a liquid will be buoyed up by a force equal to the amount of liquid displaced."

ARTERIAL GAS EMBOLISM (AGE)
A lung overexpansion injury that involves air bubbles escaping from the lungs into the pulmonary capillary bed. The bubbles can then travel to the heart and eventually follow the circulatory route to the brain. In severe cases AGE can be fatal. Treatment is immediate recompression in a hyperbaric chamber. Also known as an air embolism.

ATA
Atmospheric pressure absolute

Glossary

ATMOSPHERIC PRESSURE or ATMOSPHERE
A measure of the weight of the atmosphere at sea level, approximately 14.7 psi.

B

BAILOUT BOTTLE
See PONY BOTTLE

BCD
Buoyancy Compensator Device

BENDS
See DECOMPRESSION SICKNESS

BENJAMIN CONVERSION
A dual manifold rig designed to allow a separate regulator in-system for each cylinder. Each regulator is isolated by separate valves with a cross-over. Named for Dr. George Benjamin.

BIBS
Built-In Breathing System demand masks to deliver pure O_2 or NITROX therapy gases in chamber treatments.

BOTTOM MIX
A breathing mixture used at the deepest portion or "working depth" of a dive. See also TRAVEL MIX.

BOTTOM TIME
The interval from the start of the dive's descent until the diver's head breaks the surface following ascent. Also calculated from the start of the dive's descent until the beginning of ascent, or to the safety stop. (Some divers do not calculate the safety stop into their total bottom time.

BOYLE'S LAW
At constant temperature, the volume of a gas will be inversely proportional to the pressure sustained by it. The density will be directly proportional to it.

BRADYCARDIA
Slowness of the heartbeat.

BUDDY BREATHING
An emergency out-of-air procedure where two divers share one second-stage regulator while ascending.

BUOYANCY
The upward pressure exerted by the fluid in which an object is immersed. (See ARCHIMEDES PRINCIPLE)

C

CARBON DIOXIDE BUILDUP (HYPERCAPNIA)
An undue amount of CO_2 in the blood. A condition caused in diving by improper breathing patterns.

CARBON MONOXIDE TOXICITY
A condition that results from breathing air that is contaminated with carbon monoxide.

CARDIO-PULMONARY RESUSCITATION (CPR)
A process utilizing the combination of external heart massage and mouth-to-mouth respiration to artificially maintain the heartbeat and respiration of a victim. All divers should be certified in CPR.

CEILING
A minimum depth to which a diver may ascend without risk of decompression sickness.

Glossary

CHAMBER

See RECOMPRESSION CHAMBER

CHARLES' LAW

"If the pressure of a gas is kept constant, the volume of the gas will vary directly with the absolute temperature." The importance of Charles' Law for scuba divers is in the fact that a filled scuba cylinder will increase in pressure 4.5 psi for every degree of Fahrenheit increase. Conversely, the same cylinder will decrease in pressure 5 psi for every degree of Fahrenheit decrease.

COMPUTER DEPTH RANGE

The operational limits of a particular dive computer (DC).

CYANOSIS

A bluish discoloration of the skin that results from an oxygen deficiency in the blood.

D

DALTON'S LAW

"The partial pressure of a given quantity of gas is the pressure it would exert if it alone occupied the same volume. Additionally, the total pressure of a mixture of gases is the sum of the partial pressures of the components of the mixture."

DECOMPRESSION LINE

A line used as a point of reference and loose attachment for divers who are decompressing.

DECOMPRESSION MANAGEMENT TOOLS

Tables, wheels, dive computers, and various decompression software used to manage decompression exposures.

DECOMPRESSION REEL

A diver-carried reel with typically 300 or more feet of line, and a small LIFTBAG that can be tied off to a wreck or weighted and hung from the liftbag in the event of missing the DECOMPRESSION LINE. A standard piece of gear among many wreck/deep divers.

DECOMPRESSION SICKNESS (DCS)

A malady caused by nitrogen bubbles forming in various parts of the body when a diver ascends too quickly and/or exceeds their ceiling. Also known as the bends or Caisson disease.

DEHYDRATION

A loss of bodily fluids. In divers this can be brought about by diving with a hangover, consuming caffeinated beverages prior to diving, overexertion, or diving when ill.

DIVING REFLEX

A reaction to mammal's physiology following immersion in water. Typified by a slowing of respiration and pulse.

DOPPLER

A device used to detect bubbles in the diver's bloodstream.

DPV

Diver Propulsion Vehicle. Also known as underwater scooters.

DYSPNEA

Difficulty breathing that results from increased depth.

Glossary

E
EAD
Equivalent air depth

EBS
Emergency Breathing System

EMERGENCY SWIMMING ASCENT (ESA)
An independent, emergency ascent made upon depletion of the diver's air supply. Also referred to as an emergency out of air ascent or swimming ascent.

EXCURSION TABLES
Tables designed to allow saturated divers in a HABITAT to access deeper depths with little or no decompression obligation as long as they return to the HABITAT "storage" depth.

F
FATHOM
A nautical unit of measurement equivalent to six feet.

FFW
Feet of fresh water

FSW
Feet of salt water

G
GAUGE PRESSURE
The pressure that is indicated by a submersible pressure gauge (SPG) which is the pressure relative to ambient pressure.

H
HABITAT
An underwater dwelling for divers in saturation. Used as a base of operation. Divers may be supported for over a week for working objectives and then decompressed. This process allows more efficient time underwater and offers 'excursion" dives to deeper depths with little or no decompression.

HANG TIME
Decompression time

HELIOX
A mixed gas containing helium (He) and oxygen (O_2).

HENRY'S LAW
"If the temperature is held constant, the solubility of any gas in a liquid is directly proportional to the pressure the gas exerts on the liquid." This tells us that a liquid can absorb gas, and the more pressure placed on the liquid, the more of the gas it will absorb.

HYDROSTATIC PRESSURE
The pressure exerted underwater by the surrounding water column.

HYDROSTATIC TEST (HYDRO)
Test required every five years on scuba cylinders. The test involves pressurizing the cylinder to 5/3 of its working pressure with water used as the medium to provide pressure.

Glossary

HYPERBARIC CHAMBER

See RECOMPRESSION CHAMBER

HYPERCAPNIA

See CARBON DIOXIDE BUILDUP

HYPERLITE

Portable field chamber manufactured by SOS Ltd. (SEE Chapter 13)

HYPERVENTILATION

The process of rapidly inhaling and exhaling to purge the body of carbon dioxide, thus decreasing the natural urge to breathe. Hyperventilation is a potentially dangerous practice and can lead to shallow water blackout, unconsciousness, and drowning.

HYPOTHERMIA

A condition in which the deep tissue or core temperature of the body falls below the normal physiological range, approximately 97° F (36° C) and is the temperature at which malfunctions in normal physiology occur. If the core temperature continues to drop, serious consequences could develop.

HYPOXIA

Failure of the tissues to receive sufficient oxygen.

I

INERT GAS NARCOSIS

The intoxicating effect experienced by divers who descend to extreme depths. Nitrogen narcosis, a common form of inert gas narcosis, can be incurred at depths as shallow as 100 feet (30m), and possibly even shallower by individuals who are more susceptible.

J

JON LINE

A three to six foot line with a hand loop(s) that can be clipped around a DECOMPRESSION LINE. Named after its inventor, Jon Hulbert, a jon line serves as a dampening device for the up and down motion of the decompression line in rough seas. Also used for DPV tows.

"J" VALVE

Divers slang referring to a reserve valve on a scuba cylinder.

L

LIFELINE

A floating line trailed from a boat to provide divers something to hold onto. Also referred to as a tag line.

LIFTBAG

A bag-like device that is inflated with air and used to lift various objects from the bottom. Many models are designed with an overpressure relief valve to allow excess air to escape thus preventing damage to the liftbag.

LUNG OVEREXPANSION INJURY

An injury to the lung tissues caused by a diver ascending too quickly or holding his breath.

M

MAXIMUM DIVE TIME (MDT)

The length of time that may be spent at a given depth without being required to make a mandatory decompression stop. Also referred to as NO-STOP LIMITS and NO-DECOMPRESSION LIMITS.

Glossary

MEYER-OVERTON HYPOTHESIS

Relation of the narcotic effect of a gas to its solubility in lipid tissue.

MULTI-LEVEL DIVE

A type of dive that involves progressively shallower depths. (Also see SQUARE PROFILE DIVE)

MULTI-PLACE/MULTI-LOCK CHAMBER

A treatment chamber capable of handling two or more people and consisting of two or more pressure chambers (locks) to allow efficient transfer of staff or material without losing pressure.

N

NSS-CDS

National Speleological Society, Cave Diving Section

NIGGLE

A transient, minor symptom of DCS, often observed in cave or wreck divers.

NITROGEN

A gas that makes up approximately 78% of the air we breathe; responsible for DECOMPRESSION SICKNESS and NITROGEN NARCOSIS.

NITROGEN NARCOSIS

Loss of judgement and motor skills caused by the narcotic effect of breathing the nitrogen component of air at elevated partial pressures (i.e. depth). Condition alleviated upon ascent. Also known as "rapture of the deep".

NITROX

A mixture of oxygen and nitrogen. Standard air is NITROX. Generically, NITROX refers to oxygen/nitrogen mixtures with an oxygen percentage between 22-50%. Also referred to as SAFEAIR and Enriched Air NITROX (EAN).

NOAA

National Oceanic and Atmospheric Administration

NO-DECOMPRESSION LIMITS

See MAXIMUM DIVE TIME

NO-STOP LIMITS

See MAXIMUM DIVE TIME

O

OCTOPUS

A Type I Emergency Breathing System that is essentially an extra second stage for use if a buddy runs out-of-air. Also known as a SAFE SECOND-STAGE or bipus regulator.

OVERHEAD ENVIRONMENT

A diving environment that does not allow direct escape to the surface such as caves and wreck penetrations. Many divers consider stage decompression diving to be a form of "overhead diving" due to the obligation of the CEILING.

OXYGEN

A colorless, tasteless, odorless gas that accounts for approximately 21% of the air we breathe.

P

PARTIAL PRESSURE

The pressure exerted by each gas in a mixture of gases.

Glossary

PHYSIOLOGY

The study of the body's actions and reactions. Diving physiology is primarily concerned with the effects of water pressure on the diver.

PNEUMOTHORAX

A lung overexpansion injury that involves air bubbles escaping into the chest area and causing lung collapse. Results from ascending too rapidly and/or holding one's breath.

PONY BOTTLE

A small scuba cylinder; usually 30 cu. ft. or less. Commonly used as an EMERGENCY BREATHING SYSTEM (Type II). Also known as a BAILOUT BOTTLE.

PRESSURE RELIEF DISC

A safety device built into cylinder valves that prevents internal pressure from reaching dangerous levels. The device must be completely replaced if the disc is ruptured. Also referred to as a burst disc or overpressure relief disc.

PROPRIETARY TABLES

Private, exclusive, custom-generated tables.

PSIA

Pounds per square inch absolute.

PSIG

Pounds per square inch gauge. (See GAUGE PRESSURE)

Q

QUADS

A SET or RIG consisting of twin doubles (i.e. 4 tanks).

R

"RAPTURE OF THE DEEP"

Inert gas narcosis. Also known as nitrogen narcosis.

RECOMPRESSION

The accepted treatment for DECOMPRESSION SICKNESS and LUNG OVEREXPANSION INJURY. Treatment consists of placing the afflicted diver in a RECOMPRESSION CHAMBER and gradually increasing the pressure as per specific guidelines.

RECOMPRESSION CHAMBER

A usually cylindrical, steel chamber that is used for the treatment of DCS and LUNG OVEREXPANSION INJURY. Also referred to as a HYPERBARIC CHAMBER or CHAMBER.

REPETITIVE DIVE

Any dive following a previous dive within a particular time frame. The time frame will vary according to the decompression model used. (e.g. a repetitive dive according to the U.S. Navy model is any dive within 12 hours of a previous dive.)

RESIDUAL NITROGEN

The residual amount of nitrogen left in the body as a result of a previous dive.

RESIDUAL NITROGEN TIME (RNT)

Residual nitrogen expressed in terms of time already spent at depth.

RESIDUAL VOLUME

The quantity of air remaining in the lungs after a forceful exhalation.

Glossary

RIG
See SET

RULE OF THIRDS
A rule used primarily by cave and wreck divers that basically states that after having consumed 1/3 of your air supply you should begin your exit from the cave/wreck. The remaining 2/3 air left is used for the exit and ascent.

S

SAFETY OUTGASSING ASCENT PROCEDURE (S.O.A.P.)
A procedure that entails making a safety stop at 15-30 feet (4.5-9.1m) for 3-5 minutes at the end of every dive.

SET
A diver's equipment configuration or RIG.

SHALLOW WATER BLACKOUT
Underwater unconsciousness caused by excessive HYPERVENTILATION.

SKIP BREATHING
The dangerous practice of taking a breath and holding it for as long as possible before taking another. It is a practice that saves little if any air and can lead to a LUNG OVEREXPANSION INJURY or other pressure-related injuries.

SPG
Submersible Pressure Gauge

SQUARE PROFILE DIVE
A type of dive that involves staying at one particular depth for the entire dive and then ascending directly to the surface.

SQUEEZE
A pressure-related injury resulting from failure to equalize on descent. Air-filled cavities such as the sinuses, middle ear, and mask are most commonly affected.

STAGE BOTTLE
Extra cylinder carried with the diver or attached to the DECOMPRESSION LINE and used as a stage decompression gas. The term is also used by cave divers to denote extra cylinders "staged" in cave systems prior to deep or extended dives.

SUR D O_2
Surface decompression on oxygen. Commonly used in commercial and some high-tech diving when an on-site chamber is available. Divers exit the water and decompress in the chamber using O_2. It presents a safer, more comfortable environment for decompressing.

SURFACE AIR CONSUMPTION RATE (SAC RATE)
The rate of underwater air consumption converted to an equivalent surface rate; commonly measured in psi/minute.

SURFACE INTERVAL TIME (SIT)
The time spent on the surface between dives; must be at least 10 minutes but a minimum of one hour is suggested.

T

TACHYCARDIA
Excessive rapidity of the heart beat.

Glossary

TEST OF PRESSURE
20 minute breathing period on pure O_2 at 60 fsw (18.2 m) in a recompression chamber to observe patient for relief of DCS symptoms.

THERMOCLINE
A subsurface layer of water characterized by rapid temperature and density changes with depth.

TIDAL VOLUME
The quantity of air that is inhaled and exhaled with each breath.

TRAIL LINE
See LIFE LINE

TRAVEL MIX
The breathing mix used on descent or ascent when FO_2 varies.

TREATMENT TABLE 5
An oxygen treatment table at 60 fsw (18.2 m) for less serious "pain only" DCS. The treatment is 2 hours and 15 minutes long.

TREATMENT TABLE 6
An oxygen treatment table at 60 fsw (18.2 m) for serious DCS symptoms. The treatment is 4 hours and 45 minutes long.

TREATMENT TABLE 6A
A treatment table used for acute cases of AGE and DCS not relieved on Table 6. Involves recompression of patient to 165 fsw (50 m) on air or NITROX and subsequent re-entry to Table 6.

TYMPANIC MEMBRANE
A thin membranous partition separating the external ear from the middle ear.

TYPE I DCS
DCS involving less serious symptoms manifesting as "pain only".

TYPE II DCS
DCS involving serious symptoms typically with CNS involvement.

U

UHMS
Undersea and Hyperbaric Medical Society

UNDERTOW
Currents running toward the sea found near the bottom of a sloping beach that results from the return of water carried to the shore by wave action.

UPTD (OTU)
Unit of pulmonary toxicity dose. A method of calculating the cumulative effects of breathing oxygen.

V

VERTIGO
A loss of the sense of balance accompanied by dizziness and confusion.

VITAL CAPACITY
The maximum amount of gas an individual can move through the lungs.

Bibliography

The following compilation of books, periodicals, newsletters, and organizations is provided as a source of reference that will hopefully prove to be a valuable addition to this text. All books, periodicals, and newsletters were selected for their relevence, in one way or another, to the material covered in the preceding 13 chapters. The authors cover several subject areas that would be useful to deep divers (or, for that matter, any divers) and would provide one with a good cross-section of diving-related information. The organizations/equipment suppliers listed were chosen for their overall importance to sport divers and their of the unique information/equipment provided.

BOOKS

A Medical Guide to Hazardous Marine Life, Auerbach, P.S. (1987), Progressive Printing Co.

A Pictorial History of Diving, Bachrach,Desiderati & Matzen (editors), Best Publishing Co.

Advanced Diving: Technology and Techniques, National Association of Underwater Instructors

Advanced Wreck Diving Guide, Gentile, Gary (1988), Cornell Maritime Press

Andrea Doria: Dive to an Era, Gentile, Gary (1987), Gary Gentile Productions

Biology of Marine Life, Fourth Edition, Sumich, James L. (1988), Wm. C. Brown Publishers

Case Histories of Diving and Hyperbaric Accidents, Waite, Charles L. (1988), UHMS

Cave Diving: The Cave Diving Group Manual, Bedford, Bruce (editor), Mendip Publishing, England

Caving, A Blueprint For Survival, Exley, Sheck, NSS/CDS

Cold Weather and Under Ice Scuba Diving, NAUI/NDA Technical Publication Number 4, Somers, Lee H., Ph.D (1973), National Association of Underwater Instructors

DAN Underwater Diving Accident Manual, Divers Alert Network (1985), Duke University Medical Center

Deep Into Blue Holes, Palmer, Rob Unwin Hyman,England

Dive Computers: A Consumer's Guide to History, Theory and Performance, Loyst, with Huggins and Steidley (1991), Watersport Publishing, Inc.

Dive Rescue Specialist Training Manual, Linton,Rust, Gilliam (1986), Dive Rescue, Inc./International

Diving Accident Management Field Guide: O_2 Administration and Recompression Therapy, Gilliam, Bret C., Ocean Tech

Diving Medicine, Second Edition, Bove & Davis (1990), Grove and Stratton, Inc.

Diving and Subaquatic Medicine, Edmonds, Lowery, Pennegather (1983), Best Publishing Co.

Emergency Oxygen Administration and Field Management of Scuba Diving Accidents, Corry, James A. (1989), NAUI Publications

Field Guide for the Diver Medic, Daugherty, Gordon C. (1985), Best Publishing, Co.

Last of the Blue Water Hunters, Eyles Carlos, Watersport Publishing, Inc.

Living And Working In The Sea, Miller, James W. and Koblick, Ian G., Van Nostrand Reinhold Co.

Medical Emergencies at Sea, Kessler, William (1986), Hearst Marine Books

Men Beneath the Sea, Hass, Hans, St. Martin's Press

NITROX Manual, Rutkowski, Dick (1991), Hyperbarics International, Inc.

NOAA Diving Manual: Diving for Science and Technology, Second Edition, Edited by Miller, James W., U.S. Government Printing Office

Physiology in Depth: The Proceedings of the Seminar, Edited by Graver, Dennis (1982), Professional Association of Diving Instructors

Bibliography

Recompression Chamber Life Support Manual, Rutkowski, Dick (1991), Hyperbarics International, Inc.

Safety in Diving, Dueker, C.W. (1985), Madison Publishing Associates

Search and Recovery, Erickson, Ralph D. (1983), Professional Association of Diving Instructors

Solo Diving: The Art of Underwater Self-Sufficiency, von Maier, Robert (1991), Watersport Publishing

Stress and Performance in Diving, Bachrach and Egstrom (1987), Best Publishing, Co.

The Adventurous Aquanaut, Hauser, Hillary, Best Publishing Co.

The Art of Safe Cave Diving, Gerrard, Steve, NACD

The DAN Emergency Handbook, Lippman and Buggs (1989), J.L. Publications

The New Practical Diving, Mount and Ikehara (1979), University of Miami Press

The Physician's Guide to Diving Medicine, Shilling, Carlston and Mathias (1984), Plenum Press

The Physiology and Medicine of Diving, Third Edition, Bennett and Elliott (1982), Best Publishing Co.

The University of Michigan Diving Manual, Volume I: Diving Theory, Somers, Lee H. (PhD) (1990), The University of Michigan

U.S. Navy Air Decompression Table Handbook and Decompression Chamber Operator's Handbook, NAVSEA (1985), Best Publishing, Co.

U.S. Navy Diving Manual, NAVSEA (1980), Best Publishing Co.

Your Offshore Doctor, Beilan, Michael (1985), Dodd, Mead and Co.

ARTICLES

A New Approach to Cave Diving Emergencies, Exley, Sheck, Proceedings of the 1975 IQ

Avoiding The Bends, Gilliam, Bret C., Scuba Times Nov./Dec. 1990

Dive Computer "Post Dive" Malfunction Procedure, Emmerman, Michael N., Proceedings of 1989 International Conference on Underwater Education

Diving Florida's Springs, Caverns and Caves, Mount, Tom, Discover Diving May/June 1991

Evaluation of Decompression Sickness in Multi-day, Repetitive Diving for 77,689 Sport Dives, Gilliam, Bret C., Proceedings Journal For AAUS/DAN Conference March 1991

Extending the Working Capability and Depth of the Scuba Diver Breathing A Compressed Air Media, Gilliam, Bret C., Proceedings of the 1974 International Conference on Underwater Education

How Well Do They Do It?: A Survey of Sport Divers' Ability to Work Decompression Problems, Hill, R. Kelly, Proceedings of the XV Meeting of European Undersea Biomedical Society

If You Fly: The Diver's Dilemma Part I, Emmermen, Michael N., Discover Diving, Sept./Oct. 1989

If You Fly: The Diver's Dilemma Part II, Emmermen, Michael N., Discover Diving, Nov/Dec. 1989

Narcosis; Methods Versus Myths, Gilliam, Bret C., Scuba Times May/June 1991

One Year Database of Sport Diving Exposures: Comparison of Table vs.Computer Usage, Gilliam, Bret C., Proceedings of the 1991 International Conference On Underwater Education

Oxygen: The Princess of Gases, Crea, John, Discover Diving May/June 1991

Technical Diving, Menduno, Michael, Discover Diving March/April 1991

The Deepest Dive, DeLoach, Ned, Ocean Realm Summer 1988 '

The Diving Reflex In Man, Dircks, John W., Proceedings of the 1975 International Conference on Underwater Education

Bibliography

PERIODICALS AND NEWSLETTERS

Alert Diver
Divers Alert Network
Box 3823,
Duke University Medical Center
Durham, North Carolina 27710

AquaCorps
AquaCorps
590 SE 12th St, Suite 301
Dania Beach, FL 33004

Discover Diving
Watersport Publishing, Inc.
P.O. Box 83727
San Diego, California 92138

Diver Magazine
Seagraphic Publications Ltd.
10991 Shellbridge Way
Richmond, British Columbia,
Canada V6X 3C6

Pressure
UHMS Diving Committee
9650 Rockville Pike
Bethesda, Maryland 20814

Scuba Times
14110 Perdido Key Drive, Suite 16
Pensacola, Florida 32507

Sources
NAUI Diving Association
P.O. Box 14650
Montclair, California 91763-1150

The Slate
AAUS
947 Newhall Street
Costa Mesa, California 92627

Undersea Journal
PADI
1251 East Dyer Rd.
Santa Ana, CA 92705

Underwater USA
Press-Enterprise, Inc.
3185 Lackawanna Ave.
Bloomsburg, Pennsylvania 17815

Woman Diver
Suite 820 ST,
6631 Wakefield Drive
Alexandria, Virginia 22307

TRAINING FACILITIES

Bellingham Dive-N-Travel
{Larry Elsevier}
2720 West Maplewood Ave.
Bellingham, WA 98225
(206) 734-1770 (800) 338-6341
-Full-service dive facility specializing in NITROX training.

Hyperbarics International, Inc.
{Dick Rutkowski}
490 Caribbean Drive
Key Largo, Florida 33037
(305) 451-2551
-Advanced training programs for Nitrox diving, recompression chamber operation, dive accident management, etc. On site training chamber; also available as traveling lecture series.

ISC Management Corporation
{Ed Betts}
74 Woodcleft Ave.
Freeport, NY 11520
(516) 546-2026
-NITROX and mixed gas training, equipment outfitting.

Key West Diver: High-Tech Training Center
{Bill Deans}
MM 4.5 US 1
Stock Island, FL 33040
(305) 294-7177 (800) 873-4837
-Training programs for air and mixed gas. Equipment outfitting. Lecture and practical training anywhere in U.S.

Ocean Tech
{Bret Gilliam}
3098 Mere Point Rd.
Brunswick, ME 04011
(207) 442-0998
-Training programs for air and mixed gas. Recompression chamber operation, oxygen administration, accident management, deep U/W photography, and equipment outfitting.

Professional Scuba Association
{Hal Watts}
2219 E. Colonial Dr.
Orlando, FL 32803
(407) 896-4541
-Training in deep air diving in private Forty Fathom Grotto.

Sheck Exley
Cathedral Canyon
Rt. 8, Box 374
Live Oak, FL 32060
(904) 362-7589
-Mixed gas workshops and deep diver training in cave and cavern environments.

Submariner Research
{John Crea}
Box 1906
Bainbridge, GA 31717
(912) 246-9349
-Mixed gas workshops and deep diver training in cave and cavern environments.

Tom Mount
1545 NE 104th St.
Miami Shores, FL 33138
(305) 754-1027
-Deep diver training programs for air and mixed gas. NITROX and mixed gas courses, deep U/W photography, and equipment outfitting. Full cave and cavern courses as well.

Under H₂O Services
{Darren Webb}
5800 Lake Murray Blvd., Suite 4
La Mesa, CA 91942
(619) 464-5662
-Deep diver training programs, scientific diving services.

Undersea Systems
{Robert von Maier}
P.O. Box 3620
Escondido, CA 92033
(619) 471-8544 (619) 989-1078
-Deep and stage decompression diving instruction, U/W self-sufficiency courses.

SPECIALIZED EQUIPMENT

Dive Rite Manufacturing
Rt. 14, Box 136
Lake City, FL 32055
(904) 752-1087
-Specialized manufacturer of doubles, BCD's, line reels, lights and accessories.

English Engineering, Inc.
Route 3, Box 54
Greenville, FL 32331
(904) 948-3311
-Custom U/W lights rated to extreme depths (850+ fsw), line reels and custom DPV's.

ISC Management Corporation
74 Woodcleft Ave.
Freeport, NY 11520
(516) 546-2026
-Full engineering consulting for any high-pressure applications, air compressors, oil-free systems, etc.

Key West Diver
MM 4.5 US 1
Stock Island
Key West, FL 33040
(305) 294-7177 (800) 873-4837
-Specialized deep diving equipment, DPV's, lights and thermal suits.

Ocean Tech
3098 Mere Point Rd.
Brunswick, ME 04011
(207) 442-0998
-Consulting for specialized deep diving systems and compressor/filling systems. Oxygen equipment and recompression chambers. Vessel design, construction, operation and management.

Underwater Applications Corporation
427-3 Amherst St., Suite 345
Nashua, NH 03063
-Specialized deep diving equipment, oxygen-clean breathing systems, booster pumps, oxygen analyzers and custom tables.

CUSTOM (PROPRIETARY) TABLES

Hamilton Research Ltd.
{Bill Hamilton}
80 Grove St.
Tarrytown, NY 10591
(914) 631-9194

Submariner Research, Ltd.
{John Crea}
Box 1906
Bainbridge, GA 31717
(912) 246-9349

Underwater Applications Corporation
{Randy Bohrer}
427-3 Amherst St., Suite 345
Nashua, NH 03063

Index

A

AAUS 8, 147, 156
affects of increased pressure 131
AGE 219, 221
air management systems 117
Aladin Pro 142, 204
alcohol 63
algorithm 140, 215
alternate air source 128
Ama divers 229
American Academy of Underwater Sciences
    (AAUS) 8, 147, 156
American NITROX Divers Inc. 162, 169
Anderson, Dick 42, 43
ANDI 162, 169
Andrea Doria 31, 32, 55, 79
Andros Blue Hole 50, 54
Aqua Zepp 132
AquaCorps 13, 118, 123
arterial gas embolism 219
Australian In-Water Treatment Tables 232

B

Bachrach, Dr. Art 12, 67, 68
Bail-Out Bottle 108
Bandino, Angela 47
Behnke 113, 179
bends 229
Benjamin Cave (#4) 51
Benjamin Conversion 50, 122
Benjamin, Dr. George 17, 50, 51, 79, 121
Bennett 81
Ben's Cave 54
Bert, Paul 82
Betts, Ed 169
Beuchat 27, 142, 204
BIBS 225
BIBS mask 225, 226, 230
Big Dismal 56
Bishop Museum Deep Project 154
Bohrer, Randy 26, 308
Buccaneer 66
Buhlmann, Dr. Albert 40, 142, 145, 204

C

caisson 113, 179
Catalina chamber 226
Cayman Association of Dive Operators 11
ceiling 141
Central Nervous System O_2 Toxicity 91
chambers, portable 230
Chronic Oxygen Toxicity 96
Ciampi, Elgin 34, 35
CIS-LUNAR 176
Clarke, Dr. Eugenie 55
Clesi, Dustin 8, 50, 55
closed mixed gas rebreathing 194
CMAS 147
CNS O2 toxicity 77, 92, 93, 94, 95, 01
CNS toxicity zone 98
Cognitive or analytical narrowing 74
Conshelf II 44
Corry, Jim 218
Coston, Dave 46
Counter-Diffusion 185
Counterphobe 65
Cousteau, Jacques 21, 30, 44, 54, 58, 79
Crea, John 89, 103, 105, 199, 204, 205, 208
Croft, Bob 47, 229
Crossover Manifold/Yoke 122
custom tables 105, 207, 211

D

Dacor 132, 204
Dalton's Law 90
DAN 220, 234
DC-11 144
DCIEM 104, 204
DCIEM tables 105
DCS 105, 106, 114, 150, 200, 201, 211, 213, 234,
    214, 217, 221, 224, 226, 228, 229, 230, 234
DCS, causes 214
DCS, contributory factors 214
DCS, First Aid 218
DCS, qualification of 226
DCS, signs and symptoms 216
DCS, symptoms 217

Index

Index

Index

Index

Index